TRANSFERENCE

TRANSFERENCE

Shibboleth or Albatross?

JOSEPH SCHACHTER

THE ANALYTIC PRESS

2002   Hillsdale, NJ   London

Published by
The Analytic Press, Inc., Publishers
    Editorial Offices:
    101 West Street
    Hillsdale, New Jersey 07642

www.analyticpress.com

Designed and typeset by CompuDesign, Charlottesville, VA

Library of Congress Cataloging-in-Publication Data

Schachter, Joseph
    Transference: shibboleth or albatross? / Joseph Schachter
    Includes bibliographical references and index

    ISBN 0-88163-323-2

Printed in the United States of America
    10 9 8 7 6 5 4 3 2 1

CONTENTS

v

ACKNOWLEDGMENTS

This book is the culmination of a fifty-year evolution in my views of Freud and of psychoanalysis. My early teachers include Theodore Karwoski, an experimental psychologist who imbued me with a respect for empiricism. My interest in psychoanalysis developed in the exciting intellectual climate of Harvard's newly formed Department of Social Relations where examining concepts and assumptions was fundamental. There Robert W. White impressed me with the necessity of crediting healthy aspects of personality, of studying normal persons, and of recognizing the many nonsexual motivational systems that influence behavior.

My psychoanalytic training was at the Columbia University Psychoanalytic Center for Training and Research, founded primarily by the charismatic Sándor Rado, who by the late 1930s had eschewed libido theory and developed an adaptational theory of psychodynamics. In contrast, my training analyst, Eugene Milch, was a moderately traditional analyst, and my experience with him shaped my own treatment technique, which remained moderately traditional for many years.

Two supervisors further influenced my approach to analytic treatment. During my psychoanalytic training in the late 1950s, Barbara Ruth Easser, the first Canadian woman analyst, conceived of the treatment situation as a specialized human relationship between two people and emphasized the importance of patient–analyst interaction. Ruth went so far as to suggest that the way to understand a patient's family structure was to determine who did the dishes and who took out the garbage. Ruth was a close friend of both my wife and me until her untimely death from cancer.

More recently, Merton M. Gill had a powerful impact. He had a reputation of being prickly and tough; he made his supervisory criticisms with characteristic directness and lucidity—and repeated them as often as he felt warranted. It was abundantly clear, however, that beneath his apparent brusqueness was a boundless benevolent warmth and generativity. Although not a quick study, eventually I did learn what he meant by patient–analyst interaction and how he conceived of dealing with it.

As an author, I turned to an old friend, Gladys Topkis, for many years the "all-purpose" editor of psychoanalytic books for Yale University Press. I tentatively sent her the first few chapters; she was encouraging, reassuring me that I did have something to say and adding that my writing voice was both distinctive and attention evoking. She put me in touch with several publishers, who, in this era of curtailed psychoanalytic publication, declined my proposal. John Kerr, Senior Editor at The Analytic Press, however, responded with cautious approval and recommended we begin working together to develop the book further.

I quickly made the surprised, delighted discovery that John and I were intellectually kindred spirits in our views both of Freud and of psychoanalysis. John was especially helpful in curbing my tendentiousness and helped with many technical aspects of my writing. His suggestions and criticisms, like Gill's, were expressed directly and pointedly, and, like Gill's, without a trace of malice. In addition, I have the greatest respect for his encyclopedic knowledge of the early history of psychoanalysis. Anyone embarking on writing a first book is well advised to find an editor like John Kerr.

I would also like to acknowledge my appreciation to Paul Stepansky, Managing Director of The Analytic Press, for his intellectual adventurousness in publishing this theoretically radical book. Paul's risk taking, expressed ten years ago in his willingness to sponsor publication of innovative works and journals, has quietly been shaping and expanding American psychoanalysis.

I would like, gratefully, to acknowledge the friendly, skillful, and patient efforts of Nancy Liguori, Production Editor, and Lee Hatfield, Copy Editor, to deal with the complex manuscript with more than 500 references.

Let me add my appreciation to three colleagues who read the Conclusion and provided helpful comments, Robert Glick, Paul Mosher, and Allan Rosenblatt. I would like to add my thanks to Adolf Grünbaum who, in the process of reading my manuscript to decide if he would write comments for the book's dust jacket, generously made incisive observations and raised questions that were very helpful. Special appreciation is owed to my former patient, Pat, for very graciously granting permission to include a discussion of our work in the book.

I have saved to the last the expression of my deepest appreciation, that to my psychoanalyst wife, Judy. We have been a tight pair for well over fifty years; her help, support, and generativity long precede my work on this book. Early on, while I was in graduate school, Judy suggested that instead of being constrained in psychology I should attend medical school to enable me to pursue psychoanalysis. Later, when I was in my early forties and dealing both with midlife dissatisfactions and the limits of my therapeutic effectiveness as an analyst, I hesitated to make a change from part-time research and practice to a full-time, academic research position; Judy's encouragement, support, and help enabled me to obtain such a position. Subsequently, I returned to full-time analytic practice with new perspectives and more comfort and satisfaction with my analytic, therapeutic efficacy.

This book engendered discussions of my ideas and my writing; her comments were sometimes critical but always provided a broadened perspective. John Kerr was surprised that my manuscripts were such clean copy. I explained that every chapter—including the many drafts—had been preedited by a skillful editor, Judy. Working on this book has been intensely engaging, especially since retirement when, at times, I disappeared into the woodwork. She has been remarkably tolerant of being left so much on her own to deal with her own retirement and our move to New York. All in all, her encouragement, devotion, help, and hard work have been essential in enabling me to complete this challenging task.

Joseph Schachter, M.D., Ph.D.

TRANSFERENCE

1

Transference and the Psychoanalytic Identity

> *Valentine: "It's the best possible time to be alive, when almost everything you thought you knew is wrong."*
>
> —Tom Stoppard, *Arcadia*

Tradition, to Tevye, the poor, worshipful, God-fearing Everyman in *Fiddler on the Roof*, was sacred and beautiful. So it was to Jack Streit, who provides a telling analogy for psychoanalysts' attitudes toward the tradition of psychoanalytic theory. Jack Streit was described in his obituary (Thomas, 1998) as "a master matzoh maker devoted to keeping an ancient tradition and a family business alive on the Lower East Side" (p. C18). The obituary elaborated:

> The problem is that matzoh is so basic, a simple—and not especially appetizing—mixture of plain flour and water, that the temptation to add just a little something extra to the dough can be overwhelming. That, of course, would undercut the symbolic value of matzoh as the authentic unleavened—and unsalted and un-everything else—bread that kept the Israelites alive on their flight from Egypt. And since what began as an Exodus expedient . . . became a powerful Passover tradition, those who prepare matzoh for Passover do not fool around with the recipe (88 pounds of flour and 25.6 pounds of water for the basic Streit batch). By rights the Streit factory on Rivington Street should have been shuttered long ago, the ovens sold for scrap. But his attention was never far from the

1
~

ovens, in part because they are so old that they have needed
extensive attention. "Why is Streit's Matzoh different from all
other domestic brands? Because Streit's bakes only Streit's
Matzoh in our own ovens" [p. C18].

Jack Streit considered the tradition inviolable and his ovens sacred.
Jack Streit died Wednesday, February 4, 1998; he was 89.

The traditions of psychoanalytic theory have been profoundly
important for psychoanalysis, and, as Jack Streit realized, maintaining
tradition is closely associated with keeping the business alive.
Psychoanalytic theory, too, has been carefully nurtured even longer
than Jack Streit's ovens. It, too, has needed extensive attention, especially in recent years when formerly fundamental concepts like abstinence, anonymity, and even neutrality have begun to fall into disrepair
(Schachter, 1994). But two core principles, transference and transference interpretation, continue to be staunchly supported as a way of
distinguishing psychoanalysis from all other brands of therapy. As
Person (1993) writes trenchantly, "The development of the transference and its analysis appear to have replaced dream analysis as the
"royal road" to the unconscious" (p. 5). When there first was temptation some years ago to add a little something extra, a dash of patient-
analyst interaction, many analysts refused to "fool around" with the
recipe for fear of undercutting the tradition of transference theory.

Why has traditional theory, with transference at its core, been so
important to psychoanalysts? It was Erikson (1956, 1959, 1968), a man
who struggled with his own personal identity, who brought the importance of the sense of identity to the attention of psychoanalysis. For
many psychoanalysts, identity as an analyst is central to personal identity, perhaps to a greater degree than with many other professions.
Transference and the interpretation of transference has distinguished
the analyst from other therapists; it has come to symbolize the specific identity of the analyst.

Shibboleth was a test word used by the Gileadites to distinguish
the escaping Ephraimites, who could not pronounce the initial "sh."
Thus, *shibboleth* referred to a password that enabled an unknown to
identify himself or herself as a member of a particular group. Freud
(1914a) once referred not to the transference, but to the interpretation of dreams as "the shibboleth of psychoanalysis" (p. 57). As Person
has noted, however, the focus on dream interpretation has been
replaced by analysis of transference, and, therefore, especially in the
last decade when psychoanalysis has been battered by both internal

(theoretical) and external attacks, transference has become the shibboleth of psychoanalysis. Questioning the value of transference in our theory and practice, as this book does, potentially threatens reliance on this shibboleth.

Analysts' Uncertainty about Their Work

I think many analysts are concerned about their professional identity at least in part as a reaction to being troubled by an underlying uncertainty, sometimes acknowledged and other times either unrecognized or denied, about their analytic work. Few analysts write about this sense of uncertainty, which has many roots. Some of the roots plainly have to do with recent theory change. Meissner (1992) writes: "As the analyst gradually becomes less the "authority" and more an egalitarian participant in the patient's process of discovery, the analyst experiences a sense of uncertainty and of the unknown" (p. 1078). But a sense of uncertainty is also intrinsic to the endeavor and the more the field evolves the greater this uncertainty seems to become. Britton and Steiner (1994), referring to the bewildering variety of impressions from the patient, comment: "The resultant uncertainty and confusion is often difficult to bear, and pressure to reduce the uncertainty may influence both patient and analyst to search for a means of integrating or limiting the impressions in order to create a meaningful whole" (p. 1069). Goldberg (1997) also acknowledges the analyst's uncertainty; he refers to the need "to restore balance to our ever-present condition of uncertainty and lack of closure" (p. 14). He views the uncertainty as a function of the need to oscillate between empathy and judgment. Lichtenberg (1998) summarizes simply: "The analytic clinical exchange inevitably arouses recurrent states of uncertainty for both participants" (p. 25). Green (2000b) expresses concern that "there are sufficient signs among the ranks of psychoanalysts that this [psychoanalytic] identity is presently less assured with the evolution of our discipline. Sometimes, there is a feeling that it is threatened with fading away, if not disappearing under different influences" (p. 32).

Other sources of this lack of confidence are our failure to agree on definitions of basic concepts such as analytic process, successful termination, or a specifically analytic treatment outcome, as well as the dearth of accepted objective measures of any of these. The scathing and at times devastating criticisms of analytic theory and technique, from analysts as well as from outsiders, have contributed to the uncertainty as well. Skolnikoff (2000), discussing analytic identity, observes, "a larger doubt has arisen in the minds of many analysts with recent criticisms from outside our field" (p. 607). In addition, the recent queries about how the analyst knows what he or she knows, including recognition of the inevitable influences of the analyst's subjectivity on what he or she *thinks* he or she knows about the patient and about patient-analyst interaction, serve to further highlight the analyst's sense of uncertainty. Lastly, and perhaps most important, there is the widespread diminution in analytic practice and income (Brauer, personal communication, 1997).

Several kinds of evidence suggest that analysts do lack confidence in their analytic work, either acknowledged or covert. In regard to the latter, I would note Kernberg's astute observation (1986, 1993) that very few analysts are willing to present their own analytic work to candidates when teaching about analysis, despite the pedagogic advantages of doing so. Although numerous factors may be involved in this reluctance, including concern about maintaining confidentiality, an underlying lack of confidence in their analytic work arguably contributes to this reluctance to expose it to candidates. Concern about confidentiality does not prevent institutes from requiring that candidates present *their* analytic work in seminars. Tuckett (1994), too, noted "a relative absence of [published] process material and a great deal of apparent nervousness about presenting it" (p. 868). Because few candidates have the opportunity to hear the work of senior analysts, I developed the Senior Analyst Presentation Program. During the last five years, at each meeting of the American Psychoanalytic Association a senior analyst presented his or her own analytic work to a small group of candidates for a full day, in the manner of a continuing case presentation. This program has been appreciatively and enthusiastically received by the candidates.

Currently, only approximately 50% of newly appointed members of the American Psychoanalytic Association go on to apply for certification, which involves further, even more intensive scrutiny of their analytic work. Here too, lack of confidence in their psychoanalytic work may well be one of the factors operating.

A feeling of uncertainty can be inferred also from analysts' reluctance to participate in studies of either their past or present analytic work. Ticho (1972), and later I, observed that graduate analysts were generally unwilling to participate in studies of the outcome of analytic treatment of their former patients. Although analysts expressed numerous concerns, Ticho and I both speculate that concern about having

	Date Jul 27, 2004	Page 1
	Order Number 1000009548	

Ship To:

    RICHARD SUGDEN
    INWOOD CLINIC
    26 SHERMAN AVENUE
    NEW YORK, NY 10040

No.	Ship Via	Ship Date
00	USPS	Jul 28, 2004

cription	Qty. Ordered
BATROSS?	1

ur order!

return it to us within 14 days for a refund or credit to your
. Number (Amazon's Order Number) .

ST ACCOMPANY YOUR RETURN. ***

order, which also included the cost of shipping based on
selected.

BOOKMONGER, LTD

611 RAMSEY AVENUE
HILLSIDE, NJ 07205
E-mail: bookmongerltd@comcast.net

AMAZON.COM

Reference	Amazon's Order No.	Custo
9548	058-8895414-7486711	AMA

Picking Sequence	ISBN #	
J24E	0881633232	TRANSFERENCE: SHIBBOLETH OF

Thanks f

You must be completely satisfied with your order or you
credit card, make sure to send us yo

*** <u>A COPY OF THIS PACKING SLIF</u>

Please Note: Amazon.com has processed the payment fc
the meth<

their analytic work scrutinized by another analyst was a major factor.

Another area of analyst behavior, although complex, may also reflect an underlying lack of confidence. Commonly, analysts experience discomfort when meeting a former or present patient outside the analyst's office, whether in the corridor or in the elevator en route to the analyst's office. One recent example that I observed was of an analyst who came to unlock the front door to the office building to admit his patient. After opening the door, the analyst turned on his heel and without a word strode rapidly down the hallway to his office, leaving his patient to follow him, mutely, several paces behind. What concerns led him to behave in such an asocial, potentially humiliating fashion? After all, Freud prescribes social tact as the basis for technique. To my mind, his behavior in the hallway reflects discomfort. In that setting, where the protective analytic rules are unclear, he may be more concerned about exposing his sense of professional uncertainty. He may be less concerned in the relative security of his familiar analytic office, where he is the arbiter of analytic rules and regulations.

Finally, we might consider the results of replicated questionnaire studies (Schachter and Luborsky, 1998) about analysts' attitudes toward reading analytic research papers versus reading clinical psychoanalytic papers. A majority of clinical analysts reported high or very high levels of confidence in their psychoanalytic theory and technique. Strikingly, there was a strong negative association; higher levels of confidence were associated with lower levels of interest in reading research papers. Various hypotheses may explain the inverse relationship. The intense assaults on psychoanalysis, coupled with the widespread decrement in analysts' practice and income (Brauer, personal communication, 1997), make it difficult to take at face value analysts' reports of such high levels of confidence in their theory and technique as an indifference to research might suggest. One hypothesis is that the reported high levels of confidence represent a defensive reaction to underlying feelings of uncertainty about analytic work. The avoidance of research papers may also reflect a concern that analytic research might highlight their own covert questions and uncertainty about their analytic work.

Need for a Shibboleth

If there is a little-acknowledged lack of confidence in analytic theory and technique, the aggrandizement of a shibboleth, specifically, the theory of transference and the technique of transference interpretation, is understandable. Any criticism or threat to the symbol, such as this book, understandably may be experienced by analysts as undermining the support for analytic identity the shibboleth provides. Even though unconvincing defenses of analytic theory and techniques might actually be damaging to the psychoanalytic profession, analysts may well maintain the shibboleth regardless of cost.

Spence (1994) sounds a related note: "psychoanalytic theory may function much more as a shared fantasy that binds its followers in a common belief system *and protects them from uncertainty and doubt*" (p. 5, italics added). Earlier, Holt (1989) had asserted: "Psychoanalysts have been living in a fool's paradise, believing that the clinical theory was soundly established when in fact very little of it has been, and virtually all of that thanks to the efforts of nonpsychoanalysts" (p. 331). He noted, "It is hard to admit how little *proof* there is for any psychoanalytic hypothesis after all these years of use, when the theory seems so clinically valuable and when such a large part of the intellectual world has adopted great hunks of the clinical theory and treats it not as a set of interesting hypotheses but as received knowledge" (p. 339). Holt concluded: "American psychoanalysis has lived for so long within a snug cocoon of myth that it seems unable to go through the predictable pains of metamorphosis into a viably progressive discipline" (p. 341). A review of the Psychoanalytic Electronic Publishing Inc. (PEP) CD-ROM disc for the five years following 1989, when Holt wrote the above, indicates that not a single paper referred to his clarion call.

The thesis of this book is twofold: (1) There are good and sufficient reasons to argue that the traditional theory of transference is neither theoretically viable nor clinically useful and should be replaced; (2) There is available a substitute for transference theory that I believe is theoretically superior and may be clinically more effective. There are three major reasons that dictate replacing the theory of transference: (1) Transference theory and its keystone, infant determinism, are not testable and therefore are not theoretically viable; (2) Traditional psychoanalytic theory has failed to provide analysts with a satisfactory professional sense of confidence in the face of numerous threats to psychoanalysis; and (3) As it has been conducted heretofore, under the guiding rubric of transference theory and historical transference interpretation, psychoanalytic treatment, while apparently helpful to many, has proved to have limited therapeutic efficacy. In later chapters, I explore the first two reasons in greater detail. Here, however, I briefly take up the third reason, because it may strike many analyst readers as too severe a judgment and thereby bear quite directly on the issue of our concern about our professional identity. Because it is not the primary focus of this book, necessarily, selected results will be presented.

Therapeutic Efficacy of Traditional Psychoanalytic Treatment

Therapeutic efficacy of traditional psychoanalytic treatment is demonstrable but it is definitely limited, and that is a major reason to consider changing and improving traditional theory of technique. The subject is exceedingly complex and has a long history. The history of studies of therapeutic efficacy contains a litany of methodological problems and manifest difficulties dealing with them. For many reasons, there has never been a controlled study of the effectiveness of traditional psychoanalytic treatment with adult neurotic patients compared to placebo and to no treatment. Such a study would require that there be a pool of comparable adult neurotic patients, that these patients be randomly assigned either to psychoanalytic treatment, other treatment, or no treatment, and that independent measures be made of treatment process, treatment outcome, and long-term follow-up. The limitations of actual studies can be assessed in comparison to this ideal study.

Wallerstein (1999a) recently reviewed the entire field of psychoanalytic therapy research in a presentation to the annual meeting of the Rapaport-Klein Study Group at Austin-Riggs Center. One typical example of what were characterized as second-generation research approaches was the New York Psychoanalytic Institute studies (Erle, 1979; Erle and Goldberg, 1979, 1984) in which 40 supervised analytic patients were studied. Twenty-four (60 percent) were judged to have benefited substantially (which is consistent with findings of earlier studies), but only 17 were judged to have been involved in a proper psychoanalytic process. Of course, in the absence of controls, it is not possible to assess the power of placebo effects or other factors. Twenty-five of the patients terminated satisfactorily, but only 11 of these were considered to have completed treatment.

Wallerstein characterized as the third-generation studies of the outcome of psychoanalysis those systematic and formal psychoanalytic therapy research projects that have attempted both to assess analytic outcomes across a significant array of cases *and* to examine the processes through which these outcomes have been reached via the intensive longitudinal study of each individual case. There were two such studies: the Boston Psychoanalytic Institute studies (Kantrowitz, Katz, and Greenman, 1989; Kantrowitz, Katz, and Paolitto, 1990a, b, c) and the Psychotherapy Research Project of the Menninger Foundation (Wallerstein, 1986, 1988). In the former, 22 supervised analytic cases were selected for prospective study; nine of the 22 (41 percent) were felt to have had a successful analytic outcome, five to have had a limited outcome, and eight to be unanalyzed. Wallerstein noted that therapeutic benefit was regularly in excess of what could be accounted for by the interpretive resolution (as best as possible) of the transference neurosis. The nature of the analyst-patient match did play a role in the outcome achieved in 12 of 17 patients.

Bachrach et al. (1991) have described the Menninger Foundation Psychotherapy Research Project as "by far the most comprehensive formal study of psychoanalysis yet undertaken" (p. 878). Wallerstein summarized the results of studies of 42 patients: (1) The benefits in the more supportive therapies seemed often enough to entail just as much structural change in the patients; indeed, benefit received seemed indistinguishable from change based on the interpretive resolution, within the transference-countertransference matrix, of unconscious intrapsychic conflicts; (2) Supportive therapeutic approaches often achieved far more than was expected of them, and psychoanalysis achieved less than had been anticipated or predicted.

Another element in considering the effectiveness of psychoanalytic treatment is the fact that analysts seem to regard successfully treated patients as if they were representative of most treated patients. A possibly apocryphal story about Pavlov illustrates this same tendency toward misrepresentation. Showing a group of visitors around his laboratory, Pavlov opened a drawer in search of a "representative" record, but was unable to find one. He opened another drawer and examined more records, but again he was unable to find "it." Embarrassed, he commented, "I don't know where that 'representative' record is; I can't seem to find it anywhere." Clearly, to label that particular record representative of many was a distortion. By publishing primarily studies of successful cases without specifying the proportion of such successful outcomes the author implies that they are representative treatments. Feelings of uncertainty and inferiority may be stirred in analysts reading these purportedly representative successes.

Individual analysts don't evaluate treatment outcome in their total practice. We have no idea whether theoretically differentiated practitioners, be they traditional analysts, object-relations analysts, self psychologists, or Kleinians, differ in the proportion of patients who benefit. Significant factors in the therapeutic benefits are probably the important personality differences among the analysts as well as their convictions and passions in their work. Such differences may be partially related to choice of theory, but they are also independent of theory. Kantrowitz (1995) has noted in particular the significance of the analyst's personality in the fit of patient and analyst and their capacity to work together.

There are occasional reports of impasses in treatment or treatment failures, but mainly we learn of these informally, in a study group or over a drink with a trusted colleague. Mitchell (1997) describes one example that came via a consultation:

> I consulted with a woman who was extremely bitter about a six-year analysis she had undergone but from which she felt she derived little. She complained about the analyst's withholding stance, about his telling her nothing about what he thought or felt and turning all questions back onto the patient with the rationale that doing so kept the analysis purely on the patient's experience. This woman told me that she had become very focused on her analyst's squeaky chair, which, she decided (probably with some degree of accuracy), betrayed discomfort on the analyst's part. The patient used the squeaks to guide her productions (either associations or silences), sometimes changing what she was doing when a squeak occurred or, defiantly continuing. These wasted years of analytic stand-off seemed both ironic and tragic: the analyst was apparently convinced that he was protecting the patient's autonomy by not interacting, while that very denial created a secret, bizarre interaction that likely included some actual features of what the analyst thought and felt, expressed in an unintended fashion [p. 13].

Rangell (2000) provides another example:

> I remember a candidate who was analyzed in a training analysis but never synthesized, or put together again. I saw him progress from an integrated and successful individual, with encapsulated neurotic traits, to a decompensated person in a

> chronic anxiety state, which spilled over into social situations
> and limited his ordinary adaptedness for the remainder of his
> life until his death [p. 460].

Numerous informal stories suggest that a significant proportion of patients are not helped by analytic treatment. The literature indicates that only approximately 50 percent of analytic patients reach a mutually agreed upon termination (Hamburg et al., 1967; Schachter, 1992), and not all mutually agreed upon terminations reflect optimum or even substantial improvement. A recent questionnaire study of the candidate members of the American Psychoanalytic Association (Craige, in press) reports further evidence of the limited success of traditional psychoanalytic treatment: 28% of this highly motivated and psychologically minded group of candidate patients were "highly disappointed" with their training analyses, conducted by our most experienced analysts.

Overall, evidence is persuasive that traditional psychoanalytic treatment provides demonstrable but limited therapeutic effectiveness. This in itself is an important reason to modify the core of psychoanalytic theory and its associated technique and here we will focus on transference theory and transference interpretation—to see if we can help more patients and help patients more. Modifying this core may represent, in Kuhn's (1962) terms, a paradigm shift. Kuhn's impression, based on a famous remark by Niels Bohr, was that a paradigm shift could take place only when the senior representatives of the discipline died, making room for the next generation with new ideas. Psychoanalysis may be approaching a state in which many of those who have long been preeminent leaders have left the scene. Strange as it may sound, the theses of transference theory and transference interpretation, as these have been traditionally understood, may be destined to pass from the scene in the near future—just as the tradition of the ovens on Rivington Street may not long outlast Jack Streit's death.

Discarding Outmoded Psychoanalytic Concepts

In the history of psychoanalysis, discarded theories—like old generals—didn't die, they just faded away. Abandoned theories were not explicitly rejected; rather, they gradually were used less and less until they ceased to be used at all. I examined the frequency of use of the term libido in the title of papers in the six psychoanalytic journals included in the PEP CD-ROM through 1994. Of the 26 titles, more than half, 14, had been published prior to 1945; the maximum number, seven, was in the decade 1935–1944. The number in each of the last five decades was as follows: 1945–1954, none; 1955–1964, three; 1965–1974, four; 1975–1984, four; and 1985–1994, one (this paper dealt with the history of libido theory). I know of no explicit refutation of libido theory in these journals.

This is not to say that no such refutation exists within psychoanalysis. In the late 1930s Rado and colleagues had left the New York Psychoanalytic Institute to found the Columbia University Center for Psychoanalytic Training and Research, which was considered dangerously divergent in its psychoanalytic views—in part because it eschewed libido theory—and the Center was almost extruded from the American Psychoanalytic Association. An articulated refutation of libido theory had been written by three analysts from the Center, Kardiner, Karush, and Ovesey, in the 1950s. Their manuscript was rejected for publication by all of the psychoanalytic journals. Having no other recourse, the authors turned to a nonpsychoanalytic journal, the *Journal of Nervous and Mental Diseases*, which did publish their paper (1959).

The question of how theoretical changes occur in psychoanalysis was discussed by Eagle (1993). If analysts no longer think in accord with core Freudian propositions, how did they get to think the way they do today? He concluded that criticisms of traditional psychoanalytic theory have essentially been assimilated into so-called contemporary psychoanalysis without acknowledging the criticisms, "*without explicit acknowledgment that these earlier criticisms were valid, or that they have, in fact, been assimilated*" (p. 381).

There are a few striking deviations from the long history of allowing analytic concepts deemed no longer useful very quietly to fade away. Arlow and Brenner (1964) explicitly discarded topographic theory, Brenner (1994, 1998) articulated rejection of structural theory, and Inderbitzin and Levy (2000) recommended abandoning the concept of regression. This book is an attempt to extend the approach of these authors in specifying the bases for rejecting a psychoanalytic theory that is outmoded, an approach that I believe is far more conducive to fostering the development of theory in our profession.

Numerous analysts have already developed substitutes for transference theory, which either minimize or actually eliminate the role of childhood experience as a determinant of adult feelings and fantasies. The substitutes refer to the entire internal world that the patient brings to the analysis and all of the expressions of this world in the patient-analyst interaction. What is confusing is that these substitutes are referred to by the term *transference*, although they no longer conform to Freud's transference theory. Further, no explicit rationale is offered for discarding Freud's transference theory, which they no longer find useful, and no new terms are proposed for the substitutes for traditional transference theory.

The purpose of this book is to provide an explicit rationale for discarding Freud's transference theory, and to propose an alternative theory of technique that focuses on examining the meaning of the patient's current conscious and unconscious feelings and fantasies about the analyst in terms of their defensive and adaptive functions. The impact of the analyst's conscious and unconscious feelings and fantasies about the patient are also scrutinized and utilized in analyzing the interactions between patient and analyst and developing inferences about what I have termed the patient's "Habitual Relationship Patterns" as they are manifested primarily in relation to the analyst. Understanding the patient's current Habitual Relationship Patterns, based on observable interactions between patient and analyst in the here and now, may throw light, by extrapolation into the past, on the meaning of earlier experiences, including those of childhood, rather than the other way around. I argue that treatment based on this rationale retains the fundamentals of psychoanalysis, is superior theoretically, and may be more effective clinically.

Summary

For many psychoanalysts, holding tightly to the traditions of psychoanalytic theory buttressses their identity as analysts. They do so, at least in part, to deal with a troublesome sense of underlying uncertainty about their analytic work. Transference theory is held to be at the core of psychoanalytic theory; it has become the shibboleth of psychoanalysis. My thesis is that transference theory is not theoretically viable, may not be optimally effective clinically, and should be replaced. Review of the efficacy of traditional psychoanalytic treatment indicates undesirable limitations in the proportion of patients helped and the extent of their improvement. These limitations impel efforts to improve the psychoanalytic theory of technique so as to enhance the benefits of psychoanalytic treatment. Transference theory may have become less a shibboleth and, indeed, more an albatross.

Other analysts have found Freud's transference theory wanting and have developed substitutes for it. Unfortunately, they continue to refer to these new substitutes by the term *transference*, and fail to provide an explicit rationale for ceasing to use Freud's transference theory. This book provides an explicit rationale for discarding traditional transference theory and proposes that treatment should not focus on the putative childhood origins of the patient's conscious and unconscious feelings and fantasies about the analyst, but rather on the meaning of these current feelings and fantasies as manifested in Habitual Relationship Patterns with the analyst in terms of a defense analysis of the patient's present unconscious. Examining the analyst's conscious and unconscious feelings and fantasies about the patient provides clues to develop inferences about the patient's contributions to patient-analyst interactions in the here and now.

2

Causation in "Transference" Theory
Historical Origins

I have endeavored to demolish a convenient and attractive theory of the aphasias, and having succeeded in this, I have been able to put into its place something less obvious and less complete. I only hope that the theory I have proposed will do more justice to the facts and will expose the real difficulties better than the one I have rejected. It is with a clear exposition of the problems that the elucidation of a scientific subject begins.

—Sigmund Freud, "On Aphasia"

In the "Postscript" to the Dora case, Freud (1905) first enunciated his theory of transference (Übertragung) which he steadfastly maintained, with some variations, for the remainder of his life. His theory was an *etiological* theory that relied on an *historical* approach to the individual to explain the *sexual cause* for neurotic symptoms. Freud explains:

> What are transferences? They are new editions or facsimiles of the impulses and phantasies which are aroused and made conscious during the progress of the analysis; but they have this peculiarity, which is characteristic for their species, that they replace some earlier person by the person of the physician. To put it another way: a whole series of psychological

experiences are revived, not as belonging to the past, but as applying to the person of the physician at the present moment [p. 116].

Freud is saying that "transferences" are psychological experiences (i.e., feelings and fantasies) that originated in the past, in childhood, and are directed currently toward the psychoanalyst. In this unitary concept of "transference," Freud has merged two separate items: one is the presence of certain current feelings and fantasies that the patient directs toward the psychoanalyst, and the other is an *etiological theory* about the *cause* of these current feelings and fantasies. His etiological hypothesis is that they originated during childhood toward some person then in their lives, and subsequently they are displaced or transferred onto the analyst in the present day. Further, this transfer of feelings from the past onto the present necessarily involves *sexual* feelings.

In this chapter I explore the historical origins of Freud's focus on the etiology of the neuroses, the core of his theory of "transference." In the next chapter I examine Freud's views of the relationship between "transference," neurotic symptoms, and sexual etiology.

In the closing decades of the nineteenth century, psychiatry for the first time was brought into close contact with the mass of "noninsane," nonhospitalized men and women who we diagnose today as neurotic patients (Zilboorg, 1941). What was Freud's approach to these patients? Freud had at least three options. First, he could study the treatments of neurotics; the therapeutic approaches of Charcot and Bernheim and other practitioners emphasized hypnosis, whereas surgeons tried to cure hysterical symptoms through a variety of operations, including removal of an ovary, cauterization and surgical removal of the clitoris as well as castration. Second, he could study the pathophysiology of the neuroses—how do the symptoms operate in the minds of the patients?—analagous to performing autopsies to identify which organs were diseased. This was the path of his celebrated contemporary, Pierre Janet. Third, he could explore the *causes* of the neuroses. Freud eventually became known for his contribution in all three areas, but his intellectual passion plainly focused on this last, on etiology. It is therefore instructive to consider this choice in the context of the theories of etiology of neuroses extant at that time.

Mental diseases were primarily, though not entirely, thought to be due to brain dysfunction caused by some inherited degeneration. Magnan considered mental disease primarily hereditary. Kraepelin divided mental diseases into those caused by external conditions, which were curable, and those caused by inherent constitutional factors, which were incurable. Charcot believed hysteria was most often produced by the combination of a physical, organic morbid cause and heredity. It is true that physical traumas and stress were conceived by Charcot as triggering mental disease. Janet had even more strongly recognized the importance of unconscious factors in the formation and manifestation of hysteria, but he was unable to rid himself of the feeling that hysteria was the result of a constitutional weakness of the nervous system (Zilboorg, 1941). Overall, mental diseases, neuroses included, were still thought to be caused by organic dysfunction of the brain due to inherited predispositions.

The Focus on Etiology

I postulate that there are at least three sources of Freud's fascination with etiology: the Helmholtz school, Koch's postulates, and Darwin's theory of evolution. All three influences clearly originated from outside his consulting room—separate from experience with patients. Ernest Jones (1953) wrote of Freud's exposure to the Helmholtz school: "Freud was deeply imbued with the principles of causality and determinism, so pronounced in the Helmholtz school that had dominated his early scientific discipline" (p. 245). Newton (1995) wrote that Freud's teacher, Ernst Brücke, and Brücke's colleague, Hermann Helmholtz, "had led a revolution against the romantic vitalistic notions about human physiology that were still in currency in the mid-nineteenth century" (p. 30). They prevailed with a scientific rationalism that involved the application of quantitative materialism to the study of the nervous system. Jones described this belief: "Physical energies alone cause effects—somehow" (p. 42). In sexuality, or "libido," to use the energic term of that time, Freud evidently felt he had found a force that could be understood physically and quantitatively, even if it could only be "measured" by its presumed behavioral effects; his was an essentially tautological position that nonetheless might be heuristically valuable.

A second important source of Freud's keen interest in etiology was Koch's 1881 breakthrough in bacteriology, defining the principles for establishing the specific cause of a bacterial disease (Fischer-Homberger, 1975; Macmillan, 1976; 1991; Carter, 1980; May, 1999). If a specific etiological agent could be identified for a particular physical disease, why couldn't the same be done for neuroses? Macmillan asserts, "The framework Freud developed for establishing the causes of the neuroses was a revolutionary adaptation of Koch's postulates. Prior to Freud, no one had set out any kind of logical system by which any of the factors supposedly causing neuroses could be judged, and no one had applied principles from physical medicine to identify the specific causes" (p. 100).

In the *Studies on Hysteria* (Breuer and Freud, 1895) it was Breuer (1895) who commented about the "specifically tubercular" modifications of pulmonary tissue caused by Koch's bacillus in his discussion of the clinical picture of hysteria "which has been empirically discovered and is based on observation, in just the same way as tubercular pulmonary phthisis" (p. 187). Freud (1895b), in "A Reply to Criticisms of My Paper on Anxiety Neurosis," gives Phthisis Pulmonium as an example of a complete etiological schematic picture, whose specific cause is the Bacillus Kochii. Freud discusses preconditions: the specific cause, "which is never missing in any case in which the effect takes place, and which moreover suffices, if present in the required quantity or intensity, to achieve the effect"; and concurrent causes, "which operate alongside of the preconditions and the specific cause in satisfying the aetiological equation." Freud adds: "The schematic picture for the aetiology of anxiety neurosis seems to me to be on the same lines . . . with the specific cause a sexual factor, in the sense of a deflection of sexual tension away from the psychical field" (pp. 136, 137).

Macmillan (1991) notes that Freud first applied Koch's postulates to the cause of the actual neuroses rather than to hysteria. This application, he maintains further, was not valid. Freud believed that the sexual conditions along with the preconditions defined the sufficient conditions for the actual neuroses. Freud (1895a) wrote that the sexual factor (sexual frustration) "suffices, if present in the required quantity or intensity, to achieve the effect, provided only that the preconditions are also fulfilled" (p. 136). But, Macmillan adds,

> Freud had not examined normal subjects—"controls" if you wish—to see whether the presumed cause was at work in them. . . . He had, therefore, not provided the logical equivalent of Koch's inoculation condition. . . . All he had done was to show the presence of precondition and the specific sexual factor in each case. All that meant was that they were among

the necessary conditions. Nowhere had he demonstrated that by *always* causing the neurosis the specific factor and the pre-conditions were the sufficient conditions [1992, p. 108].

Darwin's Theory of Evolution

A third and perhaps most important outside-the-consulting-room source of Freud's attraction to the search for the etiology of the neuroses was Darwin's theory of evolution. Ritvo (1990) has written extensively on the importance of Darwin's ideas to the young Freud. Darwin formulated an etiological theory of species formation by conceiving of and studying the early history of species development. The analogical possibilities intrigued Freud, who thought that he could use a historical approach to explore the early childhood history of the individual and formulate an etiological theory of the adult's neurotic symptoms.

Ritvo has documented Darwin's influence on Freud during the latter's attendance at the *Sperlgymnasium* from 1865 to 1873. Freud later recalled that the theories of Darwin strongly attracted him during those years. Ritvo (1990) has noted: "Darwinism was at its zenith when Freud entered the medical faculty at the University of Vienna" in 1873, at the age of 17 (p. 113). Freud referred to Darwin explicitly 27 times in 17 of his writings and had 8 books by Darwin in his library in England. Freud's interest in Darwin persisted throughout his life. In 1938, shortly after his arrival in London as a refugee from the Nazi invasion of Austria, Freud was invited to sign the prestigious book of the Royal Society. Ritvo (1990) quotes from Freud's expression of pleasure in a letter to his friend Arnold Zweig:

> The most pleasing was the visit of two secretaries of the Royal Society who brought me the hallowed book of the Society to sign, as a new pain . . . prevented my going out. They left a facsimile of the book with me, and if you were at my house, I could show you the signatures from I. Newton to Charles Darwin. Good Company! [p. 198].

In addition to Freud's use of a historical approach to develop an etiological theory, Darwin's influences can be discerned in Freud's application of gradualism and continuity to his theory of "transference," his utilization of the idea of the inheritance of acquired characteristics, as well as the theory that ontogeny recapitulates phylogeny. Freud's theory of "transference" is so imbricated with the theory of evolution, as understood in the late nineteenth century, that a brief historical review of that theory is in order to illustate how it provides a framework for Freud's conceptualizations.

Let me start with a brief comment about the historical context in which Darwin himself worked. During his student days at Cambridge in the 1830s, and for a decade or two later, natural science authorities used catastrophanism to explain observable changes in the fossil record. Catastrophanism, also termed *saltation* (by leaps and bounds), in contrast to gradualism, used the change from water to steam as an example. This catastrophist approach to the problem of speciation called for sudden appearances and disappearances of species. Darwin's approach, of course, was the opposite, hypothesizing that one species gradually changed into another.

Parenthetically, when Darwin and Alfred R. Wallace presented their theory of natural selection to the Linnaean Society of London in 1858, the scientist S. Jones (1997) writes: "It had little impact. The president (a dentist interested in reptiles) claimed that the year had not 'been marked by any of those striking discoveries which at once revolutionize, so to speak, the department of science'" (p. 39).

Darwin and Wallace's evolutionary theory of natural selection held to continuity and to the related characteristic of gradualism, despite the warning by Darwin's friend T. H. Huxley that his idea of gradualism was neither necessary nor easily defensible. Darwin did not agree, and his view of gradualism is exemplified by a remark attributed to Linnaeus, "nature does not make leaps" (Lewis, 1997). Ritvo (1990) quotes Darwin as predicting that gradualism would be of even greater value for psychology: "In the distant future I see open fields for far more important researches. Psychology will be based on a new foundation, that of the necessary requirement of each mental power and capacity by gradation" (p. 109). Freud's generation was also familiar with gradualism from sources as varied as Goethe and Lamarck (p. 46).

Abrupt, major changes produce discontinuity, but gradualism, proceeding by steps or degrees, changing by fine, slight, or insensible gradations, is essential to continuity. It is this continuity that is critical to the theory of "transference," which hypothesizes direct continuity from the affections and antipathies of childhood to the attitude toward the physician. Macmillan (1991) notes that "the assumption of continuity was so central that Freud (1904) was eventually to say of the observations that he had made while filling the gaps [in the patient's associations] that they became 'the determining factor of his entire theory'" (Freud, 1904, p. 251, cited by Macmillan, 1991, p. 118).

Freud's version of Darwinism, which reduces all species development to natural selection based on gradualism and continuity, provides a framework for Freud's theory of "transferences." Paleontologists, however, have since developed more sophisticated theories of evolution. Actually, Darwin did not claim that only natural selection caused all evolutionary changes. Sulloway (1998) quotes Wallace, codiscoverer of the theory of natural selection, to the same effect. The mind, Wallace reasoned, "was capable of far more impressive feats of intellectual ability than could possibly have been useful to our ancestors living in a state of nature" (p. 34).

Stephen Jay Gould argues that reducing all species development to natural selection based entirely on gradualism and continuity is one of the great fallacies commonly made in evolutionary argument. Three additional forces are applicable to individual as well as species development. The first is the concept of punctuated equilibrium; new species originate in a geological "moment"; species do not emerge gradually over geological periods. The second focuses on the importance of nonadaptive side consequences, which he has termed "spandrels." Gould (1997) writes:

> Since organisms are . . . highly integrated entities, any adaptive change must automatically "throw off" a series of structural byproducts . . . in the case of an architectural spandrel itself, the triangular space "left over" between a rounded arch and the rectangular frame of wall and ceiling. Such byproducts may later be coopted for useful purposes, but they didn't arise as adaptations. . . . *Current utility* must not be misused to infer an adaptive *origin*. The snail umbilicus, e.g., arises nonadaptively as a spandrel—a necessary geometric consequence of growth by winding a tube around an axis. The fact that a *very few* species adapt this space secondarily as a brood chamber doesn't challenge the claim for a nonadaptive origin of the space itself. . . . Similarly, many universal features of human cognition . . . probably arise as spandrels of a general consciousness evolved for other reasons (almost surely adaptive) [p. 57].

Third, Gould points to the theoretical importance of the roles of contingency and chance in the history of life. Lewis (1997) also emphasizes the impact of random events and chance encounters on development: "We all witness this chaos in our lives and those of others" (p. 177). Jones (1997) makes a similar point about the role of chance in the evolution of species:

> In biology, sometimes things just happen. They do not demand the hidden hand of adaptation. The females of a certain moth and of the African elephant produce exactly the same complex chemical, a sexual signal known as pheromone. This attracts males of the species (which must be riskier for the moth than for the other partner in the relationship). One could no doubt think up an evolutionary hypothesis. . . . None is called for: evolution is so protean in its doings that it will sometimes do the same thing twice, just by chance. No special explanation is required [p. 41].

Within evolutionary science gradualism has clearly been discarded as invalid. As Palombo (1999) notes, "Darwin's gradualism had a major problem from the beginning. The fossil record does not support it. The fossil remains of a typical species appear suddenly, without transitional types, last for millions of years with little change, and then disappear with equal suddenness" (p. 10). Silverman (1981) and Lewis (1997) also reject the continuity and gradualism of early evolutionary theory. Thus, Gould, Lewis, Jones, Palombo, and Silverman all return to a version of the catastrophanism or saltation that predominated in evolutionary theory more than 150 years ago. Thus, the version of Darwin's theory of evolution which Freud utilized as a framework for his theory of "transferences" is no longer valid.

The Historical Approach

Ritvo quotes Haeckel (1909) from Rádl (1930), Darwin's German champion and interpreter: "Development is now the magic word by means of which we shall solve the riddles by which we are surrounded, or at least move along the road toward their solution . . . the historical approach, which Darwin had used with such world-shaking success to find a scientific solution to the problem of species, was the key to every problem" (Ritvo, 1990, pp. 17–18). Ritvo comments in regard to Darwin's influence on Freud, that the "historical approach of development and evolution is predominant" (p. 2).

Ritvo herself adds that

> Freud's youthful interest in Darwin with the idea of the impor-
> tance of the past as a clue to the understanding of the present
> . . . no doubt added to his excitement over, and receptivity to,
> Breuer's communication in 1882 of his cathartic treatment of
> Anna O. (Breuer and Freud, 1895) in which Breuer had dis-
> covered how the past determined the present: "The [past] expe-
> riences which released the original affect, the excitation of
> which was then converted into somatic phenomenon, are
> described by us as *psychical traumas*, and the pathological
> manifestation arising in this way, as *hysterical symptoms of
> traumatic origin* [p. 209].

Freud reiterates this view: "the fundamental fact [is] that the symptoms of hysterical patients are founded upon scenes in their past
lives" (Freud 1914a, cited in Ritvo, p. 19). Ritvo concludes: "For
Freud one of the most continuously useful concepts from biology
was the historical approach proclaimed by Darwin in the *Origin*"
(p. 411).

Two other views of Darwin influenced Freud. Darwin subscribed
both to the Lamarckian idea of the inheritance of acquired characteristics and the theory that ontogeny recapitulates phylogeny, referring
to the repetition of the ancestor's evolution in the development of the
embryo, larva, or child. In 1897, when Freud was no longer convinced
of the reality of the childhood seductions on which he had based his
theory of the origin of neuroses, he turned to these aspects of evolutionary theory (Sulloway, 1979).

Jones (1953) quotes Freud's (1914d) predicament:

> When this etiology broke down under its own improbabil-
> ity and under contradiction in definitely ascertainable cir-
> cumstances, the result at first was helpless bewilderment. . . .
> [but] if hysterics trace back their symptoms to fictitious
> traumas, this new fact signifies that they create such scenes
> in phantasy, and psychical reality requires to be taken into
> account alongside actual reality [quoted in Jones, pp. 266–267].

Rather than discarding his seduction theory, and acknowledging that
he did not know what caused neuroses, Freud salvaged it and retained
his hypothesis, by concluding that the fictitious trauma, the childhood

fantasy, was our phylogenetic inheritance. Freud had difficulty acknowledging that he did not know something. He believed, for example, that he knew how analytic treatment cured the patient (1937b), though many analysts believe we still don't know how a cure has come about.

Freud (1915b) believed it was "still legitimate to assume that the neuroses must also bear witness to the history of the mental development of mankind" (p. 11). Certainly by the time he published "Totem and Taboo" (1913b) Freud was committed to the idea that the Oedipus complex, the psychological core of adult neuroses, was inherited phylogenetically. This adherence enabled Freud to retain a historical view of the etiology of neurosis. Freud (1939) reiterates his conviction that

> Human beings originally lived in small hordes, each of which was under the despotic rule of an older male who appropriated all the females and castigated or disposed of the younger males, including his sons . . . this patriarchal system ended in a rebellion by the sons, who banded together against their father, overcame him and devoured him in common. . . . To this day I hold firmly to this construction [p. 131].

Kerr (1994) marvels:

> Save for Freud's justifiably great stature, and the sweet reasonableness of his prose style, the effort might have been ridiculed. Yet, this was the work that made the "Oedipus complex" central among the interpretive rubrics of psychoanalysis. . . . [O]ne also has to wonder what kind of intellectual climate [within psychoanalysis] allowed such a maneuver to go unquestioned [pp. 455–456].

At age 30, Freud felt he had to leave his research at the university in order to support his yearned for, comfortable bourgeois life with Martha Bernays. Freud diverged in his subsequent research from the main trunk of biology. He "became . . . an outsider in biology after 1886, retaining interest but no longer a student or a participant abreast of its advances as he had once been" (Ritvo, 1990, p. 52). Consequently, Freud failed to recognize the growing criticism of, and ultimate rejection of, both Darwin's gradualism and the hypothesis that ontogeny recapitulates phylogeny. The inheritance of acquired characteristics was rejected by biologists by 1930. With it went the theory of phylogenetic memory. Although psychoanalysts tried to acquaint Freud with these theoretical changes, he dismissed their appeals and stoutly maintained both Darwinian conceptions as basic to psychoanalytic theory. Ritvo (1990) observes:

> Faced at the very end of his life with this change in biological thought from that familiar to him from Darwin's writings and from his university training in evolutionary biology . . . Freud felt that he could not "do without this factor in biological evolution. . . . [Without it] we shall not advance a step further along the path we entered on, either in analysis or in group psychology. The audacity cannot be avoided. . . ." The strongest evidence he could offer in support of "the presence of memory traces in the archaic heritage" was the residual phenomena of the work of analysis which call for a phylogenetic derivation" [Freud, 1939, p. 100, quoted in Ritvo, 1990, pp. 72–73].

Sadly, Freud would not acknowledge that "the residual phenomena of the work of analysis" remained neither known nor understood, but instead maintained a phylogenetic explanation in the face of collegial and scientific judgment that such an explanation was untenable. From the first, this phylogenetic explanation was also the basis of Freud's belief that each individual progressed through a predictable series of sexual stages—oral, anal, and phallic—reflecting both gradualism and continuity.

Yet another aspect of Darwin's theory, the idea of "the struggle for existence," an external conflict, was applied to the internal workings of the individual. Internal conflict became a central Freudian tenet in understanding the psyche, and thus a focus of analytic technique. Both the centrality of internal conflict and his mnemic concept of affect— ("when a similar [primeval traumatic] situation occurs [affects] are revived like mnemic symbols" (Freud, 1926c, p. 93)—minimize, if not ignore, the external, reality adaptations of the person. Ritvo (1990) asserts: "Freud's successors have demonstrated that conflict is not the whole story for psychoanalysis any more than it has turned out to be for biology" (p. 63). Two contemporaries, Hartmann (1939) and Rado (Roazen and Swerdloff, 1995), played prominent roles in developing the recognition of the importance of external adaptation while maintaining the concept of internal conflict.

Theory of Evolution and Psychoanalytic Theory of Individual Development

There are intriguing parallels between current versions of the evolutionary theory of species development and some modern psychoanalytic theories of individual development. All three of the concepts that Gould identified as playing a role in species development also can be applied to individual development. In the psychoanalytic theory of development, "punctuated equilibrium" would refer to the view that certain changes in individual development occur relatively suddenly, rather than as a slow, gradual modification over time. Puberty would be a biological example. Further, a particular experience, either dreadfully traumatic or powerfully positive, may also profoundly impact individual development. Since the latter may be a random event, it also incorporates the role of contingency in development.

The original "transference" (childhood fantasy or feeling) may or may not have served a similar and even identical defensive purpose to that of the current "transference." An early fantasy or feeling may have developed nondefensively, that is, for some purpose unrelated to defense, or may have developed to serve an altogether different age-appropriate defensive purpose. Feelings and fantasies that originally developed nondefensively, and those that served some defensive goal, may become transformed to serve either an adaptive function or a current defensive purpose in the current "transference."

The application of these concepts to individual development is not new. Gordon Allport (1937), the internationally known social psychologist, proposed the concept of the functional autonomy of motives decades ago:

> Functional autonomy regards adult motives as varied, and as self-sustaining, contemporary systems, growing out of antecedent systems, but functionally independent of them. . . . The young man who once wanted to become a politician because of his early father fixation may become interested in politics for its own sake. . . . The life of a tree is continuous with that of its seed, but the seed no longer sustains and nourishes the full-grown tree. . . . Drives remain with us and even in complex adult motives the past is sometimes, to some degree, still alive in the present. But our task is to discover how much of the past is fire and how much of it is ashes [pp. 217–219].

A comparable conception was proposed by the analyst Hartmann (1958) in an effort to salvage libido theory: libido, the energy of the sexual drives, could be neutralized, that is, desexualized, and thereby become the energy for autonomous drives, independent of the original sexual drives. Both Allport's and Hartmann's clearly articulated concepts have been ignored, however, in discussions of "transference" in the psychoanalytic literature; "transference" has remained directly connected to its putative libidinal and aggressive childhood origins.

Sixty years later, Allport's ideas again have acquired currency. Let me turn briefly to current considerations of gradualism and continuity in individual development. Cohler and Galatzer-Levy (2000) assert that there is little value in casting the course of life in terms of a series of stages or issues to be negotiated successively across the course of life, as well as little evidence for the extent of continuity over time. Parenthetically, it should be noted that the absence of stages does not mean that the alternative is continuity; random fluctuations are one possibility.

This position, however, runs directly against the grain of our long-standing subjective experience of self. If many discontinuous mechanisms operate in individual development, how then does the individual maintain a continuing sense of self? Isn't each individual's subjective experience that his or her identity has persisted unchanged throughout development an argument for the validity of continuity? A comparable notion is reflected in Gertrude Stein's remark that "We are always the same age inside."

Other writers have also noted this difficulty in giving up the notion of continuity. Perelberg (1999) observes that "Freud pointed out the fluidity that is the hallmark of identificatory processes. This fluidity contrasts with the individual quest for a *coherent* identity, a sense of cohesiveness that is denied him by the very nature of the psychic apparatus" (p. 39). She concludes that the belief that identity can be seen as stable and coherent is illusory. This commonsense notion of the internal subjective experience of a persistent sense of individual identity belongs with other folk beliefs.

Lewis (1997), following Nozick, explains:

Imagine we have a row boat built of wood and that each year we replace one board of the rowboat with a new board. At the end of fifty years none of the original boards of the rowboat remain, and yet, at no point in this sequence of events have we said that this is not "the same rowboat," nor, for that matter, would we think that there was not a continuous change in the boat. But, if we had replaced all of the boards of the rowboat at once, we would say that "this is not the same rowboat," and that the change was not continuous. When the parts of the rowboat were slowly replaced, what we have been calling gradualism, we were willing to assume a continuous process of change, a change that did not alter the identity of the rowboat. . . . In like fashion, people are willing to assume that the changes that occur over their fifty years are continuous and therefore do not alter their identity [p. 66].

All of Japan's culturally important wooden structures, its temples and pagodas, have been replaced in this fashion. Despite these repetitive and numerous replacements the Japanese still regard them as the oldest wooden structures in the world. To them such a characterization is compelling. So, too, for the individual is the belief that he or she has always been the same self.

Summary

"Transference" comprises two elements: the patient's feelings and fantasies about the analyst, and the etiological theory of the cause of these feelings and fantasies. Though his interests included the modes of treatment of the neuroses and the exploration of how the mind of the neurotic worked, Freud's greatest intellectual passion focussed on the etiology of the neuroses; this bent was the essential precursor of how he came to conceptualize "transference" theory. His understanding of etiology, furthermore, was based on at least three influences from outside the consulting room, that is, outside his experience with patients: the Helmholz school, Koch's postulates, and most important I contend, Darwin's theory of evolution. Freud developed a hypothesis of a specific, uniform etiology of the neuroses, that of phylogenetically based childhood sexual fantasy, which he believed through gradualism and continuity directly caused adult psychopathology and the patient's unrealistic feelings about the analyst. Freud was unable to accept the later judgment of the scientific community that two of Darwin's theories—ontogeny recapitulates phylogeny and species develop gradually and continuously—are invalid.

3
Origins of Sexual Etiology

It is in the admission of ignorance and the admission of uncertainty that there is a hope for the continuous motion of human beings in some direction [progress] that doesn't get confined, permanently blocked, as it has so many times before in various periods in the history of man.

—Richard P. Feynman,
"Surely You're Joking, Mr. Feynman!"

Freud was convinced that neurotic symptoms are an expression of the patient's sexual feelings. In the "Postscript" to the Dora case (1905) he writes that sexuality

> provides the motive power for every single symptom [of hysteria], and for every single manifestation of a symptom. The symptoms of the disease are nothing else than *the patient's sexual activity* . . . sexuality is the key to the problem of the psychoneuroses and of the neuroses in general. No one who disdains the key will ever be able to unlock the door [p. 115].

What is the relationship between the patient's symptoms, conceptualized as forms of sexual activity, and "transferences," the patient's intense, unrealistic feelings toward the analyst? Freud used "transference" in its traditional form for the first time in the aforementioned "Postscript":

> It may be safely said that during psycho-analytic treatment the formation of new symptoms is invariably stopped. But the productive powers of the neurosis are by no means extinguished; they are occupied in the creation of a special class of mental structures, for the most part unconscious, to which the name of *"transferences"* may be given [p. 116].

Thus, Freud indicates, new symptomatic expressions of the patient's sexual activity are arrested and replaced by "transferences." Because symptoms are expressions of sexual activity, the substitute for symptoms, "transferences," must also be expressions of the patient's sexual activity.

That "transferences," intense unrealistic feelings toward the analyst, seemed symptomlike to Freud is not surprising. "Transferences" not only represent a "false connection" and thus are unrealistic, but like neurotic symptoms, they are unconsciously generated. This relationship between symptomlike "transferences" and sexual activity was important in Freud's early development of "transference." Lack of appreciation of this connection he made between "transferences" and sexual activity is a result of Freud's failure explicitly to articulate his view; it was left to the reader to make the inference. It is not emphasized in later "transference" theory, though Freud never discarded it.

Freud's derivation of the sexual basis of "transferences" now seems contrived and insubstantial. He asserts that patients in treatment do not develop new symptoms, but develop "transferences" instead, though he provides no evidence that one is a substitute for the other. The fact that B follows A temporally is no indication of any relationship between B and A. Further, he does not substantiate his assumption that patients regularly would be expected to develop new symptoms in treatment, though that is a necessary condition for his hypothesis that instead, patients substitute "transferences" of new symptoms. Absent evidence that patients regularly develop new symptoms in treatment, a simpler, more parsimonious view of his observation is that during treatment, patients develop "transferences" for unknown reasons that need to be explored.

For Freud (1905), "transferences" were an expression of the patient's sexual activity. But "transferences" were facsimiles of "a whole series of psychological experiences" (p. 116), not just sexual experiences. Freud described Dora enacting unrealistic feelings toward him that were other than sexual: "She took her revenge on me as she wanted to take revenge on him [Herr K], and deserted me as she believed herself to have been deceived and deserted by him" (p. 119). Were these feelings of Dora's expressions of her sexual activity?

Freud's statement that "transferences" are expressions of sexual activity is difficult, even impossible, to clarify from his writing with any certainty. Perhaps he means that the feeling or attitude is unconsciously derived from sexual feelings, in the same way that he believes that the trait of curiosity derives from unconscious wishes to explore and examine sexual activity. Whereas for some individuals such unconscious impulses undoubtedly play a role in curiosity, there may also be other than sexual sources for expressions of curiosity. Further, infants exhibit a biologically based drive for curiosity which seems unrelated to sexuality. Thus, by asserting that "transferences," such as Dora enacting her wish for revenge, are expressions of sexuality, Freud has taken behavior that can be a function of multiple determinants and reduced it to a single determinant, sexuality. He took the same unitary position regarding the generation of neurotic symptoms. While some practitioners before Freud had identified a sexual etiology as one of the causes of neurotic symptoms, Freud insisted it was the only—the exclusive—cause of all neurotic symptoms.

The Specific Sexual Etiology of the Neuroses

Freud early asserted a sexual etiology both for neuroses and for "transferences." The latter, however, was not explicitly articulated and was not elaborated by him later when he dealt with "transferences" that are not manifestly sexual in content. Freud's unitary position and conviction about sexual etiology is thus best explored in relation to the neuroses rather than in relation to "transferences."

In terms of texts, Freud (1893–1895) began discarding heredity as the etiological factor in hysteria when, in discussing his treatment of Fräulein Elisabeth von R, he focused on her motives for substituting physical feelings for mental ones. He noted that this was not the kind of questions that physicians, who assumed an etiology of inherited degeneration, were in the habit of raising. In relation to another patient, Miss Lucy R, he dismisses the role of heredity on empirical grounds:

> I am tempted to regard it as a model instance of one particu-
> lar type of hysteria, namely the form of illness which can be
> acquired even by a person of sound heredity, as a result of

appropriate experiences. . . . A neuropathic disposition, as generally understood, is something different. It is already marked out by the amount of the subject's hereditary taint or the sum of his individual psychical abnormalities. As far as my information goes, there was no trace in Miss Lucy R. of either of these factors [Breuer and Freud, 1893–1895, p. 122].

What made Freud take this large step away from the received wisdom of his time, that neuroses were caused primarily by inherited dispositions, and move to exploring other causes? He had shifted from studying the mechanisms of neurotic symptoms to probing for psychological causes, and this, he would maintain, is what led him to his theory of sexual etiology.

Earlier, in July 1883, Breuer, a distinguished Viennese physician, mentor and friend of Freud, had told Freud about his attempt to treat a hysteric woman, Anna O, by a cathartic method. As Jones (1953) reported it, the patient's belief that she had become pregnant with Breuer's baby—which was a fantasy or conversion symptom—so horrified Breuer that he hospitalized her. Newton (1995) describes Breuer telling Freud "a harrowing personal epic of a failed treatment" (p. 101). Current research, discussed later, belies the historical veracity of this account.

Two years later, in 1885, Freud visited Charcot to observe his work with hysterical patients and was quite impressed with "the great man." Freud mentioned Breuer's treatment of Anna O to Charcot, but Charcot evinced no interest. After his return to Vienna, Freud married Martha Bernays in 1886 and began a private practice devoted to patients with neurological disorders who were typically treated with the neurologist's standard repertory of hydrotherapy, electrical treatments, massage, and rest cures. Between 1887 and 1889 Freud shifted to the treatment of neurotic patients. This reflected more than a chance shift in referral patterns.

On 15 October 1886, Freud had given a paper entitled "On Male Hysteria" before the Viennese Society of Physicians. His paper was met with a distinctly cool reception to which Jones (1953) refers as follows: "When an enthusiastic, perhaps over-enthusiastic young man sets out to announce to his seniors (mostly his former teachers) that they have a lot to learn and that he is prepared to enlighten them, the inevitable response is defensive, usually taking the form of minimizing the novelty of the information and damping the exaltation of the speaker"(p. 230).

The distinctly cool reception was reprised ten years later when Freud (1914a) presented his latest discovery, the seduction theory. Freud described his own reaction to his earlier presentation on that occasion.

> I innocently addressed a meeting of the Vienna Society . . . with Krafft-Ebing in the chair, expecting that the material losses I had willingly undergone would be made up for by the interest and recognition of my colleagues. I treated my discoveries as ordinary contributions to science and hoped they would be received in the same spirit. But the silence my communications met with, the void which formed itself about me, the hints that were conveyed to me, gradually made me realize that assertions on the part played by sexuality in the aetiology of the neuroses cannot count upon meeting with the same kind of treatment as other communications. I was one of those who have "disturbed the sleep of the world" . . . and that I could not reckon upon objectivity and tolerance. . . . I was prepared to accept the fate that sometimes accompanies such discoveries . . . science would ignore me entirely during my lifetime. . . . Meanwhile, like Robinson Crusoe, I settled down as comfortably as possible on my desert island [pp. 21–22].

Freud was unable to conceive that this group of esteemed senior colleagues genuinely disagreed with his theory. He dismissed their disagreement by labelling it as irrational "resistance." Unfortunately, he took that same tack in later years in regard to disagreements by Adler, Jung, Rank, and others (Bergmann, 1997).

Wagner-Jauregg (1950), who was present on the first occasion in 1886, later recalled Freud falling into disgrace with the faculty and commented, "He was thus a neurological practitioner without patients" (p. 72). But Breuer helped Freud by beginning to refer neurotic patients whom he himself did not wish to treat.

Freud thus shifted to treating neurotic patients, and tried Breuer's cathartic method in 1888, five years after he had learned about it, in his treatment of Frau Emmy von N (Tögel, 1999). This treatment was transitional because he was also strongly influenced by Bernheim's view of the power of suggestion, and gave the patient many posthypnotic suggestions to protect her from those thoughts that were making her anxious. He also utilized the cathartic method to identify thoughts that caused distress. This patient stimulated Freud's curiosity about the workings of the hysteric's mind. On this occasion, he was rather more interested in the mechanism than in the cause of her symptoms, and he made no reference to sexual matters. This seven-week treatment, which included Freud regularly massaging this forty-year-old woman—a standard neurological treatment—was first reported by Freud (1894) as "A Case of Successful Treatment by Hypnotism. With Some Remarks on the Origin of Hysterical Symptoms through 'Counter-Will.'" Although described as a successful treatment, the patient subsequently had several relapses and required additional treatment by Freud and later by another physician. The long-term outcome does not sound felicitous in retrospect.

In 1892, Freud treated Miss Lucy R, and subsequently (1893–1895) noted that in order for hysteria to be acquired, "one essential condition must be fulfilled: an idea must be *intentionally repressed from consciousness* and excluded from associative modification" (Breuer and Freud, p. 116). In addition, he hypothesized that the cause of her symptoms of depression, fatigue, and subjective sensation of smell was unrequited love for her employer, a sexual etiology.

That same year, 1892, he also treated Fräulein Elisabeth von R, a twenty-four-year-old woman who had been suffering for more than two years from pains in her legs and who had difficulty walking. Again, Freud used the cathartic method and again hypothesized a sexual cause of her symptoms. She developed a pain in her right thigh, Freud explained, when "she succeeded in sparing herself the painful conviction that she loved her sister's husband by inducing pains in herself instead" (Breuer and Freud, 1893–1895, p. 157).

In both these patients Freud hypothesized that their symptoms were caused by repression of a *current sexual trauma*, not a childhood sexual trauma. Thus, in 1892, Freud's understanding of the symptom formation in these two patients represented the beginning of his *fundamental discovery of the power and influence on behavior of unconscious thoughts and feelings.* This discovery referred to the impact of a *current sexual trauma*, with no reference to the role of childhood sexual trauma, which became central to his later theory of "transferences." He first used the term "the unconscious" when he referred to "a premonition of an approaching condition . . . was perceived in the unconscious" (p. 76) in his treatment of Frau Emmy von N.

By 1893, Freud, in collaboration with Breuer, gave a preliminary report of the cathartic method, buoyed by a seemingly successful treatment of a hysterical patient, Frau Cäcilie M. In 1893–1895 Breuer and

Freud published "Studies on Hysteria," describing the successful treatment of six hysterical patients—including Anna O—by the cathartic method. Newton (1995) commented on the difficulty Freud had securing Breuer's agreement to collaborate, because their most dramatic clinical exhibit would be the case of Anna O. E. Jones (1953) indicated that it was only after Freud told Breuer that a patient had once importuned *him* with an embrace—and, according to Jones, offered the idea of "transference" to account for it—that Breuer was reassured (p. 250).

If it was a bold step for Freud to reject the received wisdom that the cause of neurosis was primarily organic dysfunction of the brain due to inherited predisposition, how shall we characterize his assertion and conviction that the cause of neurosis uniformly was sexual, and for hysteria specifically a repressed sexual trauma in childhood? How did Freud develop such a belief? We may never know.

Macmillan (1976) notes that in the Fliess correspondence, sexual etiology first appears in relation to neurasthenia. The concept of neurasthenia was in common use in the last quarter of the nineteenth century. It was first used by Van Deusen in 1867 and by Beard, an American neurologist, in 1871. Freud knew of Charcot's opinions of Beard's work, as well as the work itself, by the middle 1880s. For Beard, sexual excess was only one of a number of factors that produced neurasthenia. Macmillan cites: "A schematic outline, probably sent to Fliess [by Freud] at the end of 1892, contains the first proposal of a sexual etiology for neurasthenia (Masson, 1985, Draft A, possibly December 1892) . . . by early 1893 singly or jointly masturbation and incomplete coitus always produced neurasthenia (Draft B, February 1893)" (pp. 102–103). In a paper on the subject, Freud (1895a) described a girl with an obsessional neurosis who "was cured by careful surveillance which prevented her from masturbating" (p. 76). Macmillan concludes that none of the evidence Freud adduced for this hypothesis was very strong.

Today, the notion that masturbation or incomplete coitus per se is the cause of neurotic symptoms seems hardly plausible. The role of childhood sexual causes is also suspect. Yet Freud (1896a) was ready to assert unequivocally that the functional pathological modifications in the neuroses, that is, their symptoms

> *have as their common source the subject's sexual life, whether they lie in a disorder of his contemporary sexual life or in important events in his past life.* . . . I elevate these sexual influences to the rank of specific causes, that I recognize their

action in every case of neurosis, and finally that I trace a regular parallelism, a proof of special aetiological relation between the nature of the sexual influence and the pathological species of the neurosis [p. 149].

The specific etiology of hysteria, Freud maintained, was "*a passive sexual experience before puberty . . . a precocious experience of sexual relations with actual excitement of the genitals, resulting from sexual abuse committed by another person . . . [in] earliest youth—*the years up to the age of eight to ten" (p. 152).

It seems likely that Freud's early conviction about sexual etiology was not based *primarily* on patient observations, because his experience with patients had been relatively limited by 1892–1893 when he had first written to Fliess about the etiological formula. Jones (1953) refers to "some intuition in Freud that he had lighted on an important theme" (p. 248). He had begun to use the cathartic method with Frau Emmy von N in 1888, so he had had only five years of working with patients, and most of those patients probably had been treated only for a few weeks or months. In "Studies on Hysteria" (1895), written with Breuer, Freud reports treatment of six patients: one in 1888 and two in 1892; dates were not given for the other three. Frau Emmy von N was treated for approximately six weeks and Katharina was "treated" on a single occasion; duration of treatment was not provided for the other four. Self-observation was not the basis of his conviction either, because Freud did not begin his self-analysis until 1897, four years after his letter to Fliess.

Freud (1896a) reported on his sample of cases the year following publication of *The Studies*: "I have been able to carry out a complete psychoanalysis in thirteen cases of hysteria [each in a few weeks or months]. . . . In none of these cases was an event of the kind defined above [sexual abuse by another person in earliest youth] missing" (p. 152). In a follow-up paper, Freud (1896b) claimed: "In some eighteen cases of hysteria I have been able to discover this connection in every single symptom" (p. 199). It seems highly probable that this uniform finding in all eighteen patients was a consequence of covert suggestion by Freud, *and that Freud was unaware that this "finding" was a result of his unintended suggestion.* Evidence for this is provided by Freud's describing in his (1905) "Postscript" what he should have said to Dora.

"Now," I ought to have said to her, "it is from Herr K. that you have made a transference on to me. Have you noticed anything that leads you to suspect me of evil intentions similar (whether openly or in some sublimated form) to Herr K.'s? Or have you been struck by anything about me or got to know anything about me which has caught your fancy, as happened previously with Herr K.?" [p. 118].

Freud seems unaware that those words would have conveyed a powerful, covert suggestion that Dora had specific, unrecognized sexual feelings about him. Did Freud subsequently remain unaware of the impact of his unintended suggestions?

Freud had had an important experience with a patient sometime prior to his first joint publication with Breuer that is probably relevant to his conviction. It is certainly relevant, if we believe Jones's (1953) account, cited earlier, of how Freud linked sexual factors to "transference," the patient's intense, unrealistic feelings and fantasies about the physician. Freud had been treating this patient with hypnotism. He would comment (1905) in his "Postscript" that "there is usually a sort of blind dependence and a permanent bond between a patient and the physician who has removed his symptoms by hypnotic suggestion; but the scientific explanation of all these facts is to be found in the existence of "tranferences" such as are regularly directed by patients on to their physicians" (p. 117). Freud (1925) described the event with the patient as follows.

And one day I had an experience which showed me in the crudest light what I had long suspected. It related to one of my most acquiescent patients, with whom hypnotism had enabled me to bring about the most marvellous results, and whom I was engaged in relieving of her suffering by tracing back her attacks of pain to their origins. As she woke up on one occasion, she threw her arms round my neck. The unexpected entrance of a servant relieved us from a painful discussion, but from that time onwards there was a tacit understanding between us that the hypnotic treatment should be discontinued. I was modest enough not to attribute the event to my own irresistible personal attraction, and I felt I had now grasped the nature of the mysterious element that was at work behind hypnotism [p. 27].

This experience, so similar to what Freud believed had been Breuer's earlier experience with Anna O, had a profound impact. Later, Jones

(1953) remarked that "Transference phenomena had always seemed to him [Freud] impregnable proof of the sexual origin of the neuroses" (p. 242). Thus, this *inter alia* bolstered his etiological theory. Indeed, Freud (December 6, 1906) remarked in a letter to Jung: "And actually transference provides the most cogent, indeed, the only unassailable proof that neuroses are determined by the individual's love life" (McGuire, 1974, p. 13). The *only* unassailable proof for his theory of the sexual etiology of neurosis—is he referring to erotic feelings of women patients toward men analysts? How is that evidence for the *cause* of neurosis? Further, he was still using hypnosis and posthypnotic suggestion with this patient, and therefore was using the cathartic method, if he was using it at all, only to identify disturbing thoughts and feelings. At the very best he could only establish correlations between the patient's earlier thoughts and feelings and her erotic impulses toward him. A correlation does not establish causation; it was not possible for Freud to establish the cause of her erotic impulses toward him. Nor at that point was he exploring for childhood traumatic experiences.

Freud's experience with the patient who threw her arms around him and its relation to his understanding of Breuer's experience warrants further consideration. Freud later circulated a story, based on his own reconstruction, that Anna O had developed a phantom pregnancy. Breuer's experience with Anna O's pregnancy fantasy would mean that Freud's experience was similar and thereby would enhance its importance. Recent scholarship indicates, however, that whether Anna O ever had such a pregnancy fantasy is controversial. I find more convincing Esterson's (1999) conclusion that Breuer never told Freud of such a fantasy, and that the fantasy was a "reconstruction" of Freud's.

> On what did he base this reconstruction? Something Breuer told him *in another context* i.e., not directly related to Pappenheim's [Anna O] treatment. When did he arrive at his reconstruction? Long after the break in his relations with Breuer (i.e., after 1895). Clearly the suggestion that Freud learned of the event from Breuer in 1883 is without substance. In fact, both from this letter, and from his statement in the "History," it is apparent that Freud did not learn of the event from Breuer at all, and that the story derives entirely from Freud himself [p. 1238].

Esterson also quotes from Ellenberger (1972) that the Freud–Jones account of the termination of Anna O's treatment "cannot be confirmed and does not fit into the chronolgy of the case" (p. 279), while Breuer's biographer, Hirschmüller (1989), states: "The Freud/Jones account of the termination of the treatment of Anna O. should be regarded as a myth. It came into being, and was consolidated, under the influence of the advance of psychoanalytic doctrine over a period of several decades" (p. 131). I would add that further support for Esterson's conclusion is the fact that Breuer (Breuer and Freud, 1893–1895) described Anna O's cure in terms of specific symptom removal.

> I have already described the astonishing fact that from beginning to end of the illness all the stimuli arising from the secondary [dreamlike] state, together with their consequences, were permanently removed by being given verbal utterance in hypnosis . . . not until symptoms had been got rid of in this way in a whole series of instances did I develop a therapeutic technique out of it. . . . The final cure of the hysteria deserves a few more words [pp. 46–47].

It seems most unlikely that a physician of Breuer's integrity and stature would report in a scientific publication that a hysteric patient had been cured in these terms, if, as had been reported, treatment ended disastrously with a major new symptom, a fantasy of pregnancy, which required hospitalization. The patient was indeed subsequently hospitalized by Breuer, but Esterson (2000b, personal email communication) reports that in Hirschmuller's book about Breuer, there is no mention of a phantom pregnancy in Breuer's June 1882 letter to Dr. Binswanger, who was then in charge of the Kreuzlingen sanitorium to which Breuer referred the patient. It is unthinkable that Breuer would have transferred the patient to a colleague without mentioning it. Thus, Freud seems retrospectively to have constructed a picture of the termination of Anna O's treatment, in which case his own experience was not a singular one but was a replication of Breuer's earlier experience. Freud's conviction about the etiology of neurosis seems to have shaped his view of patient material—as I have postulated occurred when he made unintended suggestions about childhood sexual trauma to his eighteen consecutive hysterical patients—rather than patient material influencing his view of the etiology of the neuroses.

While we can believe that experience with this one particular patient's erotic feelings played a role, Freud's early conviction about the sexual etiology of the neuroses was stronger than could be accounted for by his experiences with other patients to that time. Recent examination of Freud's treatment of Emmy von N in 1888—her real name was Frau Fanny Moser—provides additional reason to conclude that Freud's early vision of the sexual etiology of neurosis was not primarily based on clinical material from patients. Tögel (1999) reported that in Freud's second letter to Emmy von N's daughter in 1935, he semi-apologized for his prior treatment of her mother: "But at that time I didn't understand anything and just believed in her information" (p. 1165). Tögel continues: "One of the deficiencies was that Freud believed quite naïvely almost everything that his patients told him" (p. 1167). Freud had described Emmy von N as an admirable woman of moral earnestness with humility of mind and refinement of manners, but Andersson's observation of her, quoted by Tögel, is quite discrepant: "She nearly always seems to have had lovers and erotic relationships, sometimes with doctors whom she consulted at spas, or who lived in her house as her personal doctors" (p. 11).

Thus Freud's account of his treatment of Emmy von N in the "Studies" in 1895 was based on accepting her statements at face value, and that at the time of her treatment, 1888–1889, he had not yet discovered the role of unconscious thoughts and feelings. We should note that in his 1935 letter to her daughter about her mother's treatment, Freud acknowledged: "Ten, maybe five years later, I couldn't have helped guessing that the unlucky woman fought a serious battle against her unconscious hatred for her two children and tried to defend herself by means of overtenderness" (p. 1165).

His formulation, in 1892–1893, of the theory of the sexual etiology of neurosis may have been supported by his impression of repression of *current* sexual impulses as the cause of symptoms in Miss Lucy R and in Fräulein Elisabeth von R. Alternatively, his developing conviction of the sexual etiology of neurasthenia may have influenced his "findings" of current sexual conflicts in these two patients. As noted earlier, this was the beginning of Freud's discovery of the power of unconscious thoughts and feelings. The fact that his discovery of the unconscious occurred in the sexual domain (rather than, e.g., the sphere of aggression) may explain his emphasis on the importance of sexuality in psychopathology. The association of sexuality with his fundamental discovery of the role of unconscious thoughts and feelings may have imbued sexuality with its central importance.

My psychological speculation about Freud's conviction concerning the childhood sexual etiology of neurosis is based upon the observation of analysts that they themselves are especially sensitive to concerns and conflicts in their patients that coincide with their own personal concerns and conflicts. Freud later voiced his concern that his own sexual feelings, at least toward patients, were difficult to deal with, and one of the reasons for his espousing the technical principles of abstinence and neutrality was to buttress control of such impulses (Schachter, 1994). Freud's sensitivity to his patients' unconscious sexual conflicts may have been enhanced by his own personal sexual conflicts. Further, his shift in theory from current to childhood sexual conflicts—and when he could not validate childhood sexual trauma, his subsequent inability to abandon the general hypothesis that early sexual experiences must somehow be at stake—may have been an unconscious defensive avoidance of troublesome current sexual conflicts by shifting to less uncomfortable exploration of past childhood sexuality.

However he derived his theory, he pronounced it unequivocally to the world as early as 1893. Freud (Masson, 1985) wrote to Fliess, urging him to accentuate the importance of the sexual etiology of neurasthenia: "Describe the anticipated result as that which it really is, something new; show people the key that unlocks everything, the aetiological formula" (pp. 45–46). At that time, Freud had not published a single contribution on the subject of neurasthenia or on the neuroses in general. That would change forthwith, as Freud devoted himself over the course of the next three years to establishing a differential etiological scheme that would comprise, not only hysteria and compulsive disorders, but neurasthenia and anxiety neurosis as well. May (1999) asserts: "All Freud's publications and lectures from the period 1894–1896 had the aim of establishing an aetiological theory of the neuroses and psychoses" (p. 769). Woven into this theory of etiology was a belief, which seems to have operated *a priori*, that etiologic factors in a specific case could be unearthed through personal-historical inquiry. May adds:

> Experience in practice and self-observation will have led him to assume a consistent sexual aetiology, but the certainty of his feeling of possession of the "formula" [in Freud's note to Fliess] extends beyond this. . . . I think it important to note Freud's visionary certainty and not, for example, to imply that his *leading idea* was purely empirical in character, derived from observation and thoroughly validated by observations. . . .

The conviction of having found *the* theory of the neuroses and discovered *the* root of all symptoms in sexuality had a high affective cathexis for him [pp. 776–777].

Lothane (1999), discussing the value of separating Freud's method from his theory, notes "This craving for causality, or, in medical parlance, etiology, is often conducive to the creation of a belief system, or ideology, the soul of mythology" (p. 152). Esterson (2000a) reaches a similar conclusion, which he phrases in even stronger language: "Notwithstanding Freud's description of the theory as analytic 'findings,' most of the psychosexual developmental claims consisted of his own imaginative conjectures, purportedly validated by tendentious interpretations of patients' dreams, symptoms and associations" (p. 47).

Ultimately, we cannot be certain about the origin of Freud's vision of the childhood sexual etiology of the neuroses, a vision he tenaciously retained throughout his life. Reluctantly Freud had abandoned his own scientific ambitions and perhaps he sensed the fame this theory could afford him, as fame had been awarded to Koch—whose work Freud said was received with "delirious enthusiasm" (p. 461)— and to Darwin. Freud (1896b) likened his discovery of the theory of sexual etiology to "the discovery of a *caput Nili* [source of the Nile]" (p. 203). In 1900, Freud wrote to Fliess: "I am actually not at all a man of science, not an observer, not an experimenter, not a thinker. I am by temperament nothing but a conquistador—an adventurer, if you want it translated—with all the curiosity, daring, and tenacity characteristic of a man of this sort" (Masson, 1985, p. 398). The fascination with such fame is consistent with his earlier behavior in the now infamous cocaine episode. As Swales (1989) has noted, on that earlier occasion Freud appeared to approach his work as a Faustian bargain with himself to gain worldwide fame whatever the risk and whatever the price.

The danger of proselytizing such an intense belief about the etiology of neurosis is described by Campbell (1999) in commenting about Wallace Stevens's poem "Anecdote of the Jar": "Place a jar on a hill and the entire landscape will seem to configure around it" (p. 14). Hold childhood sexual etiology up persuasively as a key to neurosis and all the clinical material of psychopathology will seem to reconfigure around it.

A Current View of Freud's Theory of the Sexual Etiology of the Neuroses

In the pitiless glare of 20–20 hindsight, Freud's insistent reach for a specific sexual etiology both of the neuroses and of "transferences" is at the same time a creative leap and asset, as well as a substantial liability. Gill's (1993) succinct judgment is that "Freud referred to a general overestimation of sex in neurosis" (p. 122). Yet, whatever misgivings we have about his theoretical focus, it was a bold and stunning step. Freud's views can be better appreciated by comparing them with those of Janet, who also recognized a role for the unconscious in hysteria, but emphasized instead the general alteration of hysterical consciousness that made unconscious ideas potent as a source of symptoms. Janet (1907) wrote that "hysteria is before everything else a mental disease consisting chiefly in an exaggeration of suggestibility" (p. xiii). Janet referred to the three stigmata of hysteria, suggestion, absent-mindedness, and alternation, and amalgamated them into a single general idea, "*retraction of the field of consciousness*" (p. 303). Janet concludes: "Their fundamental mental state is characterized by a special moral weakness, consisting in the lack of power, on the part of the feeble subject, to gather, to condense his psychological phenomena, and assimilate them to his personality" (p. 311). Essentially, it is the inability of the person to integrate the impact of a traumatic experience that generates psychopathology (van der Kolk and van der Hart, 1989); what Janet was arguing was that in hysteria the capacity for integration was too low to begin with. Nemiah (1989) has characterized it as an ego-deficit model of psychopathology.

Freud and Breuer turned this view on its head. It was the presence of the pathogenic unconscious idea that caused the stigmata and the general weakening of consciousness as well. This made the unconscious ideas, and their discharge in treatment, central.

What if our only template available to develop a roadmap for *treatment* had been, for example, the one provided by Janet. Would we have developed a current road map, and, if so, what would it look like? Although, of course, we can never know the answer, I suspect we might never have developed a road map at all, had Freud not indicated it was possible to do so by showing us one way.

As Zilboorg (1941) observed, referring to Freud and Breuer's report on hysteria (1893–1895):

It was the first time in the history of psychopathology that the cause of illness, the symptoms generated by the cause, and the therapeutic agent revealing and removing the cause were combined in one succession of factors. It is doubtful whether the full meaning of this historical fact has as yet been fully appreciated. It was this combination that made clinical psychopathology a true medical discipline for the first time in the history of medicine's struggle for the incorporation of neuroses and psychoses into its field of scientific investigation and treatment [pp. 486–487].

Newton (1995) makes a related observation discussing Freud's work with Breuer: "Freud's emphasis on the therapeutic, not just the explanatory, importance of *origins* would ever after . . . dominate his investigations of neurosis (p. 128).

Further, separate from his theoretical labors, Freud's *discovery of the power and influence of unconscious mental mechanisms*, his *clinical* acumen and sensitivity, as well as his remarkable creativity and originality created a dramatically new view of the human condition, which reshaped our understanding of ourselves and others and influenced a remarkably wide range of other disciplines.

On the other hand, the conflicting impression of Freud's *theoretical* constructions regarding sexual etiology that emerges in hindsight is a dramatic exhibition of hubris. If Freud had been less driven by ambition and had not been dazzled by Darwin's historical approach he might have been able to regard Breuer's hypothesis that hysterics suffer from reminiscences with more skepticism, considering it was not possible to determine the cause. To go from that beginning, moreover, to phylogenetic speculation about the ultimate source of such reminiscence is startling. Thomä and Cheshire (1991) cogently question "why Freud preferred making assumptions about real events in the prehistory of mankind, and in its Lamarckian heritage, to examining more thoroughly the countertransference of the analyst and the mutual seduction of any human encounter?" (p. 418). If Freud had not focused upon etiology and had not resolutely maintained his vision of the phylogenetically based sexual etiology of the neuroses—if he had not structured psychoanalytic treatment to explore for the patient's hidden childhood experiences, traumatic and otherwise, whose discovery he believed would be therapeutic—current guidelines for treatment might well be quite different. If only Freud had been able to acknowledge that we do not know the etiology of neurosis, just as we do not know what is mutative about analytic treatment, analytic treatment might have focused much earlier, as Thomä and Cheshire suggest, on the examination of the present unconscious of both patient and analyst in their current interactions with the possible promise of a more efficacious therapeutic outcome.

Such criticism notwithstanding, Freud's theory of neurosis, by implication, provided the analyst with a guideline for treatment, a guideline that heretofore had not existed. Freud thereby provided a road map for analytic technique: explore the unconscious by interpreting and reconstructing childhood longings. How shall that be evaluated if now, one hundred years later, that road map seems quite misguided? As Freud (1891) observed: "It is with a clear exposition of the problems that the elucidation of a scientific subject begins" (p. 104). That he conceived of designing a road map to explore the unconscious and developed one as an example—interpret and reconstruct childhood longings—enables us to redesign it in part or altogether. Kerr (1994), contrasting the value of Freud's clinical, technical contribution with the questionable utility of his problematic theoretical, etiological constructions, asserts that "The next generation would have to have its own genius on hand if it were really to extricate Freud's legitimate clinical insights from the vast and complex web of theory with which he surrounded them" (p. 509).

Summary

Freud hypothesized that both the patient's neurotic symptoms and the patient's intense, unrealistic feelings toward the analyst, "transferences," were expressions of the patient's sexual activity. He derived the relationship between "transferences" and sexual activity by hypothesizing that patients in treatment fail to develop new symptoms, but develop "transferences" instead. This hypothesis seems contrived and insubstantial. What Freud meant by considering "transferences" as sexual activity remains unclear.

The exploration of Freud's conviction of sexual etiology necessarily is conducted in relation to neurosis rather than in regard to "transferences." Freud's vision of sexual etiology of neurosis did not seem to be based on his relatively limited clinical experience with patients to that time, though at least one experience with a patient's erotic feelings about him clearly did influence him. Freud seemed quite unaware of how he shaped patients' material through his powerful, covert suggestions and interpretations of their presumed unconscious sexual feelings and fantasies. Freud seems to have reconstructed Breuer's treatment of Anna O by rendering Breuer's experience with a patient's erotic feelings similar to his own, thus providing a "cover," or "screen memory," that added to the importance of his own experience. Freud never explained his certitude that he had discovered the *cause* of the patient's erotic feelings toward him, rather than considering the possibility that her erotic feelings served multiple current defensive functions. The source of his vision is difficult to ascertain. I speculate it may have defensively avoided his dealing with his own current personal sexual concerns by focussing on the past. Also, it seemed to be a function, at least in part, of a driving ambition to achieve fame.

While Freud's *fundamental discovery of the power and influence of unconscious mental mechanisms* and his *clinical* acumen and creativity profoundly shaped our modern understanding of the human condition, his *theoretical* focus on *etiology* interfered with his recognizing that he does not know either the causes of neurosis or what is mutative about psychoanalytic treatment. Consequently, his conviction did provide a guideline for analytic treatment—interpret the past unconscious—but prevented psychoanalytic treatment from achieving an earlier focus on examination of the present unconscious of both patient and analyst in their current interactions. It is this latter approach that shows promise of enabling a more efficacious therapeutic outcome.

4
Problems with the Theory of "Transference"

I take this opportunity of defending myself against the mis-taken charge of having denied the importance of innate (con-stitutional) factors because I have stressed that of infantile impressions. A charge such as this arises from the restricted nature of what men look for in the field of causation: in con-trast to what ordinarily holds good in the real world, people prefer to be satisfied with a single causative factor. Psycho-analysis has talked a lot about the accidental factors in aeti-ology and little about constitutional ones; but that is only because it was able to contribute something fresh to the for-mer, while, to begin with, it knew no more than was com-monly known about the latter. We refuse to posit any contrast in principle between the two sets of aetiological factors; on the contrary, we assume that the two sets regularly act jointly in bringing about the observed result. Endowment and Chance determine a man's fate—rarely or never one of these powers alone. The amount of aetiological effectiveness to be attrib-uted to each of them can only be arrived at in every individ-ual case separately.

—Sigmund Freud, "The Dynamics of Transference"

Transference is defined by Moore and Fine (1990) as "the displacement of patterns of feelings, thoughts, and behavior, originally experienced in relation to significant figures during childhood, onto a person involved in a current interpersonal relationship" (p. 196). That the term *transference*, a shibboleth of psychoanalysis, refers not to a fact but to a *theory* has been lost to many analysts. It was lost on Freud himself. Freud (1914a) wrote:

> It may thus be said that the theory of psychoanalysis is an attempt to account for two striking and unexpected *facts* of observation which emerge whenever an attempt is made to trace the symptoms of a neurotic back to their sources in his past life: the *facts* of transference and resistance. Any line of investigation which recognizes these two *facts* and takes them as the starting point of its work may call itself psychoanalysis though it arrives at results other than my own [p. 16, italics added].

Freud noted the "facts" of "transference" and resistance emerged "whenever an attempt is made to trace the symptoms of a neurotic back to their sources in his past life." If no attempt is made to trace the symptoms of a neurotic back to their sources in his or her past life, which attempt is based on a *theory* of pathogenesis, do the same "facts" of "transference" and resistance emerge? This is not an idle query. Fonagy (1999b) asserts: "Therapies focusing on the recovery of memory pursue a false god. Psychoanalysts should carefully and consistently avoid the archaeological metaphor. . . . The recovery of memory is an inappropriate goal" (p. 220). Fonagy is here addressing himself specifically to recovered memories of abuse, but the logic of his argument applies equally to the search for the personal historical roots of a patient's "transference."

Facts are not independent entities that exist freestanding in a real universe. Facts can never speak for themselves. A fact carries weight, indeed, it only exists, as a function of a conceptual scheme or theory, and in a particular context. If the underlying conception or theory is modified, or if the context changes, the fact will be altered and may disappear. As Schafer (1994), quoted by Gay (2000), writes, "facts are facts for the time being. They are facts of a certain kind for the time being. . . . They are true for the time being" (p. 1028). This is not to say that there are no facts, but only that facts are subject to change. For example, the "facts" about Ulysses S. Grant and Robert E. Lee are currently changing (Scott, 2000). Grant is now seen as an extraordinary general whose military strategy produced proportionately fewer casualties than Lee's, as a president who worked hard to enforce Reconstruction and black equality in the South and to crush the Ku Klux Klan, and as an individual whose drinking may have been exaggerated. Meanwhile, the long-held idea that Lee opposed slavery has been discounted, and he is accused of excessive aggression in his tactics and squandering his military manpower.

There is no "fact" of "transference" as Freud uses the term. Freud fused two separate entities, the clinical phenomenon that some of the patient's intense feelings about the analyst are unrealistic, which is a widely accepted observation, with his *theory* of the cause of those feelings, which is a hypothesis and not a fact. As a result, "transference" has come to be known inclusively as "the patient's-unrealistic-feelings-about-the-analyst-that-were-caused-by-childhood-experiences," a single entity. Criticism of the term "transference" is, therefore, taken to be criticism of this fused entity, as if it represented failure to recognize the observation of the patient's intense feelings about the analyst. My criticism is directed solely at Freud's separate *hypothesis* concerning the *cause* of the patient's intense feelings. I certainly agree that patients develop intense feelings about the analyst, often feelings that cannot be accounted for by the reality of the patient-analyst relationship.

A challenge to the *theory* of "transference" is difficult for analysts to accept because it appears to threaten the whole edifice of psychoanalysis (Bachant and Richards, 1993). Over time, the theory has gradually changed, from Freud's specific hypothesis that childhood representations and impulses persist as unmodified structures that later cause adult reactions to a generalization that prior experiences influence current reactions, a hypothesis so general that it seems virtually indisputable.

Contemporaneous with this modification in theory has been a change in psychoanalytic technique, a shifting of focus from the recovery of memories and reconstruction of childhood experiences to the analysis of "transference" itself (Blum, 1999; Opatow, 1999). Why have such changes in theory and technique been necessary? Presumably because the theory of "transference" and its implications for psychoanalytic technique have fallen short. Characteristically, the history of psychoanalytic theory provides few clues to the reasons for the rejection and discarding of theories or techniques no longer deemed useful. Instead of articulating critiques, gradually the theories are simply used less and less.

Freud's Theory of "Transference"

In the *Studies on Hysteria*, Freud makes a passing but tantalizing reference to "transference" as a *"false connection."* One root of this notion has been traced to Brown-Sequard's observation of "action at a distance," that is, the fact that proximal lesions can cause distal physiological disturbances (Kravis, 1992). Then, too, Charcot observed that hysterical symptoms could be *transferred* from one side of the body to the other by the application of electricity or magnets to a patient while under the influence of hypnosis.

The process of making a *false connection* is akin to a phenomenon studied by Bernheim and others who instructed hypnotized patients to carry out certain posthypnotic actions. A patient, unaware of why he carried out some action that had been triggered by posthypnotic suggestion, creates some excuse or explanation to cover the gap in understanding. Freud (Breuer and Freud, 1893–1895) explains: "In cases in which the true causation evades conscious perception one does not hesitate to make another connection, which one believes, although it is false. It is clear that a split in the content of consciousness must greatly facilitate the occurrence of 'false connections' of this kind" (p. 67). Freud discusses that the patient becomes resistant if she "is frightened at finding that she is transferring on to the figure of the physician the distressing ideas which arise from the content of the analysis. . . . Transference [this is arguably the first appearance of the term "transference"] on to the physician takes place through a *false connection*" (p. 302). Freud gave as an example a woman who unconsciously wished that a man would give her a kiss: "On one occasion, at the end of a session, a similar wish came up in her about me. She was horrified at it" (pp. 302–303). Thus, by 1895, Freud had articulated a rudimentary theory of "transference" and focused it on *current* erotic feelings of a female patient to a male analyst.

Freud (1900) elaborated on a possibly related notion of "transference" in *The Interpretation of Dreams*: "An unconscious idea is as such quite incapable of entering the preconscious and can only exercise any effect there by establishing a connection with an idea which already belongs to the preconscious, by transferring its intensity onto it and by getting itself 'covered' by it. Here we have the fact of transference" (p. 562). This usage of "transference," to be sure, refers to an internal, purely mental "connection" and not necessarily to its possible eruption in the treatment relationship. The relevance of this usage to the explicit subsequent formulation of "transference" in the Dora case is a matter of some conjecture and perhaps further scholarly investigation will clarify it (see, especially, Makari, 1998). Of interest, it was a particular feature of Kohut's "Freudian vision" (Rubovits-Seitz, 1998) to see these usages as intrinsically connected.

The subsequent 1905 formulation in the Dora case, the first explicit description of the familiar usage of "transference" to refer to the treatment relationship, finds Freud casting the "false connection" in those historical terms that we have come to know. Transferences, he explains in the Dora case (1905), "replace some earlier person by the person of the physician. . . . a whole series of psychological experiences are revived, not as belonging to the past, but as applying to the person of the physician at the present moment" (p. 116).

Makari (1998) has tried to chart the evolution of the "transference" idea in the years leading up to the Dora case.

> After the seduction theory fell, Freud gradually rebuilt a model of neurosogenesis, hypothesizing that repressed masturbation was important in the creation of hysteria. . . . This schema explicitly called for two tiers of development, the object-unrelated/self-stimulating/autoerotic and the object-directed/alloerotic. . . . Dora's symptoms are seen as a result of her autoerotic suck-a-thumbs oral zone overstimulation and of her object-directed masturbation accompanied by incestuous fantasies. Transferences, Freud argued, replaced the true object of the fantasy with the person of the physician in two distinct ways. They could be "reprints"—autoerotic surges or projections that showed no change in the unconscious psychic content save for the substitution of self for object—or "revised editions," ingeniously created by incorporating some analogous aspect of the here-and-now person of the physician into the unconscious fantasy [pp. 1089–1090].

In the latter formulation, Freud seems to have portended Gill's reconception of "transference," emphasizing the utilization of conscious and unconscious characteristics of the analyst in the development of feelings and fantasies toward the analyst.

Freud's assumption that the patient's feeling or impulse is displaced from, or is a repetition of, a prior relationship rests on the judgment that this feeling or impulse is *distorted* with regard to the reality of the current relationship. The *distortion* is the sign of the *false connection*. Anna Freud (1936) elaborates: "By transference we mean all those impulses experienced by the patient in his relation with the analyst which are not newly created by the objective analytic situation but have their source in early . . . object relations and are now merely . . . repetitions" (p. 18).

Questions about the concept of "transference" have been raised before. "Transference," wrote Bird (1972), "is a very special mental quality that has never been satisfactorily explained. I am not satisfied, for instance, either with what has been written about it or with its use in analysis" (p. 267). Gill's (1982) even more pithy observation is that "the concept of transference is itself somewhat unclear" (p. 9). To this day, Tuckett (2000) notes, "the central concept of *transference* is a subject for dispute, being visited and revisited with little clear consensus" (p. 237).

In what follows, I consider questions arising from changes in the conceptual context in which the theory was originally developed as well as methodological problems with its validation. I also examine current concerns about and criticisms of the Oedipus complex, since the essence of the content of "transference" has been considered to be the displacement and repetition of oedipal fantasies and impulses onto the analyst.

Changes in the Conceptual Context of the Theory of "Transference"

There have been major changes in the conceptual context of "transference" since Freud first coined the term more than eighty years ago. At least three of these changes pose problems for the theory of "transference." First, "transference" was originally conceived in terms of libido theory, a theory that is no longer a uniformly or even widely accepted model for psychic functioning. Second, the notion that "transference" is resolved—that is, cured—in treatment has been abandoned. Third, "transference" was developed within a one-person model of analytic treatment, and the widespread shift to a two-person, interactional model jeopardizes its usefulness. These conceptual changes have important implications for the concept of "transference."

Freud posited libido as sexual energy divorced from structure (Fairbairn, 1944). Within the libido framework he proposed two quite different concepts of "transference"; he neither discarded one nor truly reconciled the two. The first concept was based on his observation that the patient developed strongly positive, often erotic feelings toward the analyst, which could not be accounted for by the reality of the patient-analyst relationship. Freud (1912) hypothesized that a partially frustrated person naturally directs libidinal cathexis toward every new person, including the analyst; that is to say, frustration causes the libido to enter on "a regressive course" and to revive "the subject's infantile imagos" (p. 102). In a subsequent paper, Freud (1913a) supplemented his original proposition and added that the patient "will of himself form such an attachment and link the doctor up with one of the imagos of the people by whom he was accustomed to be treated with affection" (pp. 139–140). These positive feelings of the patient for the analyst later qualified as the unobjectionable positive "transference" that aided the treatment.

Freud's (1912a) second view of "transference" rested on the observation that when the patient came upon disturbing thoughts or feelings about the analyst, he blocked them off, that is, he resisted by not following instructions to free-associate. "Where the investigation of analysis comes upon the libido withdrawn into its hiding-place, a struggle is bound to break out; all the forces which have caused the libido to regress will rise up as 'resistances' against the work of analysis" (p. 102). He added (1914c), "We . . . find . . . the compulsion to repeat, which now replaces the impulsion to remember, not only in his personal attitude to his doctor but also in every other activity and relationship" (p. 151). In this sense, "transference" was an obstacle to treatment, a substitute gratification that blocked further participation. Freud, however, provided no evidence to support the notion that childhood affectionate feelings are displaced onto the analyst *in order to* resist recollecting traumatic memories.

Anna Freud's discussion of the complexities of "transference" (Sandler, Kennedy, and Tyson, 1980) articulates the conflicting implications of Freud's two libidinal theories of "transference." She points out that if the partially frustrated patient is *displacing* libido from the parental imago, then the libidinal attachment to that imago should diminish as the libidinal attachment to the analyst increases. If, however, the libido regresses in the service of resistance and becomes attached to the analyst in a *repetition* of the attachment to the parental imago, no diminution in the libidinal attachment to the parental imago would be observed. Thus, Freud's dual conception of "transference" is theoretically unclear as to whether or not "transference" to the analyst is associated with diminished libidinal attachment to the parental imago.

A second change in context, based on posttermination observation of patients, has led to abandonment of the idea that "transference" is resolved or cured during a successfully completed analysis (Pfeffer, 1959, 1961, 1963; Schlessinger and Robbins, 1983; Oremland, Blacker, and Norman, 1975; Norman et al., 1976). Consequently, a theory of "transference" must now account for the clinical observation that although "transference" persists after analysis ends, in an effective analytic treatment its pathological impact on the patient's psychic life has been substantially diminished.

The third change in context, the theoretical shift to a two-person model of analytic treatment, has led to the realization that the analyst has an impact on the patient's "transference" (Loewald, 1971, 1986; Schafer, 1977; Gill and Hoffman, 1982; Mitchell, 1988). That is, the feelings and fantasies the patient brings to the analysis do not remain fixed and unchanged but are modified by the influence of the interactions with the analyst. "Transference" is clearly influenced by the analyst's gender (Greenson, 1967; Raphling and Chused, 1988) and most likely by numerous other analyst attributes, including the analyst's affective presence (Viederman, 1991). The analyst's impact on the patient's "transference" is used by Cooper (1987) to distinguish "transference" theories based on a one-person model from those based upon a two-person model. He refers to the concept of "transference" as displacement or repetition as the "historical view" and to the concept that interaction with the analyst shapes the patient's "transference" as the "modernist view," and he proposes a comprehensive conception encompassing both views.

These three theoretical changes in the underlying psychoanalytic context in which the theory of "transference" was developed became pressing conceptual concerns with Gill and Hoffman's (1982) assertion that "transference" cannot be said to involve distortion, but builds on selected, realistic characteristics of the analyst. This reconception creates a conundrum for the theory of "transference." Absent evidence that the impulses are unrealistic or distorted, *Freud's basis for characterizing them as false connections*, and with it, the warrant for characterizing them as "transferences"—that they are displacements from or repetitions of experiences in a prior relationship—is lost. If the patient's feelings and fantasies about the analyst are not "distorted" in Freud's sense, there is no reason to hypothesize that they were caused by childhood origins. They may be primarily *newly created* responses to the realistic qualities of the analyst. Freud's theoretical position, moreover, assumes that the analyst knows what is realistic and what is not; this putative level of discernment in the analyst forms the positivistic basis for judging what is unrealistic or distorted and, therefore, what is "transference."

Although Gill and Hoffman have discarded distortion as the basis for categorizing a reaction as "transference," they have not suggested any alternative criterion that would justify categorizing a patient's reaction to the analyst as "transference" or any way to distinguish reactions to the analyst that can be categorized as "transference" from reactions that are not "transference," but are, in A. Freud's words (1936), *"newly created* by the objective analytic situation" (p. 18, italics added).

Anna Freud (1954), quoted by Buckley (1989), commented that so much attention is paid to the "transference" that the patient's real relationship to the analyst is in danger of being overlooked:

> With due respect for the necessary strictest handling and interpretation of the transference, I still feel that we should leave room somewhere for the realization that analyst and patient are also two real people of equal adult status, in a real personal relationship to each other. I wonder whether our—at times complete—neglect of this side of the matter is not responsible for some of the hostile reactions which we get from our patients and which we are apt to ascribe to "true transference" only [A. Freud, 1954, p. 44].

A "solution" to this theoretical problem of how to determine whether a reaction to the analyst is "transference" is to *assume* that all the patient's reactions to the analyst are influenced by his or her past experience (Gill, 1994), that all reactions to the analyst are "transference." This broadening of the concept was articulated by Glover (1937): "Transference" was "all he [the patient] has learnt or forgotten throughout his mental development" (p. 43). Abend (1993) acknowledges that "transference" has been so broadened by encompassing defensive and superego elements, aggressive as well as libidinal components, preoedipal as well as oedipal factors, as to include much of psychopathology. This led Cooper (1987) to ask, "What is *not* transference?" If everything is "transference," if there is nothing that is not "transference," the usefulness of the concept is seriously compromised.

Supportive Clinical Evidence

Difficulties with the supportive clinical evidence for the traditional theory of "transference" existed from the outset. For complete recovery, wrote Freud (1910b), analysis "invariably goes back to the patient's puberty and early childhood; and it is only there that it comes upon the impressions and events which determined the later onset of the illness" (p. 41). Freud (1910a), however, ignored his own earlier statement in these same lectures when he described a woman patient who "became healthy once more" (p. 25) by reproducing the pathogenic moment which occurred quite recently in her adult life, without any recollection of childhood reminiscences.

What evidence did Freud (1910b) cite that "transference" "can only be traced back to old wishful phantasies of the patient's which have become unconscious" (p. 41)? This, he said, "is shown by every detail of its [old phantasy's] emergence" (p. 51)—presumably by the particulars of the recollection. Current studies of memory show that many factors influence recollection and recall, not least the analyst's presumptions and expectations. Freud (1899) himself was acutely aware of the general problem early on (see chapter 8, "Nachträglichkeit"). The possibility of recreating a "true" version of the life history from the analysis of "transference" has been challenged by, among others, Spence (1982), Schafer (1983), and Cooper (1987). Dennett (1991), an influential contemporary philosopher quoted by Mitchell (1997), concurs:

> Just what we are conscious of within any particular time duration is not defined independently of the probes we use to precipitate a narrative about that period. Since these narratives are under continual revision, there is no single narrative that counts as the canonical version, the "first edition" in which are laid down, for all time, the events that happened in the stream of consciousness of the subject, all deviations from which must be corruptions of the text [p. 136].

Freud (1937b) was quite clear that the analyst's "task is to make out what has been forgotten from the traces which it has left behind or, more correctly, to construct it" (p. 259). Michels (1982) cites one illustration of the dangers of such reconstruction: psychoanalytic reconstruction generated the concept of the stimulus barrier, which in turn became central to the psychoanalytic view of infancy. Stern, Michels notes, finds no stimulus barrier when he observes infants because, simply, empirical evidence is lacking.

When an analytic patient recalls the memory of a feeling or impulse in an earlier relationship which corresponds to a current feeling or impulse toward the analyst, that recollection is accepted as validation of the concept that the feeling or impulse is either displaced from the earlier relationship or is a repetition of the earlier feeling or impulse (i.e., "transference"). Bollas (1989) asserts that "the patient's conveying of the actual events . . . is actually present in the transference. . . . The fact that . . . we cannot ever know what actually happened . . . is not equivalent to the statement that nothing of the actual is present in the patient's memory or in the transference" (p. 195). Bollas fails to address the further assumption; granted that something of the actual is present in the patient's memory, we still cannot know whether it is *causally* related to the patient's current feelings and fantasies toward the analyst.

The Tally Argument as Validation

"Transference" theory hypothesizes as an initial premise that an earlier feeling or impulse is the source of a current feeling or impulse; it is assumed that if the former had not existed, the latter could not have been present. Clinical validation of this purported childhood origin is then based on Freud's (1916–1917c) claim that only interpretations that "tally with what is real [in the patient] will be therapeutically effective" (p. 452). That is, interpretations that evoke therapeutic benefit in the patient are considered correct interpretations. Interpretations that do not result in therapeutic improvement are considered incorrect, because they do not tally with what is real in the patient.

None other than Breuer (Breuer and Freud, 1893) was cognizant that, "As regards the symptoms disappearing after being 'talked away,' I cannot use this as evidence [whether the occasions and mode of origin of the phenomena were really as she represented them]; it may very well be explained by suggestion" (p. 43). Kubie (1950) and Malan (1976) have also challenged the tally argument on similar grounds. Wallerstein's (1986) investigation into treatment efficacy also confounds the tally argument from a different logical direction by reporting that supportive measures produced therapeutic benefits that were as extensive and long lasting as those produced by interpretation. Edelson (1986) offers a thoughtful and spirited defense of the tally argument but acknowledges that the psychoanalytic case study offers "stronger evidence for the scientific validity . . . for etiological explanations which involve very recent, putatively causal events . . . than it can offer for the scientific credibility of etiological explanations which involve remote, putatively causal events" (p. 111).

Poland (1992) reiterates the tally claim in modified form: "Their validity [of the products of reconstruction] is tested by their effectiveness in broadening a patient's range of thought, feeling and action" (p. 201). Here again, however, the effect does not permit an inference about cause, because it cannot identify the interpretation as the mutative agent that broadened the patient's range of thought except by fiat.

Arlow (1995) asserts an altered version of the tally argument: "After all, the methods by which one gets well must reflect in some way how the individual took ill in the first place" (p. 6). There is no evidence for this assumption, and, indeed, clinical impression suggests that the opposite is true. Analysts from widely different frames of reference, such as classical Freudian analysts, Kleinians, self psychologists, object relations theorists, and attachment theorists, all report therapeutic improvement in their patients. Since each constructs a different and distinctive narrative of how the patient took ill, the patient's improvement must be independent of the particular history of the individual.

Grünbaum (1993) discusses the tally argument in relation to neurosis. He asserts that there is no evidence that "the supposed *current* replica of the remote early event is *presently* the virulent *cause* of the patient's neurosis" (p. 157). Grünbaum savages the tally argument, maintaining that there is no convincing evidence that psychoanalytic treatment is more efficacious than other forms of treatment, and that other forms of treatment, including variations of psychoanalysis, produce therapeutic improvement. Moreover, he finds the underlying logical sequence whereby infantile causation of illness is posited uncompelling, even in the face of apparent clinical confirmation, a position he carries right to the heart of "transference" theory. "Neither the fact of being recapitulatory of a conflict, nor the fact that the setting for the recapitulation is a (bizarre) fantasy focused on the analyst, nor yet the combination of these facts shows that the reenacted scenario was pathogenically relevant in the first place as a precipitating cause!" (p. 155).

Strenger (1999) basically agrees: "Constructivism is partially motivated by the failure to come up with any strong argument that proves Freud's original idea—namely, that only interpretations that touch on the historical-causal roots of a pathology are therapeutically effective.

In *Between Hermeneutics and Science* (1991), I investigated the arguments in favor of this hypothesis extensively: unfortunately, I was not able to counter Grünbaum's claim that they are all faulty" (p. 615).

Marmor (1986) alleges that "no serious scientist today would assert that the success of any therapeutic method constitutes proof of the correctness of the theory on which the therapeutic technique was based" (p. 249). We recognize this logic in relation to physical disorders. The numerous effective treatments for hypertension include a variety of medications, sodium restriction, weight loss, and surgery. The fact that all of these therapeutic regimens benefit patients is not evidence that any of them constitutes an etiological factor. The etiology of hypertension remains unknown.

Robinson (1993), seconding Cioffi (1986), argues that Freud had actually put little weight on the tally argument, but relied, rather, on the power of narrative coherence to confer intelligibility on the data. Freud (1896b) wrote:

> It is exactly like putting together a child's picture-puzzle: after many attempts, we become absolutely certain in the end which piece belongs in the empty gap; for only that one piece fills out the picture and at the same time allows its irregular edges to be fitted into the edges of the other pieces in such a manner as to leave no free space and to entail no overlapping. In the same way, the contents of the infantile scenes turn out to be indispensable supplements to the associative and logical framework of the neurosis, whose insertion makes its course of development for the first time evident, or even, as we might often say, self-evident [p. 205].

One cannot help but admire Freud's mind!

Narrative coherence is a powerful argument, one of the more effective means to counter assertions such as those of McGinn (1999) that there is no such thing as repression and that the unconscious does not exist. Narrative coherence gathers strength not only from productions from the couch, but from a vastly larger domain including art, literature, theater, and anthropology, where psychoanalytic theory provides a plausible, meaningful understanding of a salmagundi of information. All such arguments, however, must be used with care. Narrative coherence was once used to substantiate Freud's views of paranoia: those views were mistaken. Narrative coherence was used to substantiate Freud's views of women: those views were mistaken. Narrative coherence was used to substantiate Freud's views of homosexuality: those views were mistaken. That narrative coherence may be in error attests to the remarkable mind of the narrator in creating such coherence. Further, it underscores the importance of Popper's (1972) dictum that a theory that is not falsifiable is not scientific. A theory that is compatible with everything that can happen is not scientific. Granting that caveat, nonetheless, I believe narrative coherence is the psychoanalyst's most impressive strategy for supporting its interpretive theses.

The Oedipus Complex

Since, as a practical matter, the Oedipus complex lay at the core of the traditional view of "transference," whatever criticisms are directed at the Oedipus complex apply indirectly to "transference" theory as well. Rado very early questioned the centrality of the Oedipus complex and in private he wryly commented, "It might have been better if Abraham [his analyst] had interpreted my quick temper rather than my Oedipus complex" (quoted in Roazen and Swerdloff, 1995, p. 79). Klein, too, was skeptical of the centrality of the Oedipus complex and emphasized instead a pregenital Oedipus complex (Hinshelwood, 1999). Simon (1991) writes in a way that is reminiscent of Cooper's concerns about "transference" generally: "The growing complexity of the concept of the Oedipus complex . . . has brought us to a point where the concept is . . . in danger of losing its specificity and becoming the equivalent of almost all of development and of psychopathology" (pp. 649–650). Simon adds:

> All of the questions ever raised about verification of analytic propositions either have been or could be raised about the evidence for the importance or even the existence of the Oedipus complex. From the point of view of decisive evidence, it is therefore still moot . . . the concern that our theoretical scheme, insofar as it guides our interpretations and interventions, skews or even "creates" the data. We can only see what we want to see, what our theories tell us to see" [pp. 660–661].

Simon concludes, "The Oedipus complex clearly has waned in popularity and credibility, both within psychoanalysis and within the culture at large" (p. 666).

Chodorow (1996) writes that awareness of the impact of patient-analyst interaction requires a rethinking of childhood, of the Oedipus complex, and of the relations of past and present vis-à-vis the theory of "transference."

> If psychological meaning in the clinical encounter is emergent and created through fantasy, interfantasy, collaborative and tentative transitional negotiations, transferences and countertransferences created in the here-and-now, then it cannot also be the case that an Oedipus complex, castration fears, fantasies about "the" primal scene . . . are universally given or universally determined by the conditions of early infancy or by a panhuman psychobiology [pp. 48–49].

Additional well-documented criticisms of the Oedipus complex have been mounted by Friedman and Downey (1995). They posit that masculine competitiveness, expressed in rough and tumble play in boys, is a function of genetically determined hormonal differences between boys and girls and develops independently of erotic impulses, contrary to the conception of the Oedipus complex, which regards competitiveness as a function of the erotic drive. Friedman and Downey conclude that "the fantasies of aggression and dominance in the relationship between son and father are not necessarily predicated upon the erotic desire for the mother . . . but are a manifestation of an independent psychodevelopmental line" (p. 255). They add:

> We suggest that although many children experience sexual desire during or prior to the Oedipal phase of development, many do not. They are likely to experience competitive rivalry and fear of their fathers, however. The Oedipal narrative might appear to organize their representational world. [However] abundant data from diverse areas of research indicate that the Oedipus complex does not have the type of central role in the etiology of psychopathology that Freud suggested [p. 259].

Contemporary Psychoanalysis and the Theory of "Transference"

Have the many changes from Freud's early views to the conceptions of contemporary psychoanalysis rendered moot the questions about the validity and utility of the theory of "transference"? Let me cite the views of a distinguished representative of contemporary psychoanalytic theory as evidence that the theory that childhood experiences directly cause adult characteristics persists for contemporary psychoanalysis. Gabbard (2000) was asked in an email discussion how to decide between two different types of narrative about childhood experience, oedipal or deficit/empathy. He responded as follows:

> I think we use narratives about the past to illuminate current experience and to facilitate its articulation. . . . My experience suggests that both of these narratives are of limited use but I may someday hear a patient describe experiences which will evoke one of them to assist in illuminating the patient's subjectivity. Even then I hope I would hold on to the narrative "lightly" and comfortably relinquish it if it is not useful in opening up the analytic process. Developmental research is also of assistance in encouraging new narratives of early experience which may offer approaches to understanding transference phenomena.

Although he carefully and thoughtfully qualifies the value of childhood narratives, nonetheless, he seems to believe that such childhood narratives are of value in "understanding transference phenomena." That is, he believes in an etiological approach to understanding "transference." He assumes childhood experience, reflected in a childhood narrative, has causal links with adult "transference" and therefore can provide understanding of "transference."

Another current example of Gabbard's use of childhood narratives is presented in a paper about "transference," which, Westen and Gabbard (2001) write, is not really about "transfer" at all. "Transference," they write, "involves *the heightened activation and expression of enduring patterns of thought, feeling, motivation, affect regulation, or behavior in the analytic relationship*" (p. 19). But "transference" does not include all the patient's reactions to the analyst, only those that are not "role-appropriate" or are "anomalous." That is, in Freud's terms, it is the patient's distorted or irrational reactions that constitute "transference." Although Westen and Gabbard define "transference" without explicit reference to childhood etiology, they add, unarguably, that "transferential processes *always* reflect an integration of current and past experience" (p. 40). But in their case illustration they report that "Ms. C was recreating a version of the mother-daughter relationship with him [the analyst], and he interpreted the similarity between the childhood situation and the current situation in the analytic setting" (p. 12). Here, the "integration of current and past experience" takes on an etiological cast; the patient's prior experiences with her mother are presumed to be the cause of her feelings toward the analyst: "Ms. C was recreating. . . ." Admittedly, from the clinical material this sounded eminently plausible, but it means that although childhood etiology is omitted from their formal definition of "transference," the analyst's observation seems very much a typical, traditional, historical, etiological, interpretation.

Although the authors acknowledge "the analyst's actual behavior may . . . be crucially important in activating particular representations [in the patient]" (p. 17), no picture is presented of the analyst as a person, or of his feelings or behavior. He remains an anonymous figure about whom we learn only that he became concerned about how much money the patient was spending. In contrast, they do provide an excellent picture of the patient as a person. No discussion is provided about why the patient's feelings are directed to this analyst at this time. Furthermore, there is no discussion of whether any of the analyst's feelings toward, and behavior with, Ms. C played any role in her "transferences." Indeed, the description of her treatment differs little from much earlier descriptions of analytic treatment based on a one-person model. Their paper suggests that while contemporary psychoanalysis has significantly modified theory, *clinical practice has been relatively little modified*.

In another example, Miletic, a psychoanalyst currently treating active professional and elite amateur athletes, also believes that infantile trauma causes adult psychopathology. Lipsyte (2000) quotes Miletic: "[High achieving athletes'] ability to block out pain and fear comes from their adaptive tactics to the trauma of their childhoods." Miletic believes that most people are not aware of, or discount, the *continuing* impact of their childhood trauma.

Arlow (1981), on the other hand, in a distinctive report originally published almost twenty years ago, concurred with many of the problems identified in this book with the application of "transference" theory and its impact on technique in contemporary psychoanalysis. Strikingly, he disavows the traditional etiological theory that is the basis for "transference," rejecting the view that childhood experience or trauma produces an effect that persists essentially unchanged and directly causes adult psychopathology. Arlow notes:

A thrust toward specificity and simplicity of etiology has persisted in the literature of psychoanalysis. . . . The idea that a repressed memory and the affect associated with it function as a foreign body in the psychic apparatus, which becomes the starting point for the pathogenic process, continues to exert a powerful influence on therapeutic technique. . . . Nevertheless, the appeal of specificity persists. While the recent literature has played down the importance of ferreting out and trying to attain recall of a particular, pathogenic repressed memory, the quest for specifics remains and has been transposed from the domain of individual memories to the pathogenic power of very specific object relationships. During the analysis, these relationships are not recalled as actual events; for the most part they are reconstructed by the analyst on the basis of his interpretation of the transference interaction. Quite in the manner of the repressed memory in the early theories of hysteria, the early pathogenic object relations are regarded as having been split off, internalized and structuralized—in other words, endowed with a dynamic thrust of their own. Persistently revived under appropriate conditions, they continue to exert a discreet, idiosyncratic effect upon mental functioning in adult life [pp. 333–334]. . . . It appears that we must rest in the uneasy knowledge of the limitations of our understanding and give cognizance to the multiple determination of psychopathology, including factors which to this day we probably appreciate much too little. . . . The quest for specificity of pathogenesis is an admirable one which . . . is fated for failure [p. 344].

Eagle (1993), more than a decade after Arlow, shows remarkable confluence with him as he explores the question of how theoretical changes occur in psychoanalysis. Eagle asks, do representatives of so-called contemporary theory no longer think in accord with core Freudian propositions? He concludes that the problems with etiological theory embedded in Freud's early formulations plague contemporary psychoanalysis. He discusses object relations theory, which hypothesizes that early traumatic experiences produce internalized objects and splits in the ego which generate psychopathology:

> How, short of longitudinal studies, can one adduce evidence
> for the causal chain of traumatic experiences . . . to psycho-
> pathology? Object relations theory . . . no less than Freudian
> theory, has to address the issue of the warrant for etiological
> conclusions based entirely on the productions of adult patients
> in treatment. The mere shift from repression as a pathogen to
> early traumatic deprivation and frustration that presumably
> produce splits in the ego does not attenuate the magnitude of
> the epistemological problems involved. It is difficult to under-
> stand on what basis advocates of object relations theory . . .
> believe that that theory somehow addresses or bypasses those
> of Grünbaum's criticisms of psychoanalytic theory that deal
> with its etiological claims [p. 383].

Eagle asserts the same conclusion in regard to self psychology, which
also regards as critical "the causal nexus" between infantile events and
present symptoms. Thus, to expand on Eagle's point, the epistemological burdens of "transference" theory weigh as heavily on the modern schools of psychoanalytic thought as on Freud's original theory.

The confluence of these criticisms of etiological theory of adult psychopathology in contemporary psychoanalysis independently developed
almost fifteen years apart by Arlow and Eagle, two distinguished psychoanalytic scholars of different training and experience, is remarkable.

Independent-of-Past-Experiences Responses

What is meant by a "newly created" response that is not a function of
past experience? A hypothetical illustration of an individual's "inde-
pendent-of-past-experience" response to a particular stimulus is based
on the concept of autonomous responses that are not repetitions of
specific past experiences. A particular individual may be so constituted that his response to his first experience during adolescence of
a particular form of vestibular stimulation, a roller coaster ride, is one
of pleasure—a *newly created* response. Of course, with any "first"
experience during adolescence, there must have been some prior experiences, in this instance of some forms of vestibular stimulation, but
not of this specific stimulation. Assume the adolescent had never seen
or heard about a roller coaster before this first experience. Because
this is his first experience, this response cannot have been influenced
by a similar, specific past experience. Assume that with no interven-

ing experience with a roller coaster ride, as an adult he has the same pleasurable response to a second roller coaster ride as he had to the first experience. As it was possible to account for the nature of his response to the first particular vestibular stimulus without invoking an effect of specific prior experience, so it is possible to account for his response to the second vestibular stimulus without hypothesizing a role for direct repetition of the prior experience. The most parsimonious explanation is that both responses were determined by the individual's capacity for a particular response to that specific vestibular stimulus. The same would be true of the individual's third response and his nth response. While it is possible that the second response was influenced by the first experience, there is no evidence to substantiate such a hypothesis. There is no reason to believe that if the person had not had an enjoyable first experience riding a roller coaster as an adolescent, he would have been unable to enjoy the subsequent adult experience. Parsimony suggests that the same explanation that served for the first response—the response is a function of the way the individual is constituted—would serve equally well for the second response.

Similarly, if a child has a particular reaction to intimidation by a caregiver and subsequently, as an adult, has a comparable reaction to intimidation by an authority figure, we do not know if the adult reaction is a displacement from or a repetition of the childhood experience or is determined by the individual's capacity to respond to intimidating authority figures in a certain way. In addition, we cannot know whether, even if the child had not had the childhood intimidation, the older individual might have responded similarly to an adult authority figure. The childhood experience may have influenced the adult reaction, but the only "support" for this hypothesis is an *assumption* such as Stone (1984) makes when he states that "the transference neurosis reenacts the essential conflicts of the infantile neurosis in a current setting" (p. 101). This is not to say that prior experience does not influence current behavior. Of course it does. But this can be substantiated only when we have independent evidence of the continuing effect of the prior experience in the absence of collateral causal factors.

For many patients, perhaps for all, the patient-analyst relationship is unique. It is new and different; they have never experienced one quite like it. Therefore, their adaptation, necessarily, must be at least in part a "newly created" response. What distinguishes the patient-analyst relationship is the analyst's nonjudgmental attitude, the depth of the analyst's understanding, the absence of retaliation by the analyst, and the analyst's consistent caring and emotional support. These qualities, taken together, comprise a constellation that the patient probably has never experienced. This distinctiveness of the relationship certainly plays a role in therapeutic efficacy. Since the relationship is so distinctly different from other, prior relationships, the patient's feelings cannot be simply a repetition of or displacement from an earlier historical relationship. The patient, confronted by this de novo relationship, must fashion, create, a new pattern of adaptation. This response may utilize elements of experience in a variety of prior relationships, but the gestalt of those elements will be new and unique.

If the relationship with the analyst created changes in the patient, it may well be that other, earlier relationships, unique in their own way, had also effected changes in the individual's development. These experiences, perhaps largely fortuitous, would have modified the course of development so that it did not follow a direct, continuous path.

Heritability and "Transference"

Freud credited the role of heredity on a number of occasions. In 1914 he acknowledged it as follows:

> With this sexual activity of the first years of childhood the inherited constitution of the individual also came into its own. Disposition and experience are here linked up in an indissoluble aetiological unity. For *disposition* exaggerates impressions which would otherwise have been completely commonplace and have had no effect, so that they become traumas giving rise to stimulations and fixations; while *experiences* awaken factors in the disposition which, without them, might have long remained dormant and perhaps never have developed [1914a, p. 18].

In 1937 he writes that "the properties of the ego which we meet in the form of resistances can equally well be determined by heredity as acquired in defensive struggles" (1937b, p. 241). Also in 1937 he acknowledges that patients' reactions are not a function *of only* past experience: "We have no reason to dispute the existence and importance of primary congenital variations in the ego . . . and it does not imply a mystical overvaluation of heredity if we think it credible that, even before the ego exists, its subsequent lines of development, tendencies and reactions are already determined" (1937a, p. 343). Although he referred to the "indissoluble aetiological unity" of heredity and environment, he did not, however, seem to recognize the implication of that unity. Because behavior is a function of heredity-environment interaction, if the role of heredity cannot be delineated separately, it is not possible to determine for the individual what the contribution of environment was.

The significant role of heredity in individual development recently received empirical support from a study of 1500 pairs of twins by Lykken and Tellegen (1996). These investigators conclude that about 50 percent of a person's sense of well-being—read self-esteem—is due to an inherited set point. Segal (1999) also attests to the heritability of well-being, so it seems very likely that inheritance plays some significant role in the individual's sense of well-being.

Friedman and Downey (2001) present a dramatic example of the role of heredity from the work of Wright (1997). Amy, a ten-year-old who had been adopted shortly after birth, was shy and had psychosomatic symptoms and somatic worries without cause and severe anxiety and gender confusion. Her adoptive parents both preferred her seven-year-old brother who was handsome and academically successful. Amy's adopted mother had low self-esteem and was threatened by Amy's attractiveness.

It was hypothesized that Amy was alienated in her family setting, insecure as a result of maternal inadequacies during the preoedipal period, and unable adequately to resolve oedipal phase conflicts because of defective input from both parents.

Amy's identical twin, Beth, was reared by different parents, both self-assured, supportive, and nurturant. Beth's stepbrother suffered from learning disabilities and behavioral difficulties, so Beth may have been perceived as the preferred child. Wright summarized Beth's developmental course as follows:

> In nearly every respect, however, Beth's personality followed in lockstep with Amy's dismal development. Thumb-sucking, nail-biting, blanket-clenching, and bedwetting characterized her infancy and early childhood. She became a hypochondriac and, like Amy, was afraid of the dark and of being left alone. She, too, became lost in role playing and the artificial nature of her personality was more pronounced than Amy's. She had similar problems in school and with her peers. On the surface,

she had a far closer relationship with her mother than Amy did with hers, but on psychological tests she gave vent to a longing for maternal affection that was eerily the same as her identical sister's . . . despite the difference in their environments their pathology was fundamentally the same [p. 5].

In chapter 5 I discuss three additional heritable characteristics: the predisposition to psychiatric disorder, responsivity to stress, and shyness and inhibition in response to the unfamiliar.

Stein (1981) observes that efforts to account for "transference" have, for the most part, failed to take into account both genetic endowment, on one hand, and late childhood, adolescent, and adult experiences, on the other. Only if these are considered will we "be able to prevent psychological explanations from deteriorating into a series of appealing fantasies, a kind of pseudo history based on presumed prehistoric events, which tends to operate as a defense against the discovery of something close to the genuine article" (p. 889). To add to the complexity, Emde (1988) observes: "The influence of heredity on individual differences in behavior *increases* as one goes from infancy through childhood and adolescence" (p. 26, italics added).

Hartmann, much earlier (1964), had adopted a complementary view about the role of heredity. "We have the right to assume that there are in man inborn apparatuses which I have called primary autonomy, and that these primary autonomous apparatuses of the ego and their maturation constitute one foundation for the relations to external reality" (p. xi). These "inborn apparatuses" are the origins of the newly created, relatively more specific responses that are critical to the individual's adaptation to external reality and supplement the brain's general pattern-seeking adaptive responses.

Behavior, including "transference," is always a function of the interaction of genetics with environment. Therefore, as a logical matter, so long as the individual patient's genetics are unknown, it is not possible to attribute with any certainty the cause for an individual's "transferences" to any of the individual's specific environmental experience(s) or to assess the relative proportion of trauma and constitution in that individual. Greenspan (1997) concurs.

No controversy about the predominance of nature or nurture in human development should exist. A child's constitutional makeup interacts with his emotional experience in a reciprocal manner so complex that there is no point in debating which factor contributes more. . . . There is mounting evidence that environmental influences can alter the physical structure of the brain, determining in part how genes express themselves in both biology and behavior. Even when a genetic influence has been well established, subtle environmental factors may still operate [pp. 133–134].

And vice versa. Thus, it is not possible with any certitude to determine which past environmental experiences *cause* the patients "transference" responses. Nonetheless, many analysts feel it is therapeutic for patient and analyst jointly to create a plausible narrative explicating the development of the patient's current feelings and fantasies. For example, Kennedy (1971) comments that although interpretation of the "transference" aims at showing the patient why he or she tends to function in a particular manner at the moment, a reconstruction of the past "may be brought in for purposes of adding conviction" (p. 400).

Summary

Freud's term "transference" completely fused two separate entities: the clinical phenomenon of the patient's intense unrealistic feelings about the analyst, and his theory about the *cause* of those feelings. The patient's feelings about the analyst are, virtually all analysts agree, worthy of investigation. Criticism here is directed solely at Freud's separate hypothesis concerning the *cause* of the patient's intense feelings. Theoretical changes in the context in which the development of the theory of "transference" took place pose difficulties for that theory. "Transference" was conceived as a "false connection" identifiable by the distorted or unrealistic nature of the patient's reaction. A most important, overt theoretical change occurred when Gill and Hoffman asserted that "transference" does not involve distortion, but utilizes realistic elements of the analyst; this removes the basis for categorizing the patient's reaction as a "false connection" or "transference," rather than as a newly created, realistic response to the analyst.

The attempt to substantiate the theory of "transference" by patient recall is fraught with problems, and Freud's tally argument fails to validate the hypothesis that a current feeling or fantasy is caused by a childhood feeling or impulse. Just as "transference" is influenced and shaped by interaction with the analyst, it is likely that the alleged infantile templates of "transference" have also been affected by other significant figures. Consequently, the effects of childhood experiences are likely to have been substantially modified by subsequent relationships; they would not have persisted unchanged and directly caused adult characteristics. These epistemological problems of the etiological theory of "transference" plague contemporary psychoanalytic theories no less than they do Freud's original views.

Behavior, including "transference," is a function of the interaction between the individual's genotype and experiences. Since the individual's genotype cannot be assessed, it is not possible to parcel out with any certitude the role of past experiences in causing the individual's current "transference." Nonetheless, many analysts believe that the joint creation of a plausible, explanatory narrative is therapeutic.

5

Infant Determinism
Trauma, Temperament, and Attachment

For these ideas [speculative theories] are not the foundation of science, upon which everything rests: that foundation is observation alone. They are not the bottom but the top of the whole structure, and they can be replaced and discarded without damaging it.

—Sigmund Freud, "On Narcissism"

Infant determinism is the keystone to the theory of "transference"; if it falls, the theory of "transference" cannot be upheld. Infant determinism is the cornerstone of any theory that hypothesizes that certain experiences of the infant and child have lasting effects, effects that persist continuously, essentially unchanged to adulthood, and that determine adult characteristics. Freud (1939) articulates this view:

It has long since become common knowledge that the experiences of a person's first five years exercise a determining effect on his life, which nothing later can withstand. . . . What children have experienced at the age of two and have not understood . . . at some time later it will break into their life with obsessional impulses, it will govern their actions, it will decide their sympathies and antipathies and will quite often determine their choice of love-object [pp. 125–126].

The traditional theory of "transference" relies on this hypothesis, that experiences during infancy and childhood have lasting effects that persist continuously and cause the adult patient's unrealistic feelings toward the analyst. Various contemporary schools of psychoanalytic thought also assume infant determinism, assume that these early experiences, or early relationships, are etiological in the formation of adult characteristics. Richards (2000) succinctly articulates this theory: "I would suggest that all of us agree that our wishes, fears and fantasies arise in the context of and are shaped by childhood interactions." Spezzano (2000) writes a qualified assent to Richards's assertion: "Of course we all would likely agree that our wishes, fears, and fantasies arise in the context of and are shaped, at least in part, by childhood interactions." Although widespread, this etiological hypothesis cannot be tested for a number of reasons discussed here, including the fact that analysts are limited to relying on unreliable retrospective recollections of childhood experiences from patients' reports.

Three types of psychological study are uniquely qualified to test the hypothesis of infant determinism because each utilizes defined samples of subjects, rather than self-selected patient populations, and because each studies these subjects empirically, using objective, reliable methods. The first is the study of the developmental consequences of early sexual trauma, itself the most directly relevant to the theory of "transference." The other two, that of temperament and that of attachment behavior, have the additional advantage that they empirically assess experiences during infancy and childhood and then observe the development of these subjects, either subsequently or by means of prospective, longitudinal studies. This affords an opportunity in each of these three areas of study to reject the null hypothesis regarding the theory of infant determinism.

In this chapter I propose there are theoretical reasons for believing that the continuity from infancy and childhood to adulthood, which is hypothesized by infant determinism, is not possible. Next, I consider what degree of continuity from childhood to adulthood is supported by empirical evidence in the previously noted three areas of psychological study, the consequences of early sexual trauma, temperament, and attachment behavior. Lastly, I summarize the implications of these empirical studies of development for the theory of "transference."

Critique of Infant Determinism

Thompson (1999) notes that "the belief that the child foreshadows the adult . . . is so deeply rooted in Western philosophy and North American psychology that recent voices questioning the formative significance of infancy . . . are disconcerting" (p. 280). These beliefs are evident in current affairs: Governor Zell Miller of Georgia is so convinced that playing classical music for two-year-olds makes them smarter that he is providing CDs to every new mother in the state, reports Erica Goode (1999). And in Florida, a new law requires that toddlers in state-run schools listen to classical music every day.

There are numerous roots to this widespread belief in infant determinism, which has resisted cogent criticism. People are more comfortable if they believe they can understand and explain human behavior. More specifically, at a very fundamental level, Stephen J. Gould (2000) hypothesizes that the human brain was designed for pattern recognition, that is, for detecting nonrandom associations. Just as nature abhors a vacuum, the human brain dislikes random distributions of phenomena. Gould notes that we see associations or clumps of stars in the heavens and give them names, rather than regarding them as bodies randomly distributed in space. Similarly, Gould describes how nineteenth century paleontologists assigned meaning to fossil rocks shaped like female genitalia and to those shaped like male genitalia. It took a long time for people to modify their perceptions and recognize these fossil rocks as the products of natural processes. From an evolutionary point of view, random phenomena provide no predictive information and therefore are not adaptively useful. Patterns, on the other hand, including associations or correlations, may provide adaptively useful information with potential predictive value.

Kagan (1998a) speculates that the belief in infant determinism persists in part because it is in accord with egalitarianism: with appropriate care, *all* infants could become equally successful adults. And, it makes it easier to state a cause-effect sequence. Psychoanalysts may well feel more comfortable believing that they know the childhood causes of the adult patient's unrealistic feelings and neurotic symptoms, rather than considering that they may not know what caused either.

For decades, analysts with disparate orientations and disparate agendas have warned about the inappropriateness of hypothesizing a literal, direct causation of the impact of childhood experience-fantasy on adult attributes. Some emphasize the importance of later corrective or pathogenic influences (Mahler and Kaplan, 1977), as well as noting surprising resilience following major infantile deficit or trauma (Emde, 1981, 1988; Greenspan, 1997). In an entirely different vein, selecting any predetermined time, such as childhood, as the determinant of conflict has been said to close the analyst's investigative field prematurely (Kernberg, 1987). Infant determinism hypothesizes a unitary dynamic or etiologic theme in the development of either normal personality or sexual orientation, but neither could be substantiated (Eagle, 1995; Schuker, 1996). A final encompassing conclusion from the same area of study is that development reflects a process of continual emergence, rather than a correlational replaying of the impact of early experiences (Chodorow, 1996).

Wolff (1996) presents a cogent theoretical argument that direct continuity from the child to the adult is not possible. He observes that "classic and current versions of psychoanalysis agree that the experiences of early childhood, real or imagined, are causally related to the psychological present, and that psychological development is a continuous though repeatedly transforming process" (p. 370). He presents a discussion of epigenesis and of nonlinear dynamic formulation "to establish a theoretical basis for the possibility that the psychoanalytic causal-predictive theories of mental development, even when taken on their own terms, may be fundamentally flawed, because predictions about the future in all such complex, marginally stable systems [the central nervous system of the child] may be *inherently* impossible" (p. 469). He adds that this does not imply that the past has nothing to do with the present, nor is it meant to challenge our intuition that our present selves are caused by the collective of all our past experiences.

Barratt (1996) supports Wolff's view, writing that "the possible contribution of complexity theory to this discussion is . . . that causal relationships between past and present, although deterministic instead of random, are inherently unpredictable and therefore in principle unknowable" (p. 473). He adds:

> Those who interpret the events of adult life in terms of infantile phenomena—whether objectively observed or idiosyncratically reconstructed—are engaging in grossly ideological maneuvers, the compelling quality of which is founded on a sort of myth making that reassuringly depicts continuities as a defense against acknowledgment of the nonlinear dynamic "chaos" out of which our representations of self and world are transiently constructed [p. 403].

Wilson (1996) also supports Wolff's thesis:

> As Wolff notes, similarity as a basis for attributing conceptual overlap and causality constitutes such a startlingly naïve stance toward higher-level theory construction that it makes one wince. Attributing causality between items in any perceived set merely because they possess some pattern match was known and warned against centuries ago, yet it tenaciously persists. In psychoanalytic theorizing, similarities can easily be found between two classes of items on virtually any psychological axis, but this does not tell investigators whether they are dealing with a true causal relationship or simply a more or less random overlap in the finite set of potential human actions. . . . The human mind apprehending nature all too easily confuses correlations for contingencies, when none in fact exist, a version of magical thinking found in normal mental life [pp. 454–455].

Stern (2000), one of the most eminent investigators of infants, acknowledges, in response to the question whether empirical infant observation is directly relevant to psychoanalysis, "I agree with André Green that infant observations can never prove or disprove a clinical or theoretical tenet of psychoanalysis" (p. 74). He qualifies his conclusion by stating that infant observations may be indirectly relevant in that a psychoanalytic concept, such as that of a stimulus barrier in infants, may, in the light of empirical data, be considered to have a low plausibility. Infant observation, he avers, can raise doubts about the plausibility of either clinical or theoretical psychoanalytic notions.

Fairfield (2001) argues that the irrelevance of infant observation for psychoanalytic theory is of no concern:

> A postmodern psychoanalyst would have no need whatsoever for a developmental theory, much less for any infant "observation" to back it up. Why? Because, when it comes to subjectivity, there are no raw data of observation; . . . and because, though agreeing that early experience in some way influences what comes afterward, postmoderns believe that any specific causal account is likely to be a retrodictive construct. The only purpose such a theory might serve is the pragmatic one of relieving the (modern) anxiety many patients and analysts still feel at the thought of doing without a fairly detailed story of psychological origins [pp. 235–236].

Freud's Position on Infant Determinism

In light of the foregoing, let us consider Freud's (1940) position on infant determinism at the end of his career.

> Analytic experience has convinced us of the complete truth of the assertion so often to be heard that the child is psychologically father to the adult and that the events of his first years are of paramount importance for his whole later life. . . . Our attention is first attracted by the effects of certain influences which do not apply to all children, though they are common enough—such as the sexual abuse of children. . . . Since these impressions [of childhood sexual abuse] are subjected to repression either at once or as soon as they seek to return to memories, they constitute the determinant for the neurotic compulsion which will subsequently make it impossible for the ego to control the sexual function and will probably cause it to turn away from that function permanently. If this latter reaction occurs, the result will be a neurosis; if it is absent a variety of perversions will develop, or the [sexual] function . . . will become totally unmanageable.
>
> However instructive cases of this kind [infantile sexual abuse] may be, a still higher degree of interest must attach to the influence of a situation which every child is destined to pass through . . . the *Oedipus Complex*. . . . The results of the threat of castration are multifarious and incalculable; they affect the whole of a boy's relations with his father and mother and subsequently with men and women in general. . . . The effects of the castration complex in little girls are more uniform and no less profound. . . . The whole occurrence [threat of castration], . . . may probably be regarded as the central experience of the years of childhood, the greatest problem of early life and the strongest source of later inadequacy [pp. 187–193].

Freud, as always, qualified his stance on the infant determinism of adult psychopathology. If instincts are reinforced at a later age, such as at puberty or menopause, or as a result of "fresh traumas, enforced frustrations, or the collateral influence of instincts upon one another. . . . We are not in the least surprised if a person who was not neurotic before becomes so at these times" (p. 226). These qualifications notwithstanding, Freud (1937b) stoutly maintained his theory of the infantile etiology of adult psychopathology: "It is familiar ground that the work of analysis aims at inducing the patient to give up the repressions . . . belonging to his early development. . . . We know that his present symptoms and inhibitions are the consequences of repressions of this kind" (pp. 258–259).

Another expression of Freud's belief that childhood traumatic experiences persist unchanged into adulthood is his view that the patient "is obliged to *repeat* the repressed material as a contemporary experience instead of . . . remembering it as something belonging to the past" (1920a, p. 18). In enabling the patient to recognize that what appears to be reality in the "transference" is in fact "only a reflection of a forgotten past . . . the patient's sense of conviction is won, together with the therapeutic success that is dependent on it" (p. 19). Thus, Freud reiterates his belief that it is the patient's recall of the repressed material that was the etiology of the current "transference" and that would produce therapeutic success. Here Freud essentially equates "transference" and neurosis, both of which he believes share a common sexual etiology.

Longitudinal Follow-up of Child Sexual Abuse

Child sexual abuse, Freud had written, will produce either neurosis or perversion, that is, will directly and uniformly cause adult psychopathology. Other analysts maintain considerably less linear versions of this point of view, including Levine (1997), who emphasizes "the impact on emotional development of actual childhood experience, including all kinds of trauma" (p. 316). Blum (1996) goes further, and postulates a causal role even in the absence of pattern: "The sexual abuse of children has protean effects without any uniform etiology or pathognomonic syndrome. Similar disturbances are found in nonabused individuals" (p. 1158). On the other hand, Parens (1997) points to the Oedipus complex as exacerbating some forms of abuse: "incest has specific pathogenic malignancy, because it uniquely intensifies the neurosogenic power of the child's Oedipus complex, the generative source of *neurotic* pathology" (p. 250).

Analysts offer as support for this thesis their inference that the experience of childhood sexual trauma is repeated in the "transference"—sometimes literally. For example, Davies and Frawley (1991) argue that the roles of victim, abuser, and rescuer are played out in the introjective-projective processes of the analyst-patient dyad. Levine (1997) writes, "*The experience of the treatment situation may feel like or even become the trauma.* . . . It is not unusual to discover residues of childhood sexual trauma first appearing in the quality of relationship that is being lived out in the transference rather than being reported in the patient's verbal associations" (pp. 320–321).

Pope and Vetter (1991) have suggested that about one-third of patients who had sex with therapists had a history of childhood sexual abuse, which Gabbard (1997) observes is "roughly equivalent to the incidence in the general population" (p. 379). Pope and Vetter's data indicate that two-thirds of patients who had sex with therapists did *not* report a history of childhood sexual abuse. Gabbard adds, "There is now extensive evidence that patients with childhood sexual abuse are much more prone to revictimization as adults (Briere, 1984; Russel, 1986; Chu and Dill, 1990)" (p. 380). Whether this increased risk was a function of an associated lower socioeconomic status was not examined. Further, Margolis (1997) discussed two cases where patient and analyst engaged in sexual relations and noted that both patients and analysts "had come from homes in which parents were distant, preoccupied, and sometimes quite sadistic with their children" (p. 363). He does not consider the incidence of such parental pathology—or of more marked pathology—in the histories of both analytic patients and analysts who do *not* become sexually involved with each other.

Gabbard estimates that approximately one-third of women experienced childhood sexual abuse. If the incidence of women analytic patients who have had childhood sexual abuse does not significantly exceed one-third—the prevalence in the population—this suggests that childhood sexual abuse is not likely to increase the probability of a woman seeking analytic treatment. Consistent with that impression is the report that only 20 percent of women who have been sexually abused in childhood have serious adult psychopathology (Browne and Finkelhor, 1986). Actually, Doidge et al. (1994) report that sexual abuse before age 14 was reported by 24 percent of 344 Canadian female analytic patients. Thus, the prevalence of childhood sexual abuse among female analytic patients is not only *not* greater than in the general population, if anything, it may be somewhat less. Further, it seems very likely that the majority of patients who developed an erotic transference or who became sexually involved with their analyst had *not* been exposed to childhood sexual trauma, and the majority of persons subjected to childhood sexual trauma did *not* develop significant adult psychopathology. Reports that suggest that childhood sexual trauma *caused* a particular transference reaction are inferences deduced by the analyst, which cannot be validated.

The hypothesis that child sexual abuse will directly and uniformly cause adult psychopathology was tested in an empirical study; results were reported in a thoughtful, careful, and intensive article in one of the most prestigious peer-reviewed journals of the American Psychological Association, the *Psychological Bulletin.* The authors, Rind, Tromovitch, and Bauserman (1998), employed metaanalysis, a statistical technique in which statistics from a set of studies are converted to a common metric (i.e., standard normal deviate z's) and then combined into one overall statistic. In order to examine the general population rather than a patient population, they utilized 59 usable studies of college students (36 published studies, 21 unpublished dissertations, and 2 unpublished master's theses). Prevalence rates were based on 35,703 participants and effect size data were based on 15,824 participants (3254 men from 18 samples and 12,570 women from 40 samples). Reaction and self-reported effects data were based on 3136 participants. The authors found that family environment was confounded with childhood sexual abuse (CSA) and explained nine times more adjustment variance than did CSA: "Analysis of studies that used statistical control further supported the possibility that many or most CSA-symptom relations do not reflect true effects of CSA because most CSA-adjustment relations become nonsignificant under statistical control" (p. 43).

This led to their conclusion that childhood sexual abuse was not to be understood apart from the effects of the family environment:

> [College] students with CSA were on average slightly less well adjusted than controls. However, this poorer adjustment could not be attributed to CSA because family environment (FE) was consistently confounded with CSA, FE explained considerably more adjustment variance than CSA, and CSA-adjustment relations generally became nonsignificant when studies controlled for FE. Self-reported reactions to and effects from CSA indicated that negative effects were neither pervasive nor typically intense, and that men reacted much less negatively than women [p. 22].

DeBellis (2000) provides additional data, observing that in children who experienced sexual abuse, 42 to 48 percent developed posttraumatic stress disorder. What of the 52 to 58 percent—a majority—who failed to develop posttraumatic stress disorder? DeBellis cautioned that in assessing the effects of trauma it is necessary to take account (as did Rind et al.) of many confounding variables, such as parental alcohol and drug addiction, low socioeconomic status, low education, and low intelligence.

The failure of Rind and colleagues' findings to support widespread beliefs in the predicted dire consequences of child sexual abuse stirred a great hue and cry both outside and within the American Psychological Association. Sullivan (1999) reported: "Outraged members of the religious right accused the A.P.A. of tolerating pedophilia and launched a crusade to punish the organization" (p. 40). The American Psychological Association issued a statement that the sexual abuse of children is a criminal act that is reprehensible in any context. The Association is requesting submissions of independent research, scientific comments, and public policy papers from experts on child sexual abuse for a special section in the *American Psychologist*. Further, the Association has taken the unprecedented step of seeking independent expert evaluation of the scientific quality of the article in question.

The clear failure of this large-scale, substantial, sophisticated study to find that childhood sexual abuse directly and uniformly causes adult psychopathology is a crippling blow to the theory of infant determinism, and to the theory of "transference" that is based on it.

Studies of nonsexual childhood trauma reach similar conclusions. An early adverse environment increases the probability of later disorder, but only if the adverse environment is maintained (Rutter and Rutter, 1993; Kagan and Zentner, 1996; Kagan, 1998a). If the stress of the early years continues throughout childhood and later, it is not possible to conclude that it was the early stress that was pathogenetic. Kagan (1998a) notes that despite Little Hans's childhood having been in a significantly dysfunctional family, with subsequently divorced parents, "even Freud had to recognize the resilience of 'Little Hans'—the boy with a phobia of horses. On meeting Hans a dozen years later, Freud encountered a well-adjusted youth of nineteen years who suffered from neither excessive conflict nor inhibition" (p. 112), and who, we now know, went on to a significant career.

Numerous investigations have focused on the degree of continuity observed in longitudinal studies from infancy to adulthood in subjects not selected for the presence of childhood trauma. Kagan (1998a) reports that longitudinal studies regularly find manifest inconsistency between childhood and adult functioning. This was true of Jean MacFarlane's prospective developmental study of children born in

Berkeley, California, through attainment of adulthood. On the other hand, the Abecedarian Project (Wilgoren, 1999) reported lasting effects of early day-care intervention, based on randomly assigning African-American children to full-time day-care from infancy to age five. By age 21 the experimental group consistently outperformed its peers who had not received the day-care. Inasmuch as the program also helped participants' parents throughout development, however, it was not possible to conclude that the improvement was due to the early day-care. In another study, Block (1993) did report consistency in ego-resiliency to young adulthood, though the picture was very different for girls than for boys.

Inderbitzin and Levy (2000) examined the bases of the belief that early traumatic experiences have important etiological consequences for psychopathology:

> There are now extensive data from a vast array of developmental studies and cognitive sciences challenging conventional concepts of linear development as simplistic and homogenized. . . . First, some resilient children do not develop significant psychopathology despite severe early trauma. Second, developmentalists have found more discontinuities than continuities in early development. A series of developmental transformations throughout early childhood leads to significant qualitative shifts in biological, cognitive, affective and social organization, suggesting that simple links between early and later behaviors, such as those assumed in the fixation-regression model, are unlikely to exist [p. 211].

They are unafraid to draw consequences for psychoanalysis:

> These frequent attempts to find states of mind in the past paralleling current, unexplained, adult states of mind, and then utilizing the past to explain the present by fixation or regression, are what Shapiro (1981) has referred to as a "circular path of reason that leads us to a 'no-win,' nonverifiable proposition" (p. 9). It also leads us away from analyzing [p. 216].

Numerous studies (including Rind et al.) report that continued residence in a family of poverty predicts increased difficulty in adult adjustment (Kagan and Moss, 1962). Adults raised in poverty who remain impoverished are more likely to have strokes, heart attacks, tuberculosis, and sexually transmitted diseases (Adler et al., 1994).

Temperament and Infant Determinism

Research into infant development has undergone a number of transformations as the problem of demonstrated lack of continuity has
become progressively more salient. One consequence has been to shift
the focus from the effects of infant experience to the question of the
consistency of temperament. Interest in temperament first surfaced in
the 1950s. Rutter (1987) characterized an attribute as temperament,
"If it can be defined in terms of a composite of simple behavioral styles,
if that composite has substantial neurobiological correlates and if there
is substantial consistency over time" (p. 447). Temperament, Rutter
believes, "Is best viewed in terms of simple, nonmotivational, noncog-
nitive stylistic features of which emotionality, activity and sociability
are the best validated" (p. 454). Temperamental traits, however, as
Rutter has noted, "Correlate very weakly from infancy to middle or
later childhood" (p. 446). The pioneering study of temperament by
Chess and Thomas (1990) reported that children who were classed as
difficult in their third and fourth years were judged to have achieved
a less adequate adult adjustment, though they noted that the outcomes
of a difficult temperament depended on the match between the child's
temperament and the family's expectations for the child.

One attribute of child behavior that has been intensively studied
as a temperamental trait is that of shyness or behavioral inhibition.
The inhibited type was one classification in the Dunedin investigation
(Caspi, 2000) of a cohort of 1037 individuals studied at age three and
followed until age 21. By age 21 the well-adjusted type (39 percent of
the cohort) tended to become normal, average young adults; the under-
controlled type (10 percent of the cohort) who were impulsive, rest-
less, negativistic, distractible, and emotionally labile children as adults,
reported more employment difficulties, higher levels of interpersonal
conflict at home and in their romantic relationships, had extensive
brushes with the law, and more frequently abused alcohol. The inhibited type (8 percent of the cohort) who as children were socially ret-
icent, fearful, and easily upset by strangers reported lower levels of
social support and more depression. These findings represented only
a small to medium effect size, explaining only a meager amount of the
variance in any single adult outcome. Nonetheless, despite the weakness of associations, Caspi emphasizes the numerous relationships
between temperamental qualities at age three and multiple, independently ascertained indexes of psychosocial functioning at different ages and in different settings. Caspi, however, fails to mention
socioeconomic class, potentially a major confounding variable.

Kagan (1998b) and colleagues also studied inhibited children. Kagan regarded shyness with strangers as only one feature of a broader temperamental category characterized by inhibition in the face of the unfamiliar: "Inhibited children react to many different types of unfamiliarity with an initial avoidance, distress, or subdued affect" (p. 212). Kagan notes that the parents of inhibited children are less extroverted (based on a personality question) than the parents of uninhibited children. He adds that inhibited and uninhibited profiles appear to be heritable, and concludes:

> There is consensus that some children inherit a special physiological vulnerability to some fear or anxiety states. . . . Fear [in response] to unfamiliarity or challenge is stable from early childhood to adolescence, even though the magnitude of the stability coefficient is modest. No more than one-third of children under 5 years of age who are inhibited will be diagnosed as having an anxiety disorder 10 years later. This means that most children grow towards health. . . . It is likely that an inhibited temperament makes a modest contribution to the development of the varied syndromes called anxiety disorders. Inhibited behavior is more stable in girls than in boys, and anxiety, phobias and panic attacks are more frequent among women than men. However, most inhibited children will not develop one of these psychiatric classifications. . . . About two-thirds of high-reactive, inhibited children will not develop a profile serious enough to be characterized by a psychiatrist as anxiety disorder. Predictions of a shy, restrained introverted adult personality from early inhibition is a much more likely outcome [pp. 222–223].

Studies of temperament thus yield several conclusions. A few temperamental qualities demonstrate continuity from childhood to adulthood, but the magnitude of the continuity is quite modest and is segregated in a few, small, relatively extreme groups of children. One of the most intensely studied traits, shyness and inhibition to the unfamiliar, occurs in approximately 8 to 10 percent of children and only approximately one-third of these, or 3 percent of children, demonstrate continuity to adult psychiatric disorder.

Even this limited continuity, however, fails to support the theory of "transferences," because the trait is heritable and therefore provides no substantiation to the hypothesis that the effects of childhood *experiences* persist and cause adult neuroses. Parsimony suggests that the continuity can be accounted for by the heritability of the trait; there are no data to support hypothesizing that the impact of childhood experience plays a supplementary role in the continuity. Since heritability cannot be assessed in the individual it remains impossible for the analyst to parcel out the input to adult disorder from constitution, and, consequently, to infer the role experience played. Nonetheless, despite the lack of validation, numerous analysts believe in the therapeutic impact of the mutually developed, plausible narratives about the role of childhood experience. On the other hand, appreciating the role of constitutionally based temperament may be quite useful in treatment, because it helps both analyst and patient to focus on finding patterns in the present and demarcating what can change in them.

Attachment Theory and the Theory of "Transferences"

Attachment theory shares the etiological hypothesis with "transference" theory that experiences during infancy and childhood can have lasting effects that persist continuously to adulthood, and determine specific adult characteristics. These response patterns may be adumbrated in "transference" responses. "Transference" theory hypothesizes that childhood sexual experiences cause the adult's unrealistic, intense feelings toward the analyst and the adult's neurotic symptoms. Attachment theory hypothesizes that the infant and child's internalized traumatic experiences with the primary caregiver may result in adult patterns of feelings and behavior which are likely to be replayed with the analyst, particularly with regard to separation.

Both theories, necessarily, must deal with two issues: whether continuity can be demonstrated, and whether causation, rather than correlation, can be established. The evidence in support of attachment theory especially warrants review because its literature provides us with empirical data, including those from prospective longitudinal studies.

Cassidy (1999) explains that the attachment bond is a specific type of a larger class of bonds referred to as "affectional bonds." "The attachment bond reflects only one feature of the child's relationship with the mother: the component that deals with behavior related to the child's protection and security *in time of stress*. The mother not only serves as an attachment figure, but may also serve as playmate, teacher, or disciplinarian" (p. 13; italics added).

Many attachment theorists believe that the mother's caregiving is, if not the exclusive determinant of the infant's attachment pattern, the primary determinant of that pattern. Crittenden (1995) provides a representative statement of that premise: "Maternal sensitivity is the primary determinant of quality of attachment at 12 months: sensitive mothers have secure children, inconsistent mothers have ambivalent children, and interfering/rejecting mothers have avoidant children" (p. 367). Psychological trauma can play a central role. If the caregiver exhibits "Frightened/Frightening" behavior (nomenclature of Hesse and Main, 1999) this is reflected in the infant's internalized representations of the caregiver which become the pathogenic nidus of the infant's separation and reunion responses. Although measures of the caregiver's attachment pattern are highly correlated with measures of the infant's attachment pattern, it is not clear what variables mediate that relationship (de Wolf and van IJzendoorn, 1997). Interventions that increased maternal sensitivity in the Dutch mothers of irritable infants shifted the infant's attachment toward the secure classification (van den Boom, 1994), but across all samples maternal sensitivity accounts for only a small proportion of the variance of the relationship between the caregiver's and the infant's patterns of attachment (de Wolf and van IJzendoorn, 1997).

Research measurement of the infant's attachment pattern to the primary caregiver utilizes Ainsworth's protocol, called the Strange Situation, which assesses responses of 12-month-old infants both to the presence of a stranger and reunion responses following two brief separations from the primary caregiver. Little association was found between infant temperament and the infant's pattern of separation (Vaughn and Bost, 1999).

Despite the latter negative finding, my critique of the etiological hypothesis of attachment theory, which credits maternal caregiving as the primary determinant of the infant's attachment pattern, is based on hypothesizing that at least three different heritable factors may influence the infant's response to the Strange Situation. Since these heritable factors cannot be measured, it is not possible to determine whether the caregiver's behavior is the primary determinant of the infant's response. The Strange Situation is stressful for insecurely attached, more inhibited toddlers, as evidenced by increased cortisol secretion in this group (Nachmias et al., 1996). There is evidence that such response to stress is heritable (Hewitt et al., 1991; Turner and Hewitt, 1992; Hellhammer and Wade, 1993). A second heritable factor is based on the finding that almost uniformly, children of mentally ill mothers exhibit insecure patterns of attachment (van IJzendoorn et al., 1992; National Institute of Child Health and Human Development,

1997). I hypothesize that this reflects a second inherited factor that may be operating, namely, that such children are at increased risk for inheriting a predisposition to mental disorder. A third, more controversial heritability factor, the temperamental trait of shyness and inhibition to the unfamiliar, may also be a component of the infant's response to the Strange Situation (Thompson, Connell, and Bridges, 1988; Mangelsdorf et al., 1990; Sagi, van IJzendoorn, and Koren-Karie, 1991; Calkins and Fox, 1992).

The caregiver's own attachment pattern is assessed by the Adult Attachment Interview, developed by Main, in which the mother discusses her earlier experiences with her own mother. The narrative is scored not for content, but for "lapses in the monitoring of discourse and reasoning" (Hesse and Main, 1999, p. 509), such as sudden changes in speech register or falling silent for 100 seconds mid-sentence. The rules for scoring lapses were developed empirically, selecting those maternal responses that correlated best with the infant's response to the Strange Situation. Clinically, these lapses seem to be linguistic manifestations of emotional dysregulation in response to the stress of the AAI; I postulate that they are linguistic expressions of anxiety, or depression, or both.

Consistent with this inference is Main's (1995) observation that a secure pattern of response to the AAI is rarely found in individuals suffering from psychiatric disorder or in the parents of psychiatrically disordered children; Dozier, Stovall, and Albus (1999) concur. This supports my hypothesis that those qualities of the AAI that were selectively correlated with the infant's Strange Situation classification were *also* linguistic expressions of some aspect of psychiatric disorder, reflecting heightened anxiety, depression, or both. Also consistent with this hypothesis that the AAI is also a form of mental status examination is the report (Fonagy et al., 1996) that intensive psychotherapy produced an increase in the proportion of secure classifications of the AAI. The theoretical significance of this finding that the AAI probably also measures psychiatric disorder is that it opens the possibility of genetic transmission of another heritable factor from the parent—a predisposition to psychiatric disorder in the infant. Further discussion critiques the evidence that the infant's pattern of separation is the cause of the later adult's pattern of separation.

How can we judge the continuity in attachment pattern from infancy to adulthood? The question is complicated by the fact that the instrument for measuring attachment in the infant, the Strange

Situation, is different from that used in the adult, the AAI. The former measures attachment to a specific, primary caregiver; the latter measures attachment more generally, "the state of mind with regard to attachment." There are few studies of attachment pattern from infancy to adulthood, and preliminary results appear conflicting. Main (1995) herself concludes, "In each of these studies there is sufficient unpredictability to refute any claim to early determinism with respect to adolescent or adult attachment status" (p. 448). Cassidy (2000) and Thompson (2000) concur with Main's statement about the plasticity of attachment patterns from infancy to adulthood. Crittenden (1995), too, talks about the potential for changes in development created by the interaction between experience and maturational factors.

> Genetically based characteristics do not determine quality of attachment, but, in the context of different sorts of parental behavior, they are expressed differently. . . . This interaction [between temperament and quality of attachment] is not static; it does not occur at some specific time (say infancy) and remain fixed thereafter. To the contrary, the interaction of biological endowment and circumstance is a dynamic process open to influence from all the relationships and experiences available to individuals, over the life span [pp. 388–390].

These findings can be summarized as follows: the infant's attachment patterns demonstrate conditional continuity. Only if new biological attributes do not appear during maturation, or if environmental circumstances are not markedly altered, is the attachment pattern likely to persist until adulthood. For a given infant it is not possible to predict the degree of continuity prospectively because neither the course of biological factors nor the nature of environmental circumstances is predictable.

Change in the pattern of attachment over time is a function not only of the history of past attachments, but, significantly, is a function of the impact of the current attachment relationship. Kobak (1999) observes that the predominant model of attachment theory of the 1980s and 1990s, that attachment security is largely determined in infancy and becomes an internalized part of personality that persists until adulthood, neglects Bowlby's more fruitful model in which current attachment relationships continue to be the major factor in whether a child or adult is in a secure, anxious, or distressed state regarding separation.

Kobak agrees with Thompson's emphasis on the importance of current socioemotional adaptation and writes:

> Viewing attachment as a relationship construct suggests that the validity of any measure of attachment security will depend on concurrent evidence that the individual has confidence in the availability of his or her primary attachment figure. . . . The true value of these methodologies will be realized only when working models are studied as part of the ongoing operation of the attachment system as it functions in current relationships [pp. 40–41].

We return to the issue of evaluating causation. The hypothesis of attachment theory that the impact of the infant's internalized experiences with separation from the primary caregiver is the primary *cause* of the adult's pattern of separation is not supported by the limited degree of continuity in attachment pattern from infancy to adulthood. As Crittenden asserts, the pattern of separation is a function of the interaction of biological endowment and circumstance. Because at least three heritable factors have been delineated that may influence the pattern of separation in either infant or caregiver—namely, responsivity to stress, predisposition to psychiatric disorder, and the temperamental trait of shyness and inhibition in the face of the unfamiliar—it is not possible to separate the role of experience in causing the pattern of separation. Without assessing the genotype we cannot parcel out the influences of biological endowment and of experience on the resulting pattern of attachment. The same problem has been articulated by Fonagy (1999a): "Attachment theory ignores biological vulnerabilities of the infant" (p. 449). Belsky (1999) proposes a related reservation: "Thus, security-insecurity may be a more heritably-determined feature in the case of some children and a rearing-determined one (in accordance with attachment theory) in the case of others" (p. 259).

Thus, despite the fact that, in contrast to psychoanalysis, attachment theory has been able to marshal empirical evidence, its etiological theory does not avoid the same epistemological problem, validating cause, that challenges the theory of "transference." As with "transference" theory, however, the uncertainty about "cause" does not mean that the development of plausible etiological hypotheses about attachment behavior may not be useful, as plausible explanatory narratives may be useful in psychoanalytic practice. Exploration of the parameters of interaction between caregiver and infant may illuminate some of the interactions between patient and analyst.

Summary

Infant determinism is the keystone to the theory of "transference"; if it falls, the theory of "transference" cannot be upheld. The term *infant determinism* refers to a theory that hypothesizes that certain experiences of the infant and child have lasting effects, effects that persist continuously, essentially unchanged, into adulthood, and determine adult characteristics. Three areas of psychological study have collected empirical data that enable one to test the hypothesis of infant determinism: the developmental consequences of early sexual trauma, of temperament, and of early attachment behavior. Freud's sexual theory of the etiology of neurosis is undermined by the results of empirical follow-up studies that reported that the adult effects of childhood sexual abuse were not significant when adjusted for characteristics of the family environment. Abuse was consistently confounded with family environment, and family environment explained considerably more of the variance in adult adjustment than childhood sexual abuse alone. Aside from childhood abuse, longitudinal studies of a variety of populations regularly find manifest inconsistency between childhood and adult functioning. Both negative findings, the dearth of demonstrable consequences of childhood sexual abuse and the lack of consistency from childhood to adult functioning, fail to support the theory of infant determinism.

Studies of temperament do demonstrate continuity from childhood to adulthood for a few traits, but the magnitude of the continuity is quite modest and is localized in a few small, relatively extreme groups of children. This limited continuity, however, fails to support the theory of "transferences," because the most parsimonious explanation is that these traits are heritable rather than a function of childhood experience alone. The few studies of the continuity of attachment behavior from childhood to adulthood demonstrate conflicting preliminary results. I hypothesize that the measures of attachment pattern, both in infant and adult, are confounded because at least three heritable traits—responsivity to stress, predisposition to psychiatric disorder, and the temperamental quality of shyness and inhibition in the face of the unfamiliar—interact with environmental circumstances. Because it is not possible to assess the inherited factors, the genotype, it is not possible to parcel out the role played by childhood experiences in causing the adult attachment pattern. Thus, despite empirical data, the same epistemological problem applies to attachment theory as applies to "transference" theory. Lastly, change in the pattern of attachment over time is a function not only of the history of past attachments, but importantly, of the current attachment relationship.

6
"Transference" Theory and Chaos Theory

From Parmenides to Marx, philosophers dreamed of the single principle, the single method, the single being, metaphysical or anti-metaphysical, sacred or profane, that would account for everything that exists, and bring everything that exists under a single description. [Isaiah] Berlin set out to awaken Western thought from that dream. His lifelong analysis of the idea of wholeness exposed it as a dangerous illusion. . . . He showed that it had no philosophical sense. "In the house of history," he wrote, "there are many mansions" . . . [Berlin] simply and truly detested determinisms.

—Leon Wieseltier, "When a Sage Dies, All Are His Kin"

The theory of "transference" is causal; chaos theory is not. Chaos theory illustrates how unstable dynamic systems *are not predictable*. In this chapter I argue that chaos theory is applicable to the clinical phenomena on which "transference" theory is based, and, once that applicability is recognized, "transference" behaviors are seen as neither predictable forward in time nor backward in time, that is, to those putative childhood causes of present "transference" behaviors. Chaos theory, if accepted and understood, undermines the validity of the causal nature of "transference" theory.

Unstable Systems, Time, and Certainty

Historically, chaos has not had a very good name. The birth of Christ, Bronstein (1998) writes, was considered to be a reenactment of the original act of creation out of chaos. According to the Christian order established from this birth, "All outside of the scheme of salvation belong to a taxonomy of chaos, a realm of dismal darkness and blindness, the realm of Devil" (p. 39). In the present, however, the reputation of chaos is changing, and Gore Vidal (1999) suggests: "Chaos—our current condition—may prove to be altogether too interesting to make order of (p. 39).

Bertrand Russell (1953) presaged the development of chaos theory.

> The case where one event A is said to "cause" another event B, which philosophers take as fundamental, is really only the most simplified instance of a practically isolated system. It may happen that, as a result of general scientific laws, whenever A occurs throughout a certain period, it is followed by B; in that case, A and B form a system which is practically isolated throughout that period. It is, however, to be regarded as a piece of good fortune if this occurs; it will always be due to special circumstances, and would not have been true if the rest of the universe had been different though subject to the same laws [p. 398].

I consider this to mean that any change in the conditions might modify the relationship of A to B in ways that are unknown and not predictable.

Nowotny (1998) describes the introduction of chaos theory more than a generation later:

> The enthusiastic reception of chaos theory [in the mid-seventies] can be seen as one of the subtle shifts from a regime that valued homogeneity to one that braces itself to live in a world of heterogeneity. Chaos theory captured the imagination of Western intellectuals and the general educated public alike. They see in it a striking vindication of their deeply entrenched reservations against the excessive claims of scientific predictability. Their own understanding and experience resolutely disconfirmed the predictability of human affairs in general and of public affairs in particular. If a butterfly's wing over the

Pacific could give rise to a tornado over Texas, it proved their implicit view of nonlinear dynamics to be right, even if no scholar of the humanities had ever used this term before. Epistemologically speaking, the robust link between determinism and predictability had gone [p. 94].

It is precisely that link between determinism and predictability which Freud depended on in fashioning his theory of "transference." I argue that "transference" behavior has the characteristics of an unstable, nonlinear dynamical system, and chaos theory explains why exact prediction, either forward or backward, is not possible in such a system.

Kellert (1993) describes chaos theory:

Chaos theory is *the qualitative study of unstable aperiodic behavior in deterministic nonlinear dynamical systems. . . .* A dynamical system is thus a simplified model for the time-varying behavior of an actual system. Unstable behavior means that the system never settles into a form of behavior that resists small disturbances. Unstable aperiodic behavior makes exact prediction impossible and produces a series of measurements that appear random [pp. 2–4]

Kellert elaborates: "Unpredictability results from the feature of all chaotic systems known as sensitive dependence on initial conditions . . . because even the smallest degree of vagueness in specifying the initial state will grow to confront the researcher with enormous errors in calculation of the system's future state" (pp. x–xi). Consequently, "chaotic systems require us either to revise or discard determinism" (p. 62). "Determinism is not so much proven false as rendered meaningless" (p. 74). This interdiction vitiates the old notion of determinism that Freud learned in his scientific training, which permeated psychoanalytic training until very, very recently, and which called for and found perfect predictability in principle.

Prigogine (1997) adds to the development of chaos theory a conception that has further implications for "transference" theory.

We have inherited two conflicting views of nature from the nineteenth century: the time reversible view [e.g., the addition of time and the subtraction of time have the same function in the behavior of a pendulum] based on the laws of dynamics, and the evolutionary view [time irreversible, such as the disappearance in a radioactive substance] based on entropy [p. 19].

Eddington (1958) elaborates that irreversible processes produce entropy, and this has been called the "arrow of time."

Time irreversible systems are unstable, and "instability destroys the equivalence between the individual and statistical levels of description" (p. 35). That is, unstable systems, even with complete information, can be examined only in the context of populations, not individuals: "Once we include these concepts, we come to a new formulation of the laws of nature, one that is no longer built on certitudes, as is the case for deterministic laws, but rather on *possibilities*. Moreover, in this probabilistic formulation time symmetry is destroyed" (p. 29).

Thus, recognizing each individual as an unstable system means we cannot make deterministic, causal statements or valid predictions about the individual, but are limited to probability statements about either that individual's future or past. We are accustomed to such alternatives in our daily life. For example, if you are driving along and a sign says "No shoulder ahead," that is a categorical prediction; if a sign says "May be delays," that is a probability statement, and that is what we are limited to with human individuals, Freud's theory of "transference" notwithstanding.

Psychoanalysis enables us to determine associations or correlations between feelings or behaviors within an individual, but not categorical *causes* of feelings or behaviors; associations are limited to probability statements. Fraser (1998) reaches a similar conclusion: "It is not possible to make predictions about human conduct in the service of concrete or symbolic causes without allowing for biological intentionality [in the service of biological needs] as well as for deterministic, probabilistic and chaotic contributions" (p. 13). Fraser supports Prigogine's emphasis that neither specific predictions nor statements about specific causes can be made in relation to an individual. He affirms that we are limited to a probability statement rather than to a categorical statement either about future behavior or about the past cause of present behavior. Thus, the analyst cannot properly make a categorical statement, that the patient's current separation anxiety is caused by a traumatic childhood separation experience. The analyst should be limited to stating that there is some unknown statistical possibility that the childhood experience may be causally related to the current separation anxiety.

Mosher (1990), an astute analyst, reaches the same conclusion.

Chaos theory . . . *decisively severs the tie between determinism on the one hand, and predictability of outcome on the other.* This notion is so startling and foreign that it represents what may be a major paradigm shift (in the sense of Thomas Kuhn) in our view of the world. It says, in effect, that even though deterministic laws strictly determine the behavior of a system, it may *in principle* be impossible to predict the system's behavior for more than a very short time. And, more startling, this is the way that most of the world actually works. So it's possible to have strict psychic determinism without predictability. More than possible, it's a likely conclusion [p. 96].

An Unstable System: Putting in Golf

Putting in golf, which appears to be a remarkably simple physical system, provides what turns out to be a good example of an unstable system. If a golf ball is moved in a certain direction at a particular acceleration it will end in the hole. A putting machine was developed (Pelze and Mastroni, 1989) which could always impart to the golf ball a particular acceleration and direction, but on the green many putts were missed. By moving to a brand-new, high-quality, slate-bed pool table, all putts were successful, though at a distance of eight feet the ball did not always roll into the center of the pocket, and on longer putts would have missed the pocket. Why wasn't the outcome of this absolutely reliable putting machine always predictable?

Chaos theory hypothesizes that in unstable systems, random, tiny perturbations impact the initial condition as well as various stages of the trajectory, and will have cumulative effects that result in a substantial modification of outcome. In this putting example, these tiny perturbations include whether the golf ball is perfectly spherical and perfectly balanced, how the golf ball is constructed and the material it is made of, as well as, on the golf course, inconsistencies of the green, such as footprints, ball divots, spike marks, and diseases. Even Tiger Woods, on rare occasions, will miss a four-foot putt. Since such tiny perturbations in this simple physical system can substantially effect continuity of outcome from trial to trial, extrapolation makes it easy to conceive how random perturbations in the extraordinarily complex development of a child's nervous system, subject as it is to genetic influences as well as random environmental experiences, can produce discontinuities in the child's development, and render the outcome of that development not predictable.

Can chaos theory appropriately be applied to "transference" behaviors? Do "transference" behaviors constitute a dynamic, unstable system, or are they essentially a stable system, in which case it is not appropriate to apply chaos theory to "transference" theory? Considering not just "transference" behavior, but, more broadly, certain emotional symptoms, fears, and character traits, in the absence of treatment, seem to persist for long periods, for years: that is, they seem to be a continuous, stable system. That impression needs to be qualified from several points of view because of our need to perceive apparent continuity. The first is the time-scale employed. Does the statement that a symptom has persisted for years mean it has been present in every one of those years? Has it been present in every month of each year, in every week of each year, and so forth? To whatever degree there are discernable periods of absence, we may conclude that certain perturbations affect the presence or absence of the symptom and therefore it is to that degree unstable. The smaller the unit of time of observation, for instance, hours rather than days, the greater will be the evidence of instability of the system.

Within the time-scale of a clinical treatment situation, from week to week and from session to session, most analysts are impressed that symptoms, fears, and character traits, as well as feelings and fantasies about the analyst, vary in their nature, focus, and intensity, and analysts will agree they are unable to predict these variations. This is evidential support of the thesis that these expressions of psychopathology are responding to various perturbations in unpredictable ways. It is not a large leap to conclude that the symptom complexes of psychopathology, including the distorted feelings and fantasies of "transference," may appropriately be considered expressions of unstable systems.

In addition to these intrinsic variations, the context or conditions of measurement are very likely to influence the assessment of variability. Measurements during a nontreatment period, when change is not expected, are likely to enhance an impression of stability, whereas measurements during a treatment period, when change is expected, increase the impression of change in the present. The use of different instruments will also influence the measurement.

Chaos Theory Applied to "Transference"

Repeated measurements of various "transference" feelings, such as the patient's current conscious and unconscious feelings about the analyst, including positive feelings, negative feelings, and erotic feelings, together constitute a time series of an unstable system. Chaos theory can be applied to repeated measurements of any one-dimensional time series record and, therefore, could be applied to each of these records of various "transference" feelings expressed by the patient about the analyst.

Sophisticated research measures of the patient's "transference" feelings were developed by Luborsky and Crits-Christoph (1990) to measure Freud's "transference" template, though without including any reference to putative childhood origin. These measures, called the Core Conflictual Relationship Theme (CCRT), assess "each person's recurrent central relationship pattern" (p. 4), which is derived from narratives about interactions with other people. These measures are described further in chapter 9; what is relevant to this discussion of the application of chaos theory to "transference" feelings are the questions of variations in the measurement of the initial state of "transference."

Luborsky and Crits-Christoph initially found that when judges made inferences about each patient's narratives using descriptive categories that fit each patient the best, which they characterized as the "tailor-made system," interjudge reliability was not satisfactory. Therefore, they developed a new, standard system in which each time a judge wished to make a particular kind of inference, the judge was instructed to use an appropriate word from a standard category list. When the original judges' tailor-made CCRT formulations of therapists' interpretations were coded into standard categories by three other judges, agreement was greater than 95%. Thus, the change from a tailor-made to a standard system achieved a very satisfactory reliability, at the price, however, of some sacrifice of validity.

This diminution in validity means that there will be some minor degree of vagueness or lack of accuracy in the CCRT's measure of the patient's current "transference" feelings—the initial state. Consequently, as Kellert noted, in an unstable system the smallest degree of vagueness in specifying the initial state of "transference" behavior will render prediction impossible, either forward or backward to the putative childhood cause of the current feelings. Thus, even with the achievement of a reliable measure of the patient's current "transference" feelings, it is not possible to "predict" backward what the childhood cause had been. Quinodoz (1997) makes the same point: fluctuations in the assessment of the patient's initial condition preclude prediction; human psychic activity "is above all subject to sensitivity to initial conditions," and this sensitivity "is indeed the characteristic feature of the unpredictability of human behavior and psychic functioning" (p. 704).

Chaos Theory and Backward "Prediction"

Prior to these new theories of nonlinear dynamics, analysts saw no other way to proceed than to assume a causal path from past to present—even if they simultaneously conceded there was no way to predict from the present to the future. The fact that forward prediction and backward prediction entail the same logical operation failed to impact on analytic thinking. Bertrand Russell (1953) explains:

> The law [of causation] makes no difference between past and future: the future "determines" the past in exactly the same sense in which the past "determines" the future. The word "determine," here, has a purely logical significance: a certain number of variables "determine" another variable if that other variable is a function of them [p. 396].

That is, if C varies as a function of A and B, then in a logical sense A and B "determine" C—regardless of whether A and B are future events or past events.

Even further, Kellert thus quotes Earman (1986) about the reason a belief in determinism is maintained: "if the only alternatives to determinism are final causes (e.g., divine intervention) and hazard (e.g., accident or chance) then determinism is attractive as an a priori truth or a methodological imperative of scientific inquiry" (p. 55). Clearly, and understandably, analysts would be more comfortable embracing determinism than accepting and relying on either divine intervention or chance as the organizing force in their patients' lives.

Thus, chaos theory exposes a contradiction in belief among those analysts who accept their inability to predict the patient's future behavior, but practice as if they can "predict" the patient's past behavior, that is, "predict" what childhood experiences caused the patient's present behavior. Chaos theory clarifies how forward predictions about future behavior and backward "predictions" about past behavior involve the same functions. Just as vagueness about initial conditions makes future predictions impossible, so does vagueness about present, initial conditions make backward predictions about origin invalid.

Freud himself (1920b) believed that the analyst could satisfactorily trace development only backward to its origin, while simultaneously accepted that the analyst could not predict from that origin forward to the present.

So long as we trace the development from its final outcome backwards, the chain of events appears continuous, and we feel we have gained an insight which is completely satisfactory or even exhaustive. But if we proceed the reverse way, if we start from the premises inferred from the analysis and try to follow these up to the final result, then we no longer get the impression of an inevitable sequence of events which could not have otherwise been determined. We notice at once that there might have been another result, and that we might have been just as well able to understand and explain the latter. The synthesis is thus not so satisfactory as the analysis; in other words, from a knowledge of the premises we could not have foretold the nature of the result [p. 167].

Despite his recognition of the frailty of any attempts at forward prediction from childhood events, in his last major statement in *Analysis Terminable and Interminable,* Freud (1937b) maintained a strong conviction that he could "predict" backward that childhood disorder was the cause of adult neurosis: "The next question we come to is whether every alteration of the ego [brought about by the defenses] . . . is acquired during the defensive struggles of the earliest years. There can be no doubt about the answer" (p. 240). He invoked as an example a patient who "was able to produce all the memories and to discover all the connections which seemed necessary for understanding his early neurosis and mastering his present one" (p. 217), though, in fact, later Freud had to help the patient master a part of the "transference" which had not been resolved.

Analysts have adopted such contradictory attitudes toward forward and backward prediction of patient behavior that it is useful to consider how this contradiction is comfortably maintained. When the analyst makes a future prediction about the patient's behavior, it is usually very clear whether the prediction was correct or not. When it comes to backward prediction about the origins of the patient's current psychopathology, however, there is no definite way to test the hypothesis—no clear-cut way to disconfirm it. Often both patient and analyst have an investment in enhancing the plausibility of the proposed hypothesis, and both become skilled at doing so. Subsequent associations, therefore, may support, elaborate, and enrich the hypothesis, enabling a conviction about the specific childhood origins of adult psychopathology based on backward "prediction." This may, for current defensive reasons, coexist comfortably with the recognition that future prediction is impossible.

Change is Nonlinear

Lewis (1997), a developmental psychologist, writes, "The unpredictability of human lives is undeniable" (p. 177). Work in chaos theory suggests that failure of prediction will always occur when the models of change are considered to be linear:

> There is little likelihood that change is linear. Given the large number of interactions in the course of a life history, small differences can become exaggerated into radical differences as a consequence of the large number of interactions that serve to elaborate the initial difference. The sequence of interactions is not ordered and is often random, so the differences observed could not have been predicted. . . . Any small difference in the original form, through reiteration, will appear at the end as an enormous difference [p. 179].

Remember when people in a circle whisper a statement from one to another how strikingly different it emerges at the end of the circle?

One principle of chaos theory is nonlinearity. Lewis notes: "While variables may covary in a linear fashion over part of a range of values, there is no reason to assume that they need to vary linearly over the entire range" (p. 180). Analysts may explain their inability to predict future behavior by invoking the principle of nonlinearity, though they eschew reference to nonlinearity in looking backward at their patient's childhood. He adds that chance events interfere with our inclination to view the developmental process as a continuous one:

> Chaos and catastrophe exist . . . chance encounters and accidents occur. Predictability is unlikely since the task of living organisms . . . is to adapt to their current context. . . . Such a view poses a serious threat to the world view that the developmental process is continuous and that earlier events cause

later ones. . . . Self identity requires continuity, that we see
our lives and those of others around us as a continuous
flow. . . . It is a difficult conception to give up because we are
unable and unwilling to relinquish our belief in our own identity [p. 182].

The Role of Chance in Development

Freud acknowledged that chance could profoundly influence individuals' development, but clinically he, and other analysts, remain apt to
find the hidden hand of unconscious determinism in many of the experiences that patients label as chance. Freud's fundamental discovery
was of the powerful role of unconscious forces in the individual.
Nonetheless, there are experiences and events that are completely
independent of unconscious drives and feelings and are attributable
solely to the random role of chance. To turn to some examples of the
latter, Kagan (1998a) notes: "Had Darwin's uncle not volunteered to
drive thirty miles [on horseback] to persuade Charles' father to let him
go on the *Beagle* voyage, the young Darwin would have missed the
sculpting experience of his life" (p. 148). A. O. Scott (1999), reviewing
books about the writer and poet Raymond Carver, describes the
author's accidental discovery of twentieth-century literature.

> Working as a delivery boy for a pharmacist in Yakima,
> Washington, already, at eighteen or nineteen, a husband and
> father, Carver, obsessed with the need to "write something,"
> was given copies of *Poetry* and *The Little Review Anthology*
> by an elderly customer. Just as so many of his characters find
> their lives subtly but unmistakably altered by casual, contin-
> gent happenings, so did Carver find himself changed by his
> encounter with the old man, whose name he quickly forgot
> and whom he never saw again: "Nothing remotely approach-
> ing that moment has happened since" [p. 53].

Chance has clearly affected my own life and alerted me to its importance. At age eighteen, in 1943, during World War II, I enlisted in the
Navy Air Corps and received orders to proceed to flight training, at
that time a 90-day program, due to the desperate straits of our Pacific
fleet. On the two U.S. aircraft carriers still afloat, the combat life of
those "90-day wonder" Navy pilots was measured in minutes.

My orders were cancelled at the last minute without explanation; I was upset and disappointed by the cancellation, which, in retrospect, probably spared me from death in air combat in the Pacific. After months of delay, I received new orders to proceed to the Navy Air Corps Program at Dartmouth College. Subsequently I learned that my initial orders were cancelled because Navy Air Corps regulations required that an enlistee have completed two years of college, including one year of English. A clerk reviewing my College of the City of New York transcript realized that I had completed only one semester of English. (Because upper classmen always registered first at City, the second term of English was always filled.) A less conscientious or more independently minded clerk might well have decided that such a regulation requiring a full year of English might be waived under the extraordinary circumstances of World War II, and sent me on to flight training.

My second English course exposed me to the full curriculum of a private college and shaped the remainder of my life. Earlier, no field had appealed to me, but at Dartmouth I developed a relationship with a wonderfully generative mentor, a psychology professor. I became fascinated with psychology and, as a veteran, went on to a fellowship at Harvard to work for a Ph.D. in clinical psychology in the new Department of Social Relations. I decided then to go on to medicine, psychiatry, and psychoanalysis. Additionally, while there I met the young Radcliffe student I married. Thus chance had deflected my course from death in the Pacific at age 18 to a lasting marriage and a long career in psychoanalysis. Little wonder I have been impressed with the unpredictable impact of chance on people's lives.

Chaos Theory and Development of the Nervous System

Major brain growth during the first two years of life is neither linear nor continuous (Balaban, 1998). Pally (1997) makes a related observation: "To a startling degree, it is interactions with the environment that stimulate the more precise wiring of neural connections," and he adds, "throughout life every part of the nerve cell, from soma to synapse, alters its dimensions in response to environmental stimulation" (pp. 589–591). Wolff (1996) makes related points. Some behavioral structures or functions (and their neural substrates) may play a critical role in the organism's adaptation at one point in early development and then disappear entirely, along with degeneration of their neural substrates. The central nervous system extensively remodels itself. Further, as reflected in chaos theory, under some initial conditions, minor stimuli will precipitate a radical reorganization of the neural networks, while under other initial conditions major stimuli will have no effect on them. Linear continuity of either neural networks or specific fantasies seems most unlikely. Squire (1992) notes that new perceptions are first registered in the hippocampus and subsequently are transferred for memory storage to the neocortex. This necessity for transfer is another opportunity for minor perturbations. Hilts (1997), discussing the complexities of early neural development, muses, "No wonder humans are so weird and unpredictable."

These unpredictable discontinuities, Wolff argues, render infant observations essentially irrelevant for psychoanalysis. Barratt (1996) concurs, "these neuroscientific findings do place significant limitations on the scientificity of any psychotherapy that claims to arrive by narratological reformation at a veridical comprehension of the patient's history" (p. 402).

Wolff (1998) adds, in response to further comments about his contentions:

> I am not aware of having claimed that childhood experiences have no influence on the psychological function of adults. . . . My point was therefore not to deny the possibility of continuities in psychological development, but to assert that (1) except in a crude and trivial sense, we have no idea *how* antecedent conditions in complex organisms induce novel properties not present in the antecedent condition; (2) we can probably never test probatively how variations in earlier psychological, physiological, or physical processes determine current psychological states, because the kinds of experiments that would be required to come up with even approximate answers are impossible to perform on humans; and (3) given this vacuum in our knowledge, we either fall back on correlations (too often attributing causal significance to them), or else we make up stories based on hypostasized categories that, as I tried to show, are usually based on circular reasoning [pp. 274–275].

Chaos Theory and Therapeutic Efficacy

Chaos theory does not automatically imply therapeutic nihilism. Freud and later analysts were unaware of, or disregarded, the data that many effective treatments in medicine prevail without knowledge of the cause of the disorder. Treatment of hypertension is but one example. Knowlton (1997) makes the same point: "We don't need resolution of theoretical conflicts regarding etiology to develop a system to guide medication use in combination with psychoanalysis. Rather, we must focus on phenomenology" (p. 61). We don't need to delineate the causes of adult psychopathology to be helpful to troubled patients. Future psychoanalytic work will indicate how the balance of technique, whether primarily structuring treatment according to the traditional exploration of childhood experience or primarily focusing on patient-analyst interaction in the here and now, will influence therapeutic efficacy.

Summary

The patient's feelings and fantasies regarding the analyst can be described as unstable aperiodic behavior in a nonlinear dynamic system. Chaos theory, by elucidating how even the smallest degree of vagueness in specifying the initial state of such a system renders impossible either prediction forward in time or backward in time, thereby forecloses any predicting of the earlier putative childhood cause of the present "transference." Even where relatively reliable measures of "transference" have been achieved, there is significant vagueness in measuring the patient's current feelings about the analyst—"transference"—which vitiates both future prediction and backward prediction to the putative original cause (childhood experience). For the individual, although associations (i.e., correlations) can be determined, categorical, *causal* relationships cannot; at best, only the *probability* of a relationship can be estimated. Chance experiences do occur independent of the patient's unconscious drives and feelings, and these may profoundly alter the trajectory of the individual's development. Despite the failure to know the childhood etiology of "transference," effective psychoanalytic treatment is quite possible, just as many medical disorders of unknown etiology are effectively treated.

7

The Theory of "Transference"
Problems with Clinical Application

> *Hannah: It can't prove to be true, it can only not prove to be false yet.*
>
> —Tom Stoppard, *Arcadia*

Many traditional analysts emphasize "transference" interpretations of the childhood etiology of the patient's feelings about the analyst. Usually, these interpretations seem quite plausible and often they seem to be associated with therapeutic benefit. What is the problem?

Despite the plausibility of many "transference" interpretations, methodological considerations suggest it may not be possible to validate them from the data of the analysis. The resultant degree of uncertainty renders them comparable to inexact interpretations, the efficacy of which was thought to be caused by suggestion and a placebo effect. The analyst's focus on historical "transference" interpretations centers on the childhood origins of the patient's psychopathology, which may reduce the analyst's interest in examining and analyzing the current role of suggestion and placebo effect. The latter involves scrutinizing the analyst's authority and the patient's experience of it (i.e., patient-analyst interaction) rather than primarily the patient's individual psychopathology. It would be useful to try to distinguish the mutative effects of childhood-focused "transference" interpretation, of suggestion and placebo effect, and of patient-analyst interactions.

Among the potential problems consequent to focusing intently on the preparation and presentation of historical "transference" interpretations may be the patient's experiencing them as distancing and critical. Under these circumstances the analyst may fail to attend to the nurturance of the therapeutic alliance and lose sight of the importance of the analyst's affirmation of the patient. The analyst may also tend to become less vigilant regarding the possibility that the patient's motivation for exploring childhood recollections may be in the service of defensively avoiding troublesome current conflicts. And, by concentrating on "transference" interpretation, the analyst may overlook disturbing feelings that are not expressed toward the analyst, but do surface in other relationships, such as with spouse, children, siblings, or friends.

"Transference" Interpretations

Participation in study groups and discussion of case reports enables many analysts to recognize that analysts cannot reliably agree on "transference" interpretations. Although this was empirically confirmed in four studies (Seitz, 1966; De Witt, Kaltreider, Weiss, and Horowitz, 1983; Luborsky and Schaffler, 1990; Caston and Martin, 1993), the implications of this lack of reliability for the concept of "transference" are not taken seriously and are rarely discussed in the literature. Can a fundamental concept be viable if it cannot be assessed reliably? Despite the lack of clinical reliability, Luborsky and Crits-Christoph (1990) have demonstrated that the Core Conflictual Relationship Theme (CCRT), the measure they developed as an assessment of "transference," can be measured reliably. That reliability, however, was achieved at the sacrifice of some validity—instead of codes tailor-made to the patient, standard codes had to be selected.

In addition to the problem of reliability there is the issue of veridicality of historical "transference" interpretation. There is widespread recognition that memory, either of the patient or of others, is untrustworthy; veridicality usually cannot be tested. Even if the recollection can be documented, however, this cannot establish causation, which is critical to the question of validity. Furthermore, at least two other types of problems limit the usefulness of clinical data to demonstrate the validity of interpretations based on the historical theory of "transference." First, there are the numerous inherent shortcomings in the case report as the vehicle for communicating clinical data. Second, because analysts assume the validity of the theory of "transference," they do not construct their case report to provide validating evidence. Let me begin with the former.

Methodological difficulties with the case report are ubiquitous. Wallerstein and Sampson (1971) cite evidence and Holt (1986) concludes that "retrospective data are inadequate for the testing of etiologies" (p. 243). Case reports of completed analyses remain relatively uncommon. They rarely include the advantaged perspective provided by a follow-up assessment subsequent to termination, although follow-up contacts and second analyses often indicate substantial change in the patient's view of analysis compared to that at the time of termination. Coherence in case reports has been used to support validation, but Hirsch (1967) argues that there is an inherent circularity in the interpretive process, which produces an illusion of coherence. Rubovits-Seitz (1998), however, urges that combining several methods of assessment with material from the same analysis will minimize the participant-observer's bias.

Michels (2000) emphasizes that all case histories are profoundly shaped by the author's purposes in writing them. Case histories, or more often vignettes, are embedded in papers that are constructed to support arguments. It may be, Michels comments, that uncontaminated report of clinical material is no more possible than an uncontaminated analysis. The aforementioned difficulties with case reports apply across the board; that is, they bear on the ability of case reports to support any inference, either about the etiology of the patient's psychopathology or about the usefulness of particular interventions. That is, they apply with equal force to attributions that the patient's attitude toward the analyst is in any of its particulars "transferential," or that interpreting this is mutative in terms of fostering beneficent personality change.

Tuckett (2000) notes that in regard to the subjectivity of clinical data, we risk drifting between the Scylla of naïvete and the Charybdis of nihilism. He asserts, and Michels (1994) agrees, that the essence of psychoanalysis is that the analyst, as a receptive human being, picks up data within a communication field and within a framework of meanings. Therefore, a subjective report is as indispensable to the basic data as an "objective" transcript. The analyst's attitude toward the question of the utility of clinical data, like the attitude toward the relationship between Nachträglichkeit and the theory of "transference" (see chapter 8) is probably influenced by sociocultural factors, by cognitive style—"lumpers" who feel the data are useful, and "splitters" who decry their value—and by emotional, motivational factors.

Tuckett suggests further "that the combination of presentation and discussion [with an audience] can, if the specific positions of presenter and audience are properly accounted for, produce a particular quality of validation" (p. 406). An implication of this suggestion, that the combination of presentation and discussion with others, by elucidating the impact of the analyst's subjectivity, enhances the validity of the data, is that the model of the analyst as a solo practitioner in his or her office provides less access to his or her own subjectivity compared to that of an analyst in regular, continued communication with colleagues about his or her analytic work (e.g., in a study group).

The second problem regarding the usefulness of clinical data for validation is that analysts assume that "transference," in its expanded, generally held meaning, which includes early object relations, has already been proven to be a valid concept. Therefore, analysts do not conceive it is the task of their case report to validate the theory of "transference." Consequently, "transference" descriptions are sketched in schematic, almost perfunctory ways. Tuckett (1994) decries "the very slipshod way in which we use clinical data to illustrate propositions and thereby attempt to accumulate evidence about how we understand and practice our discipline" (p. 868). Spence (1994), too, observes, "Because we are comfortable with the usual type of clinical anecdote and tend to project on to it our own assumptions, we have failed to make it conform to the usual laws of evidence" (p. 918). Consequently, he adds, "we rarely have the opportunity to take an alternate stand because we have no access to the specific data of interest" (p. 920). As Spence observes, so little data are given that often it is impossible to come up with a reasonable alternative view of the data; this would include, obviously, putative childhood roots of the "transference" feelings and fantasies.

Thus, case reports themselves do not attempt to provide clinical validation of the theory of "transference." For Freud, ultimate validation rested, or so it can be argued, on the narrative coherence of the patient's productions. If, as I and others have argued, there is reason to question the data of narrative coherence that Freud provided, then only subsequent case reports might provide such validation, but case reports after Freud fail to provide convincing data in terms of narrative coherence because the writers thought it was not necessary to do so.

My assertion is that neither Freud's reports nor subsequent case reports provide reasonably convincing validation for the theory of "transference." Adding unconvincing case reports in countless iterations does not constitute substantial validation. This leaves the fundamental theory of "transference" lacking both in reliability and validity, and opens the arena for consideration and generation of alternative theories of patient-analyst interaction.

The absence of reliability or validity of analytic data leads Phillips (1996) to comment about analysts' narratives that analysts "like everyone else have their favorite stories" (p. 35), and psychoanalysts forget "that they are only telling stories about stories, and that all stories are subject to an unknowable multiplicity of interpretations" (p. xvi). Neither the rationale for the choice of "transference" interpretation nor the search for substantiation is a major consideration of the analyst. *Assuming* that a "transference" interpretation reflects the repetition of an earlier experience, without checking for verifying recollections, impedes the search for alternative interpretations. The psychoanalyst "must be alert to what exactly [psychoanalytic theories] he uses . . . not to hear" (p. 45).

Childhood Experiences as Causes of Adult Reactions

Most "transference" interpretations are impressive in their plausibility, but methodological examination suggests that the inferences are flawed. Let us start with a single, apparently straightforward example. Jacobs (1995) characterized a patient's disturbed reaction to the analyst's absence as a "transference" reaction caused by several early experiences of abandonment. The patient's mother died suddenly when he was five years of age, and his father became so depressed that he was emotionally unavailable for an extended period. Jacobs reports that he was readily prepared to accept this explanation of the "transference" reaction as Jacobs himself felt abandoned by his own father. While this seems an eminently plausible explanation of his patient's difficulty with separation from his analyst, it is not possible to determine that the patient's early loss and abandonment were the cause of the adult separation difficulty.

Considering Jacobs's hypothesis from a larger perspective than that of a particular dyad, I find that most of my patients show evidence of separation difficulties and are disturbed when I leave. Because few of these patients report actual childhood abandonment experiences, we can recognize the ubiquity of human abandonment anxiety, and still believe that childhood abandonment is not a necessary cause of adult separation difficulty. Doidge et al. (1994) report that 23 percent of 580 Canadian analytic patients report traumatic childhood separation experiences, which means that 77 percent of analytic patients did *not* report traumatic childhood separation experiences. Numerous factors may influence a patient's report of childhood abandonment. By now, many patients who enter analysis bring with them a prior expectation that the treatment will explore for childhood origins of their present concerns, and the patient will try to cooperate with those expectations. Even without that expectation, when facing a current anxiety about separation, they may invoke a past experience to help explicate their present distress. That is, they are developing a model to help them cognitize the current discomfort in order to help them deal with it—a model that may avoid examining elements of current personal interactions. Further, there are individuals who have had severe abandonment experiences in childhood, but do not develop adult separation difficulties. Childhood abandonment, thus, is neither a necessary nor a sufficient cause of adult separation difficulty.

Michels (Panel, 1986) suggests that patients may react selectively to childhood abandonment: "From a psychoanalytic viewpoint, it is easy to understand that individuals who are largely abandoned, by objective standards, may recreate in treatment the experiences of intrusion and smothering that punctuated and interrupted that abandonment. In effect, the world of childhood reconstructed in treatment is not likely to be a valid replica of the childhood constructed from observations of children and parents" (p. 188).

The hypothesis that childhood abandonment *causes* adult separation difficulty can best be tested only with data from outside the treatment situation. One approach would be to conduct a prospective longitudinal study that takes account of hereditary factors: select a group of children who had documented abandonment experiences during some early period, such as the first five years of life. Select a control group matched for age, gender, race, and socioeconomic class, in whom no externally significant abandonment experience had occurred. Compare family histories of mental and emotional disorders for the two groups to insure at least that genetic loading for mental and emotional disorder was randomly distributed in both groups. It would be even more difficult to compare distributions of other personality characteristics to determine if they were randomly distributed in the two groups. Follow the two groups to adulthood and then test for difficulty dealing with separation. If the group with childhood abandonment did show more difficulty with adult separation, we could then conclude that the childhood abandonment *caused* the adult emotional difficulty with separation. Such a study is unlikely to be done in our lifetime or, possibly, ever.

Bowlby (1988a) provides an alternative hypothesis to explain why the majority of my patients suffer from separation difficulties. Bowlby hypothesizes that children who feel uncertain that a parent would be available, responsive, or helpful, whether because of actual, physical separation or because of poor quality caregiving, are prone to separation anxiety. Thus, Bowlby proposes an alternative, preoedipal etiology. If Jacobs's patient had had such experiences as a child, he might have developed separation difficulties even if his mother had not died. Precisely because there is no way to determine that, we cannot say that the patient's mother's death caused his adult separation difficulty. Nor do we have any way of assessing how genetic factors may have influenced his reaction to mother's death and father's withdrawal.

To move from separation anxiety to a patient's distressing belief that her analyst was not as interested in her as in his other patients, again the analyst proposes a childhood etiology. Bachant and Adler (1998) describe treatment of a woman who felt her analyst was more interested in his other patients than in her. Difficulties inhere also in their clinical illustration of "transference," which they describe as follows: "The early wishes, fears, and solutions to problems that faced us as children are now an inevitable part of us, coloring our actions, thoughts, and experience of the world" (p. 1102). They present this vignette.

Elaine was only "realistically" irritated by the ring of her analyst's phone. *Closer examination* [italics added], however, revealed that the telephone calls stimulated fantasies of impatient rival "siblings" encroaching upon her time, unable to await their turn. She assumed that her analyst was more interested in them than in herself and used these interruptions to reinforce her early idea that the best thing she could do when competing for her father's love was to "disappear," removing herself from the fray by cutting off feelings of desire to have the loved one to herself. Though it would be hard to characterize her reaction of irritation as *inappropriate* to the situation, this dynamic reveals the crucial influence of transference in structuring her ordinary interactions with others. Again and again Elaine would construct an idea of the other as not primarily interested in her and assume that what was needed in the situation was for her to retreat from any sustained involvement [p. 1103].

What is the evidence that her reported childhood sibling rivalry is the *cause* of her irritation with her analyst? First, the analyst's failure to have arranged that the phone not ring and interrupt her session can be considered to reflect an actual lack of sensitivity, if not diminished interest in her. Did the patient's behavior influence the analyst's relatively diminished sensitivity and interest? I agree with the authors that the irritation is a healthy, appropriate reaction. Second, the dynamic was revealed upon a *closer examination* that may well have been guided by the analyst. An analyst who has a conviction that childhood feelings influence current interactions would expect to find evidence of such childhood feelings and therefore actively probe for such evidence. A compliant patient may produce material that satisfies the analyst's expectations. Third, if the patient had failed to respond with irritation, would the analyst have probed for the childhood roots of the absence of irritation? Fourth, at most there is evidence of correlation, but no evidence of causation. If the patient had recalled a childhood experience that could be validated in which she reacted to sibling rivalry by withdrawal, the most that can be concluded is that there is a correlation, that is, there was a withdrawal response as a child and there is a withdrawal response as an adult; there is no evidence that the childhood response caused the adult response. There is no way to determine whether, if there had never been such a childhood response, there might have been the same adult response. Fifth, another possibility is that the withdrawal response may be a reaction formation. As a child she may have reacted to one or more sibling-rivalry experiences by ferociously winning out with traumatic emotional consequences, and then she changed to a withdrawal response as a reaction formation, which she recreates over and over. If a reaction formation is operating, her "memory" of childhood withdrawal would be a product of the same construction as her adult withdrawals.

These examples illustrate Prigogine's (1997) assertion that causal relations cannot be derived from an individual; from an individual, what can be developed, at best, is a statistical probability statement about the possibility of a causal relationship.

Conceptions of the Patient's Erotic Feelings about the Analyst

The patient's erotic feelings about the analyst seemed to Freud—and therefore to subsequent generations of analysts—unexpected, inappropriate, and unreasonable, and the expression, par excellence, of "transference." Because Freud early had developed an etiological theory of adult psychopathology, he applied this theory to the etiology of the adult patient's erotic feelings toward the analyst, which were hypothesized to have originated in, and been caused by, childhood erotic feelings toward a loved person. Therefore, the patient's feelings were labeled erotic "transference." Gabbard (1994) describes this view: "Embedded in the notion of transference is the idea that the love for the analyst is actually a derivative of a childhood wish for someone else, and that the patient is trapped in a repetitive pattern that will recur with any therapist or analyst" (p. 1087). Stoller (1979) also believed in the childhood origin of erotic "transference." He, however, believed that at the center of most erotic excitement was the desire to harm or degrade, and that the hostility that generates sexual excitement is "an attempt, repeated over and over, to undo childhood traumas and frustrations that threatened the development of one's masculinity or femininity" (p. 6).

Other analysts variously attest the childhood oedipal origin of the patient's erotic feelings toward the analyst. Kernberg (1994) describes the role of the oedipal feelings as follows:

> Working through transference love signifies working through the renunciation and mourning that normally resolve the oedipal situation, but also the acknowledgement of the permanent nature of the oedipal structuring of reality as a consistent frame for all future relationships. . . . This does not imply reducing all future love relationships to the oedipal situation; it does imply the influence of the oedipal structure in framing the new experiences in an individual's and a couple's love life. . . . The intensity of erotized transferences in patients with hysterical personality structure represents an instance of classic transference love: a defensive, sexualized idealization of the analyst often hides significant unconscious aggression derived from oedipal disappointment and unconscious oedipal guilt [pp. 1138–1141].

Levine (1998) is more encompassing and notes that it is commonplace in psychoanalysis to *assume* that a patient's unfulfilled longings and desires, especially those that arise from the formative years of early childhood, may serve as the unconscious focus around which intense feelings of love and desire (toward the analyst) may develop. Our analytic engagement, he adds, includes a passionate, affect-filled re-creation in the transference of the patient's important positive and negative oedipal, as well as preoedipal, conflicts and configurations.

Viederman (1995) described his treatment of a woman who developed "an erotic paternal transference" (p. 1174) and subsequently recalled a childhood sexual molestation, the occurrence of which was later confirmed by a family friend. "Transference," Viederman observes, "is the only sure method of re-experiencing the past, albeit in modified form" (p. 1189). Despite overwhelming plausibility, the fact that her childhood molestation was verified does not establish either that it was the *cause* of her erotic "transference" or that her erotic transference was a repetition of the molestation experience.

Thus, analysts typically derive the origin of the patient's erotic feelings toward themselves from the patient's childhood love relationships. For methodological reasons, these views should be questioned. It is not possible to assess the role of genetic factors in any patient's recall of a response to childhood experience from the data of the analytic treatment. Further, childhood sexual abuse is reported by 20 to 25 percent of women (Bukerton, Hall, and Williams, 1991). Gabbard (1997) estimates the prevalence at approximately one-third. If childhood sexual abuse is a *sufficient* cause of adult anxiety and erotic feelings toward the analyst, then all patients with childhood sexual abuse should demonstrate this in treatment. Also, if childhood sexual abuse were a *sufficient* cause of adult psychopathology, the percentage of women analytic patients with childhood sexual abuse should be far greater than the 20 to 25 percent or 30 percent prevalence in the general population. Actually, Doidge and colleagues (1994) report the prevalence of childhood sexual abuse in 344 Canadian female analytic patients as 24 percent. Conversely, if only 20 to 25 percent of female patients in analysis report childhood molestation (this is the same prevalence as in the general population), it would suggest that childhood sexual molestation does *not* increase the probability of entering psychoanalytic treatment. As noted earlier, Rind, Tromovitch, and Bauserman (1998) reviewed a large number of studies of college students and concluded that childhood sexual abuse could not be evaluated and understood apart from the effects of the family environment. That is, the relations between childhood sexual abuse and young adult adjustment generally became nonsignificant when studies controlled for the effects of family environment.

The theory of the childhood origin of erotic "transference," passed by iteration through so many successive generations of analysts, is no longer regarded as a theory, but, rather, as an established fact, so much so, that I know of not a single *contrary case report* in the vast analytic literature which questions the validity of this theory of the origin of the patient's erotic feelings toward the analyst. Despite questions raised in the last decade about the centrality of the Oedipus complex and its etiological role in adult psychopathology (Simon, 1991; Downey and Friedman, 1995), no doubts have been expressed about the childhood roots of erotic "transference."

How can the analyst conceive the widely accepted observation that many—not all—adult patients develop intense erotic feelings about the analyst, usually but not always when the analyst is of a different gender? I think we need to start by acknowledging that, after observing the phenomenon for 100 years, *we do not know why patients develop these feelings.* Further, I question whether trying to understand the *cause* of these erotic feeling should be the first priority. More important, I suggest, is to try to understand the functions and the meanings of these feelings in the patient's unconscious economy.

The thesis that it is not possible to validate *etiological* "transference" interpretations with data from the analytic treatment situation is not new, but this limitation continues to be disregarded. As Tuckett (1994) observes, "We have had a collective tendency to ignore questions of validity concerning our psychoanalytic understanding in the clinical setting" (p. 866). It is not possible to *know* that childhood experiences *caused* adult reactions for the reasons discussed in this book, including the impossibility of assessing the possible role of hereditary factors. As Chodorow (1996) notes, "Many of us seem not ready to give up assumptions about the determinative importance of childhood in adult psychic life. . . . It seems hard for us not to assume or make explicit the actual past roots of present-day psychical reality" (pp. 39–40).

Inexact Interpretation, Suggestion, and the Placebo Effect

Can there really be problems in such applications of the historical theory of "transference" when patients who have been given plausible "transference" interpretations often show therapeutic gains? Providing "transference" interpretations probably contributes to the analyst's confidence that he or she presumably knows what caused the patient to be sick, and knows the mutative factors in analytic treatment. The analyst's confidence may well play a salient role in facilitating therapeutic gains. Here we are entering the realm of inexact interpretation, if not of outright suggestion.

The fact that analysts cannot *know* what childhood experiences caused adult reactions means that for the past 100 years all historical, etiological "transference" interpretations have been of untested validity. They have been, in Glover's (1955) term, inexact interpretations. Glover defined an inexact interpretation as one that did not uncover the specific fantasy system. When "specific childhood experience" is substituted for "specific fantasy system," then analysts have been providing inexact interpretations to patients because validated, exact interpretations were not possible. Like M. Jourdain, analysts have been talking "prose"—making inexact interpretations—all their professional lives.

Glover recognized that inexact interpretations may produce therapeutic improvement "in the symptomatic sense" (p. 356), but he argued that such improvement, based on suggestion in various guises, is not *analytic*: "inexact interpretation, whether therapeutically effective or not, is a form of suggestion" (p. 381). The therapeutic effect of suggestion is like that which "can be achieved by encouraging a stranger to feel friendly" (p. 130), and is due to "an increase in the effectiveness of repression" (p. 355). Analysts' concerns, Glover notes, that "deep down at the core of the analytic relation the factor of reassurance through rapport may be decisive . . . is surely groundless . . . provided, of course, the interpretations are accurate" (p. 372). But we can never be certain interpretations are accurate. He adds, pointedly, *"When therefore any two analysts or groups of analysts hold diametrically opposed views on mental mechanisms and content, it is clear that one of them must be practising suggestion"* (pp. 381–382). The current widespread diversity of analytic theory and technique implies, according to Glover, that many groups are practicing suggestion. Further, his assertion that inexact interpretation produces improvement in a way not considered *analytic* must give us pause, if, necessarily, all historically based etiological interpretations are inexact interpretations. The hoary accusation that analytic interpretations are disguised suggestions rears its head and deserves a more serious response than it has so far received (Meehl, 1994).

Freud himself used the word "suggestion" in two quite different ways, or rather, he held two different views as to whether it was consequential in analytic treatment. One meaning was the direct, specific urging to some course of action or thought. Freud (1925) asserted "I do not believe even now that I forced the seduction-phantasies on my patients, that I 'suggested' them. I had in fact stumbled for the first time upon the *Oedipus complex*" (p. 34). Freud (1926a) urged as a general guide: "We don't use this personal influence, the factor of 'suggestion' to suppress the symptoms of the illness, as happens with *hypnotic* suggestion" (p. 190). Freud (1913b) elaborates: "Often enough the transference is able to remove the symptoms of the disease by itself, but only for awhile. . . . In this case the treatment is a treatment by suggestion, and not a psycho-analysis at all" (p. 143).

Elsewhere, Freud (1926b) virtually equated suggestion with "transference":

> Transference is a proof of the fact that adults have not overcome their former childish dependence [on parents]; it coincides with the force which has been named 'suggestion'; and it is only by learning to make use of it that the physician is enabled to induce the patient to overcome his internal resistances and do away with his repressions. Thus psychoanalytic treatment acts as a second education of the adult [p. 268].

Yet, Freud was explicit about suggesting ideas to the patient:

> The patients cannot themselves bring all their conflicts into the transference. . . . We tell the patient about the possibilities of other instinctual conflicts, and we arouse his expectation that such conflicts may occur in him. . . . What we hope is that this information and this warning will have the effect of activating in him one of the conflicts we have indicated [p. 233].

Freud believed that as the child is motivated to learn and grow out of love for his or her parents, so will the patient be motivated to learn out of love for the analyst and work at undoing his or her repressions. He acknowledged that psychoanalysis involved a measure of suggestion: "It is perfectly true that psychoanalysis, like other psychotherapeutic methods, employs the instrument of suggestion (or transference). . . . It is used to induce the patient to perform a piece of psychical work—the overcoming of his transference resistances—which involves a permanent alteration in his mental economy" (pp. 42–43). He was willing to acknowledge a role for suggestion because he felt there were two safeguards that would limit or eliminate it. One safeguard was his tally argument (1917): "[the patient's] conflicts will only be successfully solved and his resistances overcome if the anticipatory ideas he is given [by the analyst] tally with what is real in him. Whatever in the doctor's conjectures is inaccurate drops out in the course of analysis" (p. 452). As discussed earlier, the tally argument fails to withstand critical scrutiny.

The second safeguard Freud (1912a) implied was the complete dissolving of the transference.

> To this extent we readily admit that the results of psycho-analysis rest upon suggestion; by suggestion, however, we must understand . . . the influencing of a person by means of the transference phenomena which are possible in his case. We take care of the patient's final independence by employing suggestion in order to get him to accomplish a piece of psychical work which has as its necessary result a permanent improvement in his psychical situation [pp. 105–106].

The "piece of psychical work," which would undo the effects of suggestion and establish the patient's independence, was the resolution of the "transference." Freud (1917) later made this explicit.

> We put an end to such successes [symptom remission that set in too soon] by constantly resolving the transference on which they are based. It is this last characteristic which is the fundamental distinction between analytic and purely suggestive therapy, and which frees the results of analysis from the suspicion of being successes due to suggestion. . . . At the end of an analytic treatment the transference must itself be cleared away; and if success is then obtained or continues, it rests, not on suggestion, but on the achievement by its means of an overcoming of internal resistance, on the internal change that has been brought about in the patient [p. 453].

At the time that was written, Freud's psychoanalyses typically lasted six months. The idea that a treatment of that duration could completely dissolve the transference could only have been hypothetical. Years later, Freud (1937b) acknowledged that some residue of "transference" persists even after long-term, successful analysis. Freud's hope for a means of demonstrating that the therapeutic effects of analytic treatment were not based on suggestion never materialized.

Suggestion and the placebo effect in psychoanalytic treatment have not, by and large, been the focus of interest of many analytic theorists;

Glover (1955), Marmor (1986), Meehl (1994), Mosher (1999), and Levy and Inderbitzin (2000) are exceptions. The PEP CDRom through 1994 lists 24 papers with "suggestion" in the title. Six dealt with hypnotic suggestion; 21 of them were from 1966 or earlier. No papers were reported with "placebo" in the title. Marmor (1986) notes that what the analyst shows interest in, the kinds of questions he asks, the kinds of data he chooses to react to or ignore, and the interpretations he makes, all have significant suggestive impact on the patient. Gill (1991) observes that whatever the analyst does is invariably saturated with suggestion. As an example, not proffered as suggestion by the author, is Schlesinger (1995) thinking of saying to a patient, "It is all right for you to act and feel in these odd ways, but I insist that you know about what you are doing" (p. 685). Schlesinger characterizing the patient's neurosis as "odd" may well constitute a powerful suggestion that it is *not* all right to continue with those ways, that they should be changed to healthier, more appropriate ways.

Spence (1995) argues, from the results of a sophisticated empirical study of audio recorded analytic data, that suggestion could not account for the finding that interpretations during hours when there were indications of greater patient-analyst relatedness had more impact on the patient than interpretations during hours when there appeared to be less patient-analyst relatedness. This finding, however, has no bearing on whether suggestion plays a role in other aspects of the analytic situation, nor was a relationship shown between the measure of interpretation impact and therapeutic gain. Spence's study did not test whether any of the analyst's interpretations may have implied a suggestion that the patient change the relevant feeling or behavior to a different, healthier form. Thus, he does not address the question of whether suggestion plays a role in producing therapeutic improvement.

Levy and Inderbitzin (2000) assert that the traditional, one-person model of analytic treatment subsumes the analysis of "suggestive factors" through consistent "transference" analysis. Thus, they elaborate Freud's hope that resolution of the "transference" will ultimately remove or markedly diminish the role of suggestion in analytic treatment. They differentiate suggestion, a mode of irrational influence, into *suggestive*, "referring to influence from the analyst that depends on unconscious factors in the patient" and *analytic*, "referring to interpretive influence relying on the patient's rational, conscious collaboration" (p. 743). They regard suggestion and "transference" as intimately linked; "transference" is conceived traditionally as "replicating significant relational experiences—especially those arising during childhood" (p. 750).

This concept of suggestion is inappropriately narrow because its locus is almost entirely within the patient. The only contribution by the analyst that they include is "the analyst's commitment to a theory of technique" (p. 753). They therefore fail to acknowledge that the analyst's personal values and personality—what I later term "Habitual Relationship Patterns"—may not only influence the analyst's commitment to a theory of technique, but also may subtly but pervasively influence many of the patient-analyst interactions, as described by Marmor. Their failure to acknowledge the pervasive and profound role of the analyst in suggestion, and their term "suggestive factors," are best exemplified in their concept that patients can "free associate," presumably free of the analyst's influence. A thesis of this book is that with a different analyst, the patient's "free associations" will be fundamentally different, because of the analyst's influence.

Although no psychoanalytic studies have focused on suggestion, a review of a multitude of studies in psychological therapeutics led Shapiro and Shapiro (1997) to conclude, because of the predominance of nonspecific effects and the absence of proof of specific effectiveness and other attributes, that the psychotherapies have the characteristics of placebo treatments. Mosher (1999) concurs, remarking about "the growing currency of the notion that the major effect of *every* treatment for most mental disorders is largely due to either *placebo* effects *and/or* to so-called *non-specific* effects." I think we, as psychoanalysts, need to swallow hard and begin to examine, to try to understand and conceptualize, the role of suggestion, of placebo effects, and non-specific effects in analytic treatment. These subjects should be included in psychoanalytic curricula.

Suggestion and the Analyst's Authority

Glover had concluded that the therapeutic power of suggestion rests upon a strong "transference" authority. Hoffman's (1991) social-constructivist view, while apparently emphasizing mutuality in patient-analyst interaction, actually is based equally squarely on the superior authority of the analyst, which, Hoffman notes, is constructed by the patient's idealization and by the ritualized asymmetry of the psychoanalytic situation. Mutuality need not be inconsistent with inequality.

On the other hand, Brenner (1996) denies that the analyst's authority enters into, or should enter into, the analytic process.

The facile dismissal of the placebo effect and suggestion as disposed of through analysis of "transference" prevents us from facing the likelihood that important problems with clinical application of the theory of "transference" may be rooted in the concentration of both patient and analyst on developing mutually accepted narratives about the causes of the patient's psychopathology. Such concentration leaves little interest in addressing and exploring the role of placebo effects and suggestion, based on the patient's current experience of the analyst's authority.

Greenberg (1996) summarizes the theoretical view: "Interpretation, putatively free of interactive contaminants, was the 'pure gold' of analysis; cure by interaction—of which suggestion was the historical and conceptual prototype—was the 'base metal' of psychotherapy" (p. 27). To the extent that unvalidatable etiological "transference" interpretations operate like inexact interpretations, they are likely to affect the patient, in part, on the basis of the analyst's authority and the consequent power of suggestion. Freud (1910c) comments that "we had much to expect from the increase in authority which must accrue to us as time goes on" (p. 146). Hoffman proposes, à la Freud, that the loving authority of the analyst, like that of the parent earlier, enables a process of resocialization. And here we reach a paradox. The analyst's authority and the analyst's related sense of confidence may be important to achieving therapeutic gain and, at the same time, reduce the analyst's interest in, and energy for, further exploration of all the meanings of the patient's feelings and fantasies, including especially the patient's experience of the power of the analyst's authority-based suggestion. Application of the theory of "transference," in which the analyst reports knowing what made the patient ill as well as what will make him better, would tend to enhance the patient's idealization of the analyst. My contention is that, instead of the analyst telling the patient that he or she knows the causes of the patient's psychopathology, acknowledging that the analyst cannot be sure what experiences made the patient ill should tend to minimize the patient's idealization of the analyst, to reduce the analyst's authority and, thereby, the impact of the power of suggestion.

Cooper (1994) asserts that the mutative effects of analytic treatment derive not so much from the authority-based, explicit interpretations as from the complex minutiae of the analyst's moment-to-moment interactions with the patient:

The analyst's relative tolerance, his devotion to attempting to understand the patient, the atmosphere of stability and safety inculcated through the peculiar imbalance of the analytic setting, can be conceived of as the conveyance of an analytic fact to the patient—the fact that it is possible to relate to an object that will not conform to the objects of his inner world nor to the projection of that inner world onto objects in the outer world. This analytic fact, formulated through our attitude, is often weightier than the content of our formulation at any given moment. . . . our actual behavior in the analytic setting presents the patient with facts that are as significant as those we are also formulating in every transference interpretation [pp. 1112–1113].

Yalom (1980) earlier asserted similarly that "viewing the therapist-patient relationship primarily in terms of transference [unrealistic and distorted feelings] negates the truly human, and truly mutative, nature of the relationship" (p. 404). Meissner (1996) makes a related point; it is the empathic bond between patient and analyst that empowers the analyst's interpretation, enabling its mutative effect on the patient.

"Transferences," referring to the patient's feelings and fantasies about the analyst, probably include newly created reactions to actual characteristics of the analyst as well as unrealistic, distorted responses. The latter, of uncertain origin, serve current defensive functions and meanings for the patient. The former feelings and fantasies are included in the therapeutic alliance, and as Cooper describes, are importantly mutative. Freud (1912a) felt that unconscious positive feelings "invariably go back to erotic sources" (p. 105) and must be analyzed, but the patient's conscious friendly and affectionate feelings toward the analyst are "unobjectionable . . . and . . . the vehicle of success in psychoanalysis exactly as it is in other methods of treatment" (p. 105). Those of the patient's "transference" feelings that were considered distorted should be analyzed in the sense of delineating their unconscious defensive functions and meanings, and, perhaps, in addition, in developing plausible hypotheses about their historical origins and causes.

As I indicated at the outset of this chapter, several other problems of a practical nature may arise as a result of applying the theory of "transference." Let me review these again. For one, the analyst may be so focused on preparing and presenting "transference" interpretations that he or she may fail to attend to the nurturance of the therapeutic alliance and to utilize the value of the analyst's affirmation of the patient. Indeed, "transference" interpretations may well be experienced by the patient as critical and therefore have a negative—in contrast to an affirmative—impact on the patient.

Another potential difficulty is that the analyst's concern for generating historical "transference" interpretations may reduce his or her vigilance for the possibility that the patient's motivation for the exploration of childhood experiences may be in the service of defensively avoiding troublesome current conflicts. If those conflicts involve disturbing feelings about the analyst in the here and now, the analyst, who may also find the issues uncomfortable—such as dealing with the analytic fee—may unwittingly collude with the patient, and direct their exploration to the past.

An additional difficulty is that, for a variety of reasons, certain of the patient's difficulties may not become engaged with the analyst, but may be expressed in relations with others—spouse, children, siblings, or friends. A focus on "transference" interpretation may result in the analyst overlooking these concerns of the patient, since they fail to involve the analyst.

Summary

Analysts who assume the validity of the traditional theory of "transference" make relatively little attempt to validate it, often applying it clinically in a casual and stereotyped manner. Further, methodological problems, including the impossibility of assessing the role of hereditary factors, preclude the possibility of validating an *etiological* "transference" interpretation about the specific childhood origin of adult behavior with data from the analytic treatment situation. The lack of either reliability or validity of the theory of "transference" constitutes grounds for considering and generating alternative hypotheses about patient-analyst interaction.

To the extent that unvalidated etiological "transference" interpretations operate like inexact interpretations, their impact on the patient may be due, in part, to the power of suggestion. Although traditional analytic theory attributes the primary mutative effects of treatment to historical interpretation, and to "transference," interpretation in particular, alternative views regard as efficacious the impact of the analyst's loving authority as reflected, at least in part, in covert suggestion and placebo effect. Focusing on historical "transference" interpretation may result in the analyst's failure to explore the role of suggestion and placebo effect, experienced by the patient in relation to the analyst's authority. In addition, the analyst may fail to attend to nurturing the therapeutic alliance, may avoid dealing with current conflicts in favor of exploration of the past, which may be defensive, and may miss important feelings of the patient that are not directed toward the analyst, but emerge in other relationships.

8
Nachträglichkeit

> *This advice was sanctioned by Dr. Kimble, on the ground that it was well to try to do what could do no harm—a principle which was made to answer for a great deal of work in that gentleman's medical practice.*
>
> —George Eliot, *Silas Marner*

The "historical" view of "transference," as labelled by Cooper (1987), was last articulated by Freud in 1937, and focused on analytic reconstruction of objective childhood memories and fantasies that the patient had transferred onto the analyst. A new theory of "transference" was effectively introduced 45 years later when Gill and Hoffman (1982) asserted that the patient's feelings and fantasies, directed toward the analyst, were responses to actual characteristics of the analyst; "transference" was not distortion based on displacement or repetition of a childhood experience. Cooper terms this the "modernist" theory of "transference." According to this theory, the actual characteristics of the analyst influence the patient's "transference," and it is likely that other significant persons at various stages of the patient's development had also evoked, influenced, and modified memories and fantasies; these changes are closely akin to what is referred to by the concept of *Nachträglichkeit*. It is not surprising that attention to the "modernist" theory has rekindled interest in the long disregarded concept of Nachträglichkeit, a process of memory formation and, especially, reformation throughout life.

Nachträglichkeit, a concept long abandoned by Freud and ignored in *Psychoanalytic Terms and Concepts* (Moore and Fine, 1990), has recently been given new currency in psychoanalysis, particularly by Modell (1990, 1995) who believes it contributes to a valuable broadening of "transference." Modell and I start from the same set of observations, namely, we accept Gill and Hoffman's assertion that the actual characteristics of the analyst influence the patient's feelings and fantasies about the analyst, the patient's "transferences." Consequently, "transferences" encompass more than simply repetitions of unmodified traumatic childhood experience-fantasy, which was Freud's (1937a, 1940) final conception of "transference." Clearly this change in the view of the analyst's influence poses a problem for Freud's "historical" theory of "transference." Modell and I turn to different, conflicting resolutions.

It is the thesis of this chapter that Nachträglichkeit is inconsistent with Cooper's "historical" theory of "transference" and cannot broaden it. My assertion is that, properly understood, the two concepts, Nachträglichkeit and "historical transference," are contradictory. That is to say, if we accept the general application of memory-retranscription, as described by the concept of Nachträglichkeit, then we can't continue to hold on to the "historical" interpretation of "transference"— and vice versa. We must choose one or the other as Freud did.

Freud's Concept of Nachträglichkeit

Reading and understanding Freud is sometimes difficult, and nowhere is that more evident than when trying to understand his conceptions of Nachtäglichkeit and "transference." It is not so much that he is not clear, but rather that he is so persuasive. In reading Freud, one finds that in one paper he presents an altogether persuasive account, and in another paper, with no reference to the earlier one, he presents an equally persuasive account that directly conflicts with the earlier account. He usually makes no reference to the difference between the papers, nor to his reasons for change. The logic of his writing is almost irresistible. The award of the Goethe Prize for literature is readily understandable.

In the period 1892–1897, during which Freud developed his concept of Nachträglichkeit, he was especially concerned with sexual feelings and fantasies, his own as well as those of his patients. In 1892, Freud had hypothesized that the symptoms of two of his hysteric, women patients were caused by repression of a current sexual trauma—he had discovered the power of unconscious thoughts and feelings. By 1896 he "discovered" that "neurotic symptoms originated in *the subject's sexual life, whether . . . in a disorder of his contemporary life or in important events in his past life*" (1896a, p. 149). Nachträglichkeit critically involves the interaction between present and past in the unconscious.

Modell (1990) notes that Nachträglichkeit first appeared in a letter from Freud to Fliess on December 6, 1896. This was a time when Freud, aged forty, was concerned about regulating his own sexual feelings and impulses toward women patients (Anzieu, 1986; Glenn, 1986; Moi, 1990), a persistent problem as he, himself, subsequently acknowledged to Jung (McGuire, 1974, Letter 145F, pp. 230–231). This may have partially motivated his self-analysis on which he embarked in 1897 (Anzieu, 1986). Initially, he hypothesized that it was actual seduction that was responsible for the childhood sexual trauma that was the root cause of adult neurosis, a formula that would have applied to himself as well. Did he have a "memory" of being seduced by his father? An elliptical comment to Fliess suggests he may have, but nothing is certain. In any event, the theory was short-lived, as in that same year, 1897, he realized that patients' memories of seduction—and perhaps his own, as well—were not veridical.

Initially, Freud described Nachträglichkeit solely in relation to memory. The implications of this concept for his theory of "transference" were not considered until later. He defined Nachträglichkeit as:

> the material present in the form of memory-traces being subjected from time to time to a *re-arrangement* in accordance with fresh circumstances—to a *re-transcription*. . . . I should like to emphasize the fact that the successive registrations represent the psychical achievement of successive epochs of life. Every later transcript inhibits its predecessor and drains off the excitatory process from it. A failure of translation—this is what is known clinically as "repression" [1896c, pp. 233–235].

In the same letter, Freud elaborates the special category of sexual memories:

> There is *one* case, however, in which the inhibition [when the memory recurs] is insufficient. If [memory] A, when it was current, released a particular unpleasure and if, when it is reawakened, it

releases fresh unpleasure, then this cannot be inhibited. If so, the memory is behaving as though it were some current event. This case can only occur with sexual events, because the magnitude of the excitations which these release increase of themselves with time (with sexual development). Thus a sexual event in one phase acts in the next phase as though it were a current one and is accordingly uninhibitable. What determines pathological defense (repression) is therefore *the sexual nature of the event and its occurrence in an earlier phase.* [p. 236].

In yet a third paper from the same year, Freud (1896d) adds:

The reactivated memories . . . never reemerge into consciousness unchanged: what becomes conscious as obsessional ideas and affects, and take the place of the pathogenic memories so far as conscious life is concerned, are structures in the nature of a *compromise* between the repressed ideas and the repressing ones. . . . First, something contemporary is put in the place of something past; and secondly, something sexual is replaced by something analogous to it that is not sexual [p. 170].

Freud (1899) wrote a paper about screen memories which was later recognized to be clearly autobiographical, and dealing with his own adolescent love experience. The editor's note to the paper "Screen Memories" comments that Freud wrote in an unpublished letter to Fliess that he was immensely pleased by that paper during its production, which he then saw as a bad omen for its future life (p. 301). Strachey also noted that it was curious that the type of screen memory mainly considered in the paper—one in which an early memory is used as a screen for a later event—almost disappears from later literature. What has come to be regarded as the "regular" type—one in which an early event is screened by a later memory—is only barely alluded to here (p. 302). Freud believed that although a sexual event could cause unpleasure in a young child, the child did not have the capacity to inhibit that unpleasure as "before the age of 4 there is no repression yet" (p. 236).

Freud's original concept applied not to memory in general, but to the small class of memories associated with the unpleasure of a childhood experience-fantasy. The translation or retranscription was not an intrinsic characteristic of memory, but was conducted for a specific psychological purpose, that of displacing or draining off the libido associated with the memory.

This model of memory later in life becoming connected through associations to an earlier memory is called a "screen memory." Why does it get connected to a memory of a *childhood* event or scene? "For the sake of its innocence, perhaps," replies Freud (p. 317). He reiterates, "these falsified memories too, must have originated at a period of life when it has become possible for conflicts of this kind and impulsions toward repression to have made a place for themselves in mental life—far later, therefore, than the period to which their content belongs" (p. 322). But, to repeat, this kind of screened memory from early in life is not the central focus of the paper. Rather Freud is principally concerned with processes whereby memories ordinarily become transformed with further development.

In the screen memory paper (1899) Freud writes:

It may indeed be questioned whether we have any memories at all *from* our childhood: memories *relating to* our childhood may be all that we possess. Our childhood memories show us our earlier years not as they were but as they appeared at the later periods when the memories were aroused. In these periods of arousal, the childhood memories did not, as people are accustomed to say, *emerge*; they were *formed* at that time [p. 322].

He adds that screen memories "are altogether analogous to the formation of hysterical symptoms" (pp. 320–321). Freud's description of screen memories is complicated. A disturbing childhood experience may be repressed and become associated with a neutral childhood experience; the memory of the latter is the screen for the former. Alternatively, a repressed childhood experience may become associated with a neutral later experience, and, again the memory of the later experience is a screen for the former.

Thomä and Chesire (1991) elaborate Freud's analogy that the processes of screen memories are comparable to those of hysterical symptom formation. One conception is that the memory trace of traumatic experiences with their associated passivity and helplessness constitute a *disposition* for neurosis, which becomes activated later in life by certain stimuli. A second is that the pathogenic effect of the memory trace has been generated *de novo* by later experiences, which brought about a reconstrual, a rearrangement, a retrospective fantasy that was pathogenic. May (1999) describes the latter conception as follows: "Pathological defensive processes resulting in symptom formation occur after the period of sexual maturation if an internal conflict is connected associatively with an instance of sexual abuse experienced in childhood" (p. 771).

Freud (1914a) later explained further that fantasies at a later age which become connected to earlier fantasies "were intended to cover up the auto-erotic activity of the first years of childhood, to embellish it and raise it to a higher plane. And now, from behind the phantasies, the whole range of a child's sexual life came to light" (p. 18).

Freud's sense of a bad omen for the future life of this "screen memories" paper may have reflected an underlying feeling that he would subsequently abandon his view that we don't have any memories at all from our childhood. More than 35 years later (1937a), he expressed the conviction that such memories existed and could be delineated by a construction made by the analyst.

"Transference" and Nachträglichkeit

Freud's (1905) treatment of Dora includes the first reference to the implications of Nachträglichkeit for his theory of "transference." "Transferences," Freud explains, are new editions or facsimiles of impulses and fantasies, of a whole series of psychological experiences, which replace some earlier person by the person of the physician.

> Some of these transferences . . . are merely new impressions or reprints. Others are more ingeniously constructed; their content has been subjected to a moderating influence—to *sublimation,* as I call it—and they even become conscious, by cleverly taking advantage of some real peculiarity in the physicians' person or circumstances and attaching themselves to that. These then will no longer be new impressions but revised editions [p. 116].

Here Freud elucidates his early theory of "transference" which is that an early psychological experience can be revived unchanged as a reprint, *or* transformed, as in Nachträglichkeit—which he here terms "sublimation." The latter, which takes advantage "of some real peculiarity in the physician's person or circumstances," antedates, by almost a century, Gill and Hoffman's contribution (1982), which Cooper (1987) characterizes as the modernist conception of "tranference." Freud (1905) added that Dora "*acted out* an essential part of her recollections and phantasies instead of reproducing it in the treatment" (p. 119).

More than a decade later, Freud (1917) further expands the role of retranscription, described initially in relation to Nachträglichkeit, explaining that the presence of a strong father transference does not necessarily imply

> that the patient had suffered previously from a similar uncon-
> scious attachment of libido to his father. [That is, "transfer-
> ence" is not necessarily a repetition of childhood feelings.] His
> father-transference was merely the battlefield on which we
> gained control of his libido; the patient's libido was directed
> to it from other positions. . . . Not until after the transference
> has been resolved can we construct . . . the distribution of
> libido which had prevailed during the [earlier] illness
> [pp. 455–456].

At that time, however, analyses were comparatively very brief, so resolution of "transference" that Freud refers to arguably could only have
been hypothetical. Lacking resolution, the implication is that we are
left unsure of what the original feelings, fantasies, or experiences were.

Freud (1918) also used the concept of retranscription or construction in discussing the treatment of the Wolf Man, a young man
then in his early twenties who was completely incapacitated and
dependent on other people. Using this patient's dreams as a form of
memory, Freud describes construction in two senses: a construction
by the patient (at age four he constructed a primal-scene memory from
age one-and-a-half) and construction by the joint efforts of patient and
analyst (scenes "are as a rule not reproduced as recollections, but have
to be divined—constructed—gradually and laboriously from an aggregate of indications") (p. 51).

Freud considered the Wolf Man's "memory" at age four of having
seen the primal scene at age one-and-a-half to be a construction,
because he believed it was unlikely that the child at one-and-a-half
actually witnessed his parents having sexual intercourse. Freud, however, believed the report of this specific memory at age four. He did
not consider the possibility that *this* putative "memory" from age four
was itself a current construction, serving a role in the "transference."
The patient reported that his sister had begun fondling his penis when

he was three-and-a-quarter years old, and that at age four he developed an animal phobia. Freud's interpretation was that his sister's stimulation evoked the primal scene memory, which then activated castration anxiety; libido was repressed and replaced with the animal phobia.

In discussing this treatment, Freud seems in a transition point between his early theory, that repression of libido transforms it into anxiety, and his later theory (1926c), that anxiety is generated by the ego as a signal of danger. In discussing the Wolf Man (1918) he wrote: "The ego, by developing anxiety, was protecting itself against what it regarded as an overwhelming danger" (p. 112).

Freud (1917) still emphasized that early experience was transformed in its expression in "transference":

> The patient's illness . . . is not something which has been rounded off and become rigid but that it is still growing and developing like a living organism. . . . the whole of his illness's new production is concentrated upon a single point—his relation to the doctor. . . . Thereafter it is not incorrect to say that we are no longer concerned with the patient's earlier illness but with a newly created and transformed neurosis which has taken the former's place. . . . All the patient's symptoms have abandoned their original meaning and have taken on a new sense which lies in a relation to the transference [p. 444].

In addition to these numerous references to transformations of the original traumatic childhood experience-fantasy, Freud in several instances (1914c, 1915) described exact replications or repetitions of the original experience-fantasy with no indication of transformation. Thus, in various papers through the years until 1933, Freud seemed to consider that the childhood experience-fantasy could *either* be transformed or repeated unchanged. Thomä and Cheshire (1991) noted "deferred action," Strachey's translation of *Nachträglichkeit*, continued to appear as a term in the *Standard Edition* until 1933, but not thereafter. In 1930, and again in 1937, 1939, and 1940, Freud referred only to the concept of repetition, arguing that the analyst's construction, or reconstruction, would expose unchanged the content of the *original* memory, fantasy, or experience. Freud (1937a) wrote:

> All of the essentials [of memory] are preserved; even things that seem completely forgotten are present somehow and

somewhere, and have merely been buried and made inaccessible to the subject. . . . His [the analyst's] task is to make out what has been forgotten from the traces which it has left behind or, more correctly, to construct it. . . . His work of construction, or, if it is preferred, reconstruction, resembles to a great extent an archaeologist's excavation of some dwelling-place that has been destroyed and buried or of some ancient edifice. . . . what the analyst is dealing with is not something destroyed but something that is still alive [pp. 258–260].

Thus, the memories persist unchanged, are "still alive."

Freud (1940) similarly notes that "the transference reproduces the patient's relation with his parents" (pp. 176), without mentioning transformation. In these papers from 1930 to 1940 it is difficult to judge whether his failure to mention transformation is deliberate, but to repeat, the term Nachträglichkeit was not used after 1933. This later view that there was a permanent record of memories of traumatic childhood experience-fantasy and that analytic work could uncover their content became the foundation of the classical view that constitutes the "historical" theory of "transference."

Modell's Concept of Nachträglichkeit

For Modell (1990), "Nachträglichkeit refers to traumatic or unassimilated memories that are later revised" (p. 62). He also asserts: "It follows then that the re-creation of the nuclear complex in the transference may not necessarily be a repetition of experience or a re-creation of a fantasy. . . . Transference . . . unquestionably belongs to the class of phenomena described under the heading Nachträglichkeit" (p. 17). The focus on whether transference is a repetition of the past or a newly formed creation, Modell maintains, "misses the point of the complex cyclic relation between affective memories and fantasies that are evoked by current reality" (p. 17). He conceives that the original memory or fantasy cycles through each of the subsequent stages of development and is thereby transformed at every stage. Yet Modell fails to acknowledge an implication of this conception of Nachträglichkeit: the same original memory cannot cycle through each developmental stage. Rather, the original memory is revised in the first developmental stage, and it is this revised memory that is presented to the next developmental stage, where it is further revised. After many such revisions it is no longer possible to identify the original memory with certainty. In addition, looking back during analysis, the patient's report of a memory, prior fantasy, or prior experience is arguably a construction, itself revised as a function of the patient's situation at that time, especially his or her interaction with the analyst. Therefore, there is no way of knowing with any certainty whether an expression in the "transference" is a repetition or even a retranscription of an original childhood memory or fantasy. Only treating a patient as a child or an adolescent, and tuning in on fantasies at that stage of development, would enable the treating analyst of the young adult subsequently to ascertain how those fantasies were later presented and to determine how the fantasies had been transcribed.

Disregarding his realization that "transference" is never resolved (1937b) and that it is not possible to ascertain with certitude what the original distribution of libido (memory or fantasy) had been, Freud returned to his early formulation that there was a permanent record of specific memories and that analytic work could uncover or reconstruct their content. This formulation thus became the foundation of the classical view that constitutes Freud's theory of "transference." This definition of "transference" is inconsistent with Nachträglichkeit, which acknowledges that memory is transformed during different stages of development as well as by the influence of the current context—patient-analyst interaction—and accepts that the original memory or fantasy cannot be known with certainty.

Analysts differ in their views of the current relationship between the terms "transference" and Nachträglichkeit. Laplanche and Pontalis (1973), who credit Lacan with reviving interest in Nachträglichkeit, write: "The first thing the introduction of the notion [of Nachträglichkeit] does is to rule out the summary interpretation which reduces the psychoanalytic view of the subject's history to a linear determinism envisaging nothing but the action of the past upon the present" (pp. 111–112). They note that Freud believed that it is the revision of traumatic past events that invests them with pathogenicity, a view that enjoys some textual support vis-à-vis memory as pathogenic, but which is decidedly inconsistent with my reading of Freud's final view of "transference." Baranger, Baranger, and Mom (1983), whose belief in the repetition compulsion as a clinical expression of the death instinct requires the explicit repetition of childhood memories, write: "If one takes Freud's expression 'nachträglichkeit' seriously, the discontinuity of psychoanalysis with respect to any developmental psychology cannot fail to be evident" (p. 6). Thomä and Cheshire (1991) criticize

Strachey's translation of Nachträglichkeit as *only* "deferred action." They conclude, as I do, that "the very concept of Nachträglichkeit should in fact forbid reducing the history of the subject to a mono-causal determinism that pays attention only to the direct influence which actual events in very early infancy may have on the present" (p. 418).

Is the Childhood Experience/Fantasy Unchanged or Transformed?

Freud himself (1926c) examined this question.

With regard to the repressed instinctual impulses themselves [considered to have been stimulated by childhood experience-fantasy], we assumed that they remained unaltered in the unconscious for an indefinite length of time. But now our interest is turned to the vicissitudes of the repressed and we begin to suspect that it is not self-evident, perhaps not even usual, that those impulses should remain unaltered and unalterable in this way. . . . has the portion of them in the unconscious maintained itself and been proof against the influences of life that tend to alter and depreciate them? In other words, do the old wishes, about whose former existence analysis tells us, still exist? . . . the old repressed wishes must still be present in the unconscious since we still find their derivatives, the symptoms, in operation. [But this] does not enable us to decide between two possibilities: either that the old wish is now operating only through its derivatives, having transferred the whole of its cathectic energy to them, or that it is itself still in existence too. If its fate has been to exhaust itself in cathecting its derivatives, there is yet a third possibility. In the course of the neurosis it may have become re-animated by regression, anachronistic though it may be now [p. 142].

In the text, Freud does not decide between these possibilities.

Modell speculates that Freud discarded Nachträglichkeit because it was not consistent with his theory of the death instinct and its expression, the repetition compulsion. My own hypothesis is that Freud abandoned it for several other reasons. First, he no longer needed Nachträglichkeit to transform libido into anxiety, because in 1926 he abandoned that theory. Second, I think Freud recognized, exactly as Modell (1990) did, that the implication of Nachträglichkeit is that "the recreation of the nuclear complex in the transference may not necessarily be a repetition of experience but a recreation of a fantasy" (p. 17). Freud would have had to dispense with what he saw as the core of analytic work, the analyst's reconstruction in the "transference" of the patient's objective traumatic memories (1937a). Third, for Freud, since a powerful mutative element in treatment was the patient's conviction of the truth of the reconstruction, theoretically, there could be no such conviction unless the original memory could be identified. Without objective memories to reconstruct, the "historical" theory of "transference" is undermined.

I suspect that the most important implication for Freud was that continuing to acknowledge Nachträglichkeit meant abandoning his "historical," etiological theory of "transference" and thereby relinquishing his life-long goal of discovering the cause of neurosis via the treatment. Unless some residue from childhood persisted unchanged throughout life, how could childhood experience-fantasy be discovered to be the cause of adult neurosis? If nothing from childhood persisted to adulthood how could the first five years of life be determinative of the adult, how could the child be father to the man? More puzzling is the converse question: Why did Freud remain comfortable, at least until 1933, with conceiving that "transference" could involve *either* transformation (Nachträglichkeit), or unchanged repetition of the etiological childhood condition, without grasping that this contradictory view essentially undermined his theory of "transference?"

Modell, I believe, in resurrecting Nachträglichkeit, is reflecting his awareness and acceptance of a change in psychoanalytic technique encompassing the analyst's influence on "transference." Treatment now focuses on analyzing the "transference" conceived of as the patient-analyst interaction in the here and now, rather than focussing on hidden childhood memories. This departure from Freud's recommendations for technique presses Modell to assimilate this change by representing Nachträglichkeit as a "broadening" of "transference." He thereby encompasses the change in technique within Freud's theory of technique.

Edelman's (1989, 1992) current laboratory-based neurophysiological theory of memory, like Nachträglichkeit, denies the possibility of veridical recall of an early memory. He hypothesizes that what is stored in the brain is not a precise representation of the original experience, but the potential to refind the category or class of which the event is a member. Modell recognizes Edelman's view that memory is transformational, not replicative; memory involves recategorization. But he does not address the issue that this conception of memory is inconsistent with Freud's last view of "transference," in which the analyst reconstructs the patient's objective memories. Parenthetically, Edelman's theory differs from Nachträglichkeit in that he postulates no psychological purpose to the transformation; rather, that is the way the mind works, and it does so with all memories, not just traumatic ones.

Consistent with, and supplementary to, Edelman's conception of memory is the work of Nader, Shafe, and LeDoux (2000) who studied rats' recall of fear conditioning, and concluded that memories become labile and open to revision every time they are recalled. Once a memory is recorded, it does not remain forever fixed. Retrieving a memory involves mingling the representations of the past with the percepts of the present (Tulving, 1983). Thus, the recall of a memory is influenced by the individual's current state.

Different Views of the Relation between Nachträglichkeit and "Transference"

What influences analysts' disparate views of the relation between these terms? Modell and I, for instance, see the relation quite differently. My answer to this question relates to my belief that overriding categorical attitudes influence views of psychoanalytic theory. Siegel (1999) usefully categorizes attitudes toward phenomena and toward concepts as follows: "The temptation to focus on two distinct modes of processing has its historical roots. Philosophers have long noted the differing styles of knowing about the world; they have contrasted creative, synthetic, emotional, intuitive and nonconscious patterns with those of critical, analytic, intellectual, rational, and conscious modes of thought" (p. 178).

This polarity in cognitive style places "lumpers" at one extreme and "splitters" at the other. Lumpers focus on and emphasize similarities between phenomena; they embrace ambiguity. Splitters look for and highlight differences; they disdain ambiguity. In this context, Modell is a lumper because he regards "transference" as a form of Nachträglichkeit and minimizes the differences between these concepts. I maximize the differences between them and regard "transference" and Nachträglichkeit as inconsistent. Modell (1990) writes, "The current interest as to whether the transference is a repetition of the past or a newly formed creation . . . misses the point" (p. 17). Epistemologically, to me, that is the point; he dismisses a difference that I consider significant. Again, Modell writes, "Freud understood . . . the transference neurosis . . . to be a repetition of the past and at the same time a newly created illness . . . the paradox implicit in mental phenomena" (p. 128). His inclusive paradox is my distinction.

Psychoanalysis has its share of both lumpers and splitters. A theorist like Wilson (1996) can be classified as a lumper when he states that psychoanalysis "is an inexact theory still evolving" (p. 455) and that "one of the most important tasks facing psychoanalysis is how to set the table so that new ideas can be properly and carefully considered, in order that psychoanalysis might . . . become an ever evolving entity, cartwheeling along with the times while preserving its essence" (p. 456). Another lumper, Seligman (1996), writes: "Some of the particular tenets of 'Freudian' analysis . . . are falsified by direct infant observation, but the overall edifice can be improved, rather than overturned by the new data. . . . Reevaluating such [traditional] ideas to bring them into harmony with the breadth and dynamism of contemporary psychoanalysis would strengthen them both intellectually and ideologically" (pp. 438–439). And finally, Sandler and colleagues, authors of *Freud's Models of the Mind: An Introduction*, are also lumpers when they see themselves "ignoring inconsistencies and variations [in order to present] a rounded out picture" (p. 167, quoted by Spillius, 1999, p. 828).

Psychoanalytic splitters include Wolff (1996) and Renik (1996). Grünbaum (1997), at the extreme, is the splitter par excellence because he considers meaningful distinctions grounds for rejecting much of the psychoanalytic enterprise. In philosophy, Isaiah Berlin, who deplored all unifying systems, is the ultimate splitter.

Aren't both extremes of cognitive style equally useful? A splitter responds: "It depends." Lumpers, like Freud, are most valuable when a new paradigm is being developed, and the splitters, who carp on differences and inconsistencies, are a hindrance. On the other hand, splitters are most useful when an old paradigm is being dismantled and a new one is being developed. At that time, lumpers, who minimize and overlook inconsistencies, constitute a resistance to abandoning the old paradigm. These polar positions will influence an analyst's assessment of the value of the present psychoanalytic paradigm.

Cognitive style, obviously, is only one among the many variables that influence attitudes toward psychoanalytic theory in general and probably contribute to the currently widespread diversity of views regarding psychoanalytic theory. Changes in the profession of psychoanalysis during recent decades, including the impact of decreased psychoanalytic practice and income, as well as enrollment of different sectors of the professional population, may have played a role in this increased diversity by enabling more splitters to express and publish their views. Other factors, such as trends in the outside culture, may play a role as well, but they are too diverse to go into here.

"Transference" or Nachträglichkeit: What Difference Does It Make?

The choice between Nachträglichkeit and the theory of "transference" has substantial implications for analytic technique. The historical theory of "transference" directs the analyst to reconstruct memories of specific childhood traumatic experiences and fantasies. Their recollection, or the conviction of the validity of the reconstructions, is regarded as the mutative factor producing therapeutic improvement. Freud (1918) described the implication of the theory of "transference" for technique: "After the infantile fantasies had been disposed of . . . it would be possible to begin a second portion of the treatment, which would be concerned with the patient's real life" (p. 50). Kardiner (1977) commented that at the termination of his six-month analysis with Freud in 1918, Freud advised him to continue the analytic work on his own, and work out the relationship of his infantile fantasies to his current life. Clearly, Freud had not worked out the relationship of Kardiner's infantile fantasies to his current life.

The concept of Nachträglichkeit, with its implications of many earlier transformations, results in relatively little focus on the reconstruction of childhood traumatic memories. Rather, emphasis is placed on patient-analyst interaction in the here and now and on providing increased understanding of the meanings of the patient's habitual reactions, whatever their origin. Cooper (1987) made a similar distinction in comparing the historical view of "transference" with what corresponds to a view informed by Nachträglichkeit, the modernist view.

> The historical view is more likely to regard the infantile neurosis as a "fact" of central importance for the analytic work, to be uncovered and undone. The modernist view regards the infantile neurosis, if acknowledged at all, as an unprivileged set of current fantasies rather than historical fact. From this

modernist perspective, the transference resistance is the core
of the analysis, to be worked through primarily because of the
rigidity it imposes on the patient, not because of an important
secret it conceals [pp. 81–82].

Thus, the historical approach explores memories and constructs narratives; the Nachträglichkeit-modernist approach examines the personal meanings of the patient's current feelings and fantasies. While
many analysts agree with Freud (1937a) that the joint construction of
a narrative with the patient seems therapeutic, the relative mutative
effects of narrative construction, of the impact of the patient-analyst
relationship, and of the power of suggestion remain to be delineated.

Summary

Gill and Hoffman introduced a new theory of "transference" by asserting that the patient's feelings and fantasies toward the analyst were
responses to actual characteristics of the analyst, rather than a repetition of childhood feelings. Cooper termed this the "modernist" theory of "transference," and it is this modernist theory that is congruent
with the concept of Nachträglichkeit, Freud's original conception of
the transformation of the memory of traumatic experience-fantasy.
Modell tries to accommodate the revisiting of Nachträglichkeit to
Freud's "historic" theory of "transference" by representing
Nachträglichkeit as a concept that broadens the theory of "transference." Both Nachträglichkeit and Edelman's theory of memory imply
that validation of an original past memory, fantasy, or experience is
not possible, while Freud's last version of the theory of "transference"
privileges the analyst to validate the existence of the original memory,
fantasy, or experience. I repeat: Nachträglichkeit is inconsistent with
"transference," not broadening of it; we must choose one term or the
other, as Freud did.

   Attitudes toward the relation between Nachträglichkeit and "transference" vary widely among analysts and are influenced by cognitive
style, among other factors. Different styles aside, the joint construction of narratives by patient and analyst, the impact of the patient-analyst relationship, and the power of suggestion are all generally
acknowledged to provide therapeutic benefit. The contribution of each
remains to be delineated.

9
Habitual . . . What?
An Alternative to "Transference"

The Renaissance teaches us that the book of knowledge is not to be learned by rote but is to be written anew in the ecstasy of living each moment for the moment's sake. Success in life is to maintain this ecstasy, to burn always with this hard gem-like flame. Failure is to form habits. To burn with a gem-like flame is to capture the awareness of each moment; and for that moment only. To form habits is to be absent from those moments. How may we always be present for them?— to garner not the fruits of experience but experience itself?

—Tom Stoppard, *The Invention of Love*

The term "transference" is readily deconstructed into two elements: first, the patient's feelings and fantasies about a current person—most often the analyst—and second, a theory that childhood experiences are the etiology of these feelings and fantasies (Malin, 1998). This theory is neither necessary nor useful for successful treatment, and in this chapter I propose the term, "Habitual Relationship Pattern" for the nontheoretical element of "transference," the patient's feelings and fantasies about a current person. As for how this change affects the analyst's theory of technique, in the next chapter Mitchell's (1997) "self-reflected responsiveness" is proposed as the guideline for examining the patient's Habitual Response Patterns in treatment.

Treatment Focus on the Here and Now

Once the term "transference" has been deconstructed into its two elements, we have the option of discarding the theory of the childhood
origin of adult feelings because its disadvantages outweigh its advantages. No, I don't think "the child is father to the man"—perhaps the
child is great grandfather to the man, or perhaps great, great grandfather to the man.

A number of commentators writing from quite different points of
view independently have urged that treatment should concentrate on
exploring the meanings of the patients' feelings and fantasies in the
here and now, rather than exploring for childhood origins. Such a position is not so unconventional as it may first appear. For example, Levy,
in a panel discussion of Kohut's *The Analysis of the Self* (Panel, 1995b),
remarked that one of Kohut's ideas that he found useful is that there
is an ahistorical way of conceptualizing "transference" and of linking
"transference" to defects in psychic structure, rather than to past experience in relationships. Brooks Brenneis (1999) warns that the interest in pursuing reconstruction of childhood experiences or traumas
on the part of either patient or the analyst may serve the defensive
purpose of fleeing from a currently emotionally disturbing situation
between patient and analyst: "When . . . the dynamics of the analytic
situation impose a kind of pressure to believe in these reconstructions
[of childhood abuse], this may well signal the need for a careful investigation of contemporary analytic experiences that have possibly been
transported to the past" (p. 198).

Writing from a more philosophical vantage point, Sass (1999) considers the traditional analytic focus on childhood a deviation, but he
regards it as a desirable one that serves to take us away from the present and its attendant existential anxieties, "distracting us from the
potentially devastating realization of our own finitude and mortality"
(p. 906). I do not share Sass's rather dark view, virtually devoid of hope.

In a summary statement on the subject, Fonagy (1999b) argues
that analysts should avoid the archaeological metaphor; the recovery
of memory is an inappropriate goal. In a discussion, Mollon (2000)
questioned whether Fonagy was "advocating a completely ahistorical
form of psychoanalytic technique, in which the analyst makes only
here-and-now interpretations and carefully avoids any allusion to childhood?" (p. 168). Fonagy (2000) responds to Mollon:

Recovered memories should . . . be treated with suspicion; potentially they are byproducts of focussing on specific patterns of transference relationship, especially when trying to establish an historical explanation for current difficulties. Recovery of memories is of great significance, not as explanations for current patterns but as material that serves to enlighten us further about the nature of the transference relationship. . . . [I] did not suggest that creating meaning in terms of [the patient's] *childlike ways of relating* [to the analyst], was not a helpful part of the analytic process. It is the concretisation of this aim that is risky. Identifying transference patterns as the past is explored is qualitatively different from exploring the past in order to understand transference [p. 169, italics added].

Thus, Fonagy suggests that a recovered memory is not of intrinsic interest for its own sake; it is, rather, useful as a signal that some process is taking place between patient and analyst and that the memory recovery is serving some current unconscious function for the patient. Patients express *childlike ways of relating* to the analyst within the domain of here-and-now interactions, and, arguably, these expressions are apt to be more affect-laden than discussions of childlike ways of relating from long ago.

These quotations from Fonagy are consonant with my belief that the meanings of the patient's Habitual Relationship Patterns, primarily as displayed in the patient-analyst relationship, should be the analytic focus, rather than the putative childhood origins of these feelings and fantasies. The meanings of the Habitual Relationship Patterns can be explored in the context of the defensive functions these conscious and unconscious fantasies currently serve. Repetitive observations of the undesirable consequences of these patterns, such as emotional discomfort, distress, or constriction of life style, motivate the patient to try to modify these patterns.

To a noteworthy extent, the change I am advocating has already gotten underway in Kleinian circles. For example, Ponsi (1999), discussing issues of definition and terminology, considers discarding the term "transference."

Does it make sense to discard the term and concept of transference, given that by now to a great extent it is meant in a

different sense than Freud's? It is a challenging task to discard
and revise a concept such as transference but it seems to me
it is just as challenging for every author to explain every time
how he/she intends to use this term. . . . In practice, what most
often occurs in post-Kleinian analyses—but not only in these—
is a privileged exploration and interpretation in the here-and-
now, both horizontally and vertically, both in extent and in
depth, *whereas the link with past history is left in the background.* . . . Going by this, I wonder whether this type of "transference" exploration and interpretation wouldn't be better
defined as exploration and interpretation of interaction (email,
italics added).

I agree with Ponsi that these feelings and fantasies toward the analyst
should be given a name other than "transference" in order to shed the
theoretical assumptions that Freud himself connected to the concept
of "transference." Patients can be helped to change these feelings therapeutically without knowing what caused the feelings in the first place.
And what is so useful about painstakingly delineating what, putatively,
those early origins were? Try to put aside Freud's expectation, and ask
yourself why *you* think that recalling the putatively causal memory
will remove its present distressing effect. And why also assume that
the particular pattern of feelings originating in childhood was characterized by the same unconscious meanings and defensive functions
that are attributed to them in the present? For example, does it seem
likely that a particular pattern of sexual feelings will have the same
unconscious meanings and serve the same unconscious defensive functions when the person is 80 years old, when the person is 60 years old,
when the person is 40 years old, when the person is 20 years old, when
the person is five years old, and when the person is one year old? If
not, if the unconscious meanings and defensive functions are different, perhaps quite unrelated, why is determining the origin of value to
the patient who is trying to change a disturbing, *current* pattern of
feelings?

The Patient's Habitual Relationship Pattern

Once the etiological aspect of "transference" is discarded, we are faced
with shifting focus to that other element of "transference," the patient's
current feelings about other persons, especially those directed toward

the analyst. We all have organizations of feelings and fantasies, conscious and unconscious, that shape our interactions with individuals we characterize in various ways—as authorities, underdogs, allies, critics. We have long observed that the analytic situation exposes these patterns in a palpable and powerful way that both patient and analyst can perceive. Freud (1937b) notes that the adult ego "finds itself compelled to seek out those situations in reality which can serve as to be able to justify, in relation to them, its maintaining its *habitual* modes of reaction" (p. 238, italics added). As Cooper (1987) observed, there is a question whether maintaining current, habitual defenses takes precedence over concern about the original danger. I here propose to refer to these organizations of feelings by the term *Habitual Relationship Pattern*. The patient's Habitual Relationship Pattern will be influenced by the state of patient-analyst interaction at that time.

The locus of the term Habitual Relationship Pattern clearly is the patient. An alternative locus, suggested by Ponsi, is "exploration and interpretation of interaction." Much can be said for her proposal because there is no patient without an analyst, and, operationally, it is the interaction that is dealt with in the treatment. Treatment, however, focuses primarily on the patient, and, therefore, I prefer the term Habitual Relationship Pattern, which has "relationship" as its central parameter, indicating that the pattern always involves interactions with others.

The concept of Habitual Relationship Patterns involves little or no connection with, or interest in, the *etiology* of these feelings and fantasies. Malin (1998) concurs with this attitude of disinterest, noting that "affect and cognition may be explored psychoanalytically, but metapsychological propositions about their etiology have no immediate clinical relevance" (p. 760). There are three reasons for this lack of clinical relevance: (1) effective treatment can be provided without knowledge of etiology; (2) it is impossible to assess the veridicality of any hypothesis about etiology from analytic data; and (3) the relevance of etiology is unclear because the current dynamic function of the pattern may be different from, and have become independent of, its initial function.

Conceptual Forebears of Habitual Relationship Pattern

It was rather humbling to learn that my current ideas about analytic theory and technique, which I thought of as innovative, had been described almost word for word more than 60 years ago by Karen Horney (1939):

> The concept of transference—divested of the theoretical con-troversies as to whether transference is essentially a repeti-tion of infantile attitudes—contends that observation, understanding and discussion of the patient's emotional reac-tions to the psychoanalytical situation constitute the most direct ways of reaching an understanding of his character structure, and consequently of his difficulties. It has become the most powerful and indeed the indispensable, tool of ana-lytical therapy. I believe that quite apart from its value to ther-apy, much of the future of psychoanalysis depends on a more accurate and a deeper observation and understanding of the patient's reactions. This conviction is based on the assump-tion that the essence of all human psychology resides in under-standing the processes operating in human relationships. The psychoanalytical relationship, which is one form of human relations, provides us with unheard-of possibilities in under-standing these processes. Hence a more accurate and profound understanding of this one relationship will constitute the great-est contribution to psychology which psychoanalysis will even-tually have to offer [pp. 33–34].

She elaborates: "I differ from Freud in that, after recognition of the neurotic trends, while he primarily investigates their genesis I prima-rily investigate their actual functions and their consequences" (p. 282).

Following Horney there are numerous other conceptualizations antedating my own which are essentially consonant in one or more respects. For example, Arlow (1969) describes persistent, constantly active, highly organized unconscious fantasies that vary in ease of accessibility to consciousness. These fantasies and external stimuli constantly interact with each other; the fantasies provide the "mental set" in which the stimuli are integrated, that is, infused with meaning. These fantasies are grouped together around certain basic childhood wishes and experiences, according to Arlow, while the self-represen-tations in the fantasies help make up the individual's identity.

Bowlby's idea of internal working models has much in common with my notion of Habitual Relationship Pattern. Fonagy (1999a) notes Bowlby was troubled by the lack of attention paid to infants' actual experiences with caregivers by both Freud and Klein, and asserted

(Bowlby, 1969, 1973) that representations of others and of the self were organized into internal working models (1980, 1988b) to deal with adaptation to social relationships. These internal working models served to interpret, regulate, and predict the behavior and feelings of the significant other person to whom the individual was attached, as well as the individual's own attachment-related behavior and feelings. If appropriately revised in relation to developmental and environmental changes, they facilitate adapting to future social, attachment relationships. Repeated, unchanged operation of these internal working models, however, tend to render them less conscious or inaccessible to consciousness as they become *habitual* and automatic, resulting in some loss of flexibility and adaptibility.

Closely related is Stern's (1985) concept of Representations of Interactions that have been Generalized (RIGs). He suggested that infants have a capacity to aggregate experiences and distill an average prototype. These prototypes, or RIGs, he asserts, constitute a basic unit for the representation of the core self. Stern has not followed the longitudinal development of the infants whose observation formed the raw material of his conception, so he is unable to comment about how subsequent development and experience may have continued to shape these RIGs.

Another concept analogous to my notion of Habitual Relationship Pattern is Dorpat and Miller's (1992) concept of a schema, which is "a bound, distinct and unitary representation of an interaction with the environment . . . [which] functions as a template for organizing and interpreting lived experience" (p. 111). They note, in agreement with Stern, that "Organizing schemata are the blueprints for maintaining a cohesive sense of self" (p. 118). They assert that "transference is not a biologically determined drive to repeat the past ad infinitum for its own sake; rather it is an expression of a human striving to organize experience and to create meanings" (p. 216). They add that "transference manifestations do give the analyst a glimpse of what a childhood relationship was like . . . not because an idea or emotion from the past has been displaced onto the present, but because the schemata that were organized in the past continue to be functionally effective or remain available for periodic mobilization" (p. 221).

I want to also mention Lichtenberg, Lachmann, and Fosshage's (1992) concept of model scenes that organize and help the dyad understand how the individual deals with his or her own motivational systems. Model scenes are jointly constructed by patient and analyst from memories of events and occurrences at any phase of development in the patient's life. Since they may convey the essence of an adult's relationships and motivations, they are especially useful to illuminate "transferences." Reviews of model scenes enable the integration into a cohesive self-organization of the living experiences of motivations representative of past and present.

There are similarities, too, with the work of Horowitz (1995), who describes structures that function to preserve continuity of both self-organization and relationships which he terms *person schemas*. He utilizes a configurational analysis that looks for interactions of wish, fear, and defense at each of four levels: (1) the phenomena to be explained; (2) analysis of states of mind; (3) inferences that are made about the internalized self and other schemas from role-relationship models; and (4) shifts in terms of habitual styles of defensive control of states and schemas. He also formulated a role-relationship-model configuration that organizes inferences about the interactions of wishes, fears, and defenses.

Independently, Luborsky, in the laboratory, and I, through my work in the consulting room, have fashioned impressively similar conceptions of "transference." Luborsky started with efforts to measure therapeutic alliance and, over a period of more than 20 years, has developed the Core Conflictual Relationship Theme (Luborsky and Crits-Christoph, 1990) as a measure of Freud's "transference" template. Inferences about "each person's recurrent central relationship pattern . . . rely on three facets of narratives about interactions with other people: (1) the type of wishes, needs, and intentions concerning the other person; (2) responses from the other person; and (3) responses of the self" (p. 4). These components found across the sample of narratives are combined to determine the measure. The rater first makes a tailor-made inference from the relationship episode, and then, to enable measures of reliability, translates it into standard categories that can be reliably measured independently by different judges.

Luborsky and Crits-Christoph note that although current memories of relationship episodes with parents show similarity with relationship episodes about other people in the present, "the degree of similarity of the early and late relationship episodes does not prove causality but is consistent with the supposition that the later pattern was prefigured by and may have originated in the earlier one" (p. 312). They note that Arlow viewed the Core Conflictual Relationship Theme "as an offshoot of a more basic substrate composed of unconscious fantasies. . . . The heart of both the unconscious fantasies and the Core Conflictual Relationship Theme of the narratives may be fruitfully conceived of as related expressions of the pervasive central relationship patterns that are expressed when wishes are activated toward other people and even to the self" (Luborsky and Crits-Christoph, 1990, p. 6).

The focus on those central relationship patterns *without any necessary assumption of the childhood etiology* of these patterns links the Core Conflictual Relationship Theme with Habitual Relationship Patterns; both try to characterize the dimensions of a pattern without attempting to ascertain its etiology.

The most recent forebear is that of Brickman (2000), who describes "a unifying concept of habitual behavior patterns reflected in modular neural networks" (p. 1). He has developed "the acronym CARD—Contingent Affect-imbued Relational Disposition—to denote a theoretically and clinically inferable neuro-psychoanalytic conceptual template which can serve as an imageable focus for clinical inquiry" (p. 19). He adds that because affect is a key organizer of relational experiences, the hypothalamus, amygdala, and midbrain are significant components of these networks. He explains that "the behavioral consistency which is the hallmark of characterological 'structure' can be re-thought as neurally encoded CARDS which have persisted in the face of repeated environmental—chiefly relational—challenges" (p. 29). In treatment, patients attempt to replace maladaptive relational innervative patterns by engaging the therapist in a mutative relationship. Durable behavioral change would reflect altered neural innervation patterns.

The Nature of Habitual Relationship Patterns

Habitual Relationship Patterns refer to organizations of conscious and unconscious fantasies, feelings, and attitudes toward significant others and toward self that persist over time. They structure and integrate the gamut of interpersonal and other experiences, and color perceptions to provide them with meaning. The concept is functionally the same as Fosshage's (1994) organization model of "transference," without the distracting terminological link to an older, outmoded conception: *"the primary organising patterns or schemas with which the analysand constructs and assimilates his or her experience of the analytic relationship.* Schemas can be activated internally (with shifts in motivation and self-states), or externally (by the analyst and others)" (p. 271).

The Habitual Relationship Patterns that are the focus of treatment are those that refer to ways of relating to others that involve significant irrational elements. This is comparable to Freud's conception that the patient's feelings and fantasies about the analyst that should be considered to be "transference" are those that are distorted, that is, irrational, not those that are appropriate reactions to actual characteristics of the analyst. There are healthy Habitual Relationship Patterns with few if any irrational elements. They are usually of little interest because they do not appear to be troublesome either to the patient or to the analyst.

How are the organizations of Habitual Relationship Patterns characterized? Do they take the form of representations? Are identification and introjection included? Do they involve drives? Habitual Relationship Pattern deliberately is conceived as a generic construct. I don't want to propose a standard characterization. The dynamics of the irrational aspects of a Habitual Relationship Pattern can be formulated in whatever theoretical terms and concepts the analyst is comfortable. I tend to structure the Habitual Relationship Pattern in terms of defenses, but other ways are possible. Levine and Friedman (2000), discussing intersubjectivity as a point of view, also note that it does not require the analyst to adopt any particular theory of mind: "Instead, we focus upon the importance of unintended, unconscious, spontaneous and mutually constructed interactive components that constitute and contribute to each participant's experience in the analysis" (p. 71). The term Habitual Relationship Pattern was selected in an attempt to encourage the analyst to avoid etiological theorizing in structuring the patient's mind.

One example of a Habitual Relationship Pattern is Kernberg's (1975) description, which does incorporate an etiological explanation, of narcissistic, promiscuous men "who unconsciously seek revenge against the oral, frustrating mother through pseudogenital relationships with women" (p. 42). Character traits, too, such as hysterical, obsessive-compulsive, and narcissistic attributes, are Habitual Relationship Patterns involving the relationship with the self as well as with others.

Let me present an example of a Habitual Relationship Pattern of a patient, Pat, whose treatment I describe more fully in a subsequent chapter. Whenever faced with a really difficult problem, Pat's Pattern was to withdraw from the possibility of receiving help from others, and to elect to resolve it, for better or worse, on his own. Although ordinarily both comfortable and skillful about delegating authority and responsibility to others, under duress he cannot turn to others for help. One sustaining result of this Pattern was his unusual adeptness at problem solving. Several times during his analysis he failed to mention a significant concern he was dealing with until he had resolved it alone, for example, a conflict about whether to fire someone.

In one session I informed him that I was planning to retire in a little more than a year. His immediate conscious reaction was to feel sad, but in the next session he, uncharacteristically, found little to talk about. We agreed that he was reacting to the difficult problem my retirement presented by again feeling he had better find a way to deal with it on his own, with no help from me. His Pattern of withdrawing from possible help was related to several unconscious fantasies. One was that if he accepted help, he would become obligated to reciprocate, and thus vulnerable to the anticipated exorbitant demands he would be unable to fulfill. He then risked exposure to shame and humiliation.

A second was related to his realization that he had had some wish to terminate the analysis. This stirred a fantasy that his doing so would hurt me and only he could deal with this. The same concern and guilt had been activated in relation to his former wife. He had wanted to leave her, but felt she depended on him and that his leaving would be very destructive to her. He, on his own, dealt with his guilt then by becoming so provocative with her that she decided to divorce him. He had made it appear that she was rejecting him rather than that he was leaving her. This conflict recurred with me. His unconscious fantasy about the intensity of his destructive power, a manifestation of his fantasy about the destructive potential of his rage, generated concern and guilt about damaging me. Even though he wanted to terminate treatment, there was also evidence of unconscious anger that I did the leaving.

When the multiple meanings of these Habitual Relationship Patterns are elucidated in relation to the analyst, they can be applied retrospectively to develop hypotheses about the patient's relationship to earlier figures in the patient's life. "Transference" is turned upside down, reversing the logic used with traditional, historical "transference," in which reconstruction of earlier feelings and fantasies "explains" current feelings and fantasies toward the analyst. The affect experienced in the here-and-now patient-analyst interactions creates a presence that facilitates understanding that is often lacking in discussing relationships in the distant past. Those feelings and fantasies from the Habitual Relationship Patterns directed toward the analyst and other current persons in the patient's life may be extrapolated toward persons earlier in the patient's life, and used to develop a hypo-thetical personal narrative for the patient.

Such an example of a hypothesis about a relationship in the past, extrapolated from a current Habitual Relationship Pattern, is described briefly, and reprised in more detail in a later chapter. The aforemen-tioned analytic patient, Pat, was currently conflicted about devoting himself to golf for his own pleasure, rather than to any more "serious" or "worthy" enterprise. He unconsciously dealt with this internal con-flict by projecting one side of the conflict onto me, picturing me as opposed to golf and its competitive, playful pleasures. As far as I could tell, although not a golfer, I was not critical of his involvement in golf, though I had some difficulty understanding its predominant role in his life. Thus, he had transformed an uncomfortable internal conflict into an external conflict between himself and me. In adolescence, Pat had also pictured his father as opposed to his playing golf. Extrapolating from our understanding of how he was dealing with the current con-flict, we hypothesized that in adolescence he had been conflicted about whether to make playing golf his professional goal. He dealt with this same issue in adolescence as he did in his analysis, projecting one side of the conflict onto his father, picturing his father in opposition, and thereby transforming an internal conflict into an external one with an authority figure.

A Rationale for the Analyst's Technique

What is the analyst's rationale for a technique not based on that archae-ological model in which the analyst explores for buried memories of traumatic childhood experiences that putatively caused the adult's emotional disorder? Friedman (1996) describes the dilemma: "It is hard to picture how an analyst would work who no longer believes in hunt-ing for something that is already there to be discovered" (p. 261). To be left without a rationale is, indeed, disconcerting.

An alternative rationale is based on the idea that the more infor-mation available about the person who is the object of the patient's feelings, the greater the possibility of understanding the patient's feel-ings and fantasies about that person. The analyst, as participant-observer in the treatment situation, has access to observations, both objective and subjective, both conscious and unconscious, about one person with whom the patient interacts—the analyst himself or her-self—as well as direct observation of the patient's affects and behavior. When the patient relates experiences with other individuals, past or present, and describes the feelings and behavior of these other individuals, the patient's report about them and about the patient's own feelings and fantasies are screened through, and influenced by, the current dynamics of the patient-analyst relationship. A more solid ground for developing inferences about the patient's feelings and fantasies toward the analyst is based on a field-theory approach, focusing on patient-analyst interactions in the here and now. A spectrum of analysts now emphasize focusing on what, in the intersubjective moment of the here and now, has stimulated the patient's fantasies and reactions (Gabbard, 1998; Shengold, 1998; Tyson, 1998).

Michels (1998), in discussing a report by Arlow, essentially agrees with the point previously noted by Fonagy, while offering an alternative conception from Arlow's of understanding patient verbalizations about the childhood origins of their psychopathology. Arlow (1998) described two patients, one of whom recalled an intense trauma early in life, while the other remembered a series of minor stresses, but no major trauma. Arlow conceptualized these clinical examples as different types of origins of adult psychopathology. Michels suggests that instead of viewing these reports as containing veridical, etiological information, they should be considered to be symbolic statements that contain information about current patient-analyst interactions. That is, patients' productions should not be considered literal statements about actual past events, but rather, figurative comments that allude to and provide information about the current experience of interaction with the analyst in metaphorical terms. Inferring the symbolic significance of the patient's statement provides an understanding of the patient's present experience with the analyst.

Kerr (2000, personal communication) notes that Freud's famous rule dictating the need for "transference" analysis—you cannot destroy anyone in effigy or in absentia—suggests that such "transference" analysis is just that, an attempt to destroy someone in effigy. Although the patient may be "reliving" childhood experiences and relationships in the "transference," which is what Freud maintained was happening, at some level in the patient there is the realization that the analyst is not *actually* the parent or the significant other. The neurotic "transference" in these terms has the unreal quality of an "as if" relationship; it is more an effigie than a reality. This distinction is exemplified by the difference between a psychotic "transference," in which the patient believes the analyst *is* the patient's parent or significant other, and a neurotic "transference," in which the patient believes the analyst is *like* the patient's parent or significant other. The implication is that, contrary to Freud, it is in the actual, realistic relationship between patient and analyst, between these two flesh-and-blood persons, that the patient's troubling fantasies and feelings can be really "destroyed" or resolved. To go backward to the past, and toward a putative child-hood etiology of these here-and-now feelings, Kerr asserts, is to do precisely what Freud warned against, that is, settle for an attack on an effigy.

Summary

I propose discarding the etiological theory element of "transference" and renaming the nontheoretical portion, comprising the patient's feel-ings and fantasies about others, as Habitual Relationship Patterns. Numerous conceptual forebears of Habitual Relationship Patterns are described, from Horney to, most recently, Brickman. One example of a Habitual Relationship Pattern is that of a patient who, when con-fronted with a particularly difficult problem, withdraws from others, feeling he must deal with it entirely on his own. Extrapolating from such Patterns to earlier relationships enables the development of hypotheses about historical narratives regarding the patient's earlier development. In place of exploring the memories of traumatic child-hood experiences presumed to have caused "transference" responses, I propose that treatment focus on delineating the current conscious and unconscious defensive meanings of the patient's Habitual Relationship Patterns as they manifest themselves primarily, but not solely, in relation to the analyst. This focus provides the analyst with the most information, both objective and subjective data about the per-son who is the object of the patient's feelings, the analyst himself or herself.

10
A Theory of Technique

Both analyse and transference are treacherous words, treacherous because analysts of the same and different persuasions use them in association with too many different conceptions of childhood development; of psychopathology; of repetition and its basis, functions and modes; of the uses of counter-transference in defining transference; of the so-called real relationship with the analyst; of appropriate kinds and degrees of analytic activity; and so on. . . . Consequently, to agree that we analyse transference amounts to little more than agreeing that we use the same words for whatever it is that we do.

—Roy Schafer, "The Search for Common Ground"

How do we work analytically if, when we discard the traditional concept of "transference," we discard the associated traditional theory of technique in which the analyst explores for and reconstructs traumatic childhood experiences-fantasies that were the putative origins of adult neuroses and of the patient's unrealistic feelings and fantasies about the analyst? What are the implications for a theory based on technique of my conception of Habitual Relationship Patterns? Can the analyst operate atheoretically? Is the concept associated with a particular theory of technique or is it compatible with different theories of technique?

Guidelines for analytic treatment compatible with the concept of Habitual Relationship Patterns are here presented. The role of regression in treatment is reviewed and the mutative effects of analysis discussed. Finally, criteria for characterizing a treatment as psychoanalytic are described.

The Role of Theory in Technique

Pine (1994) acknowledges that in his book (1990) he had implied that "the clinician can be just a naïve naturalist observer walking through the world of clinical psychoanalysis creatively and refreshingly spotting interesting phenomena" (p. 213). The analyst cannot operate in a theoretical vacuum, and now Pine recognizes that how we describe and categorize things reflects theory. Sandler (1990) believes that multiple models and multiple part theories exist in the minds of analysts. Theories are useful; phenomena cannot be defined without them, but they also constrain by inevitably excluding certain phenomena, which Pine refers to as "tunnel vision" (p. 219). Analysts' attitudes toward theory can be considered to vary from theoryophile to theoryophobe. Theory is important and influential for the theoryophile; in field-theory terms, it is a strong vector. Theory is less important and exerts less influence for the theoryophobe, and thus, in field-theory terms, is considered a weak vector. Another factor that influences the role of theory is the discrepancy between public theory and private theory (Mayer, in Panel, 1995a); public theory is reported in the analyst's writing and presentations; private theory shapes the analyst's interventions in the treatment.

Pine asserts that theories differ in their suitability for dealing with various clinical phenomena, and urges, as do Hoffman (1996) and Akhtar (2000), that the analyst use the theory best suited for the particular phenomenon. This assumes that the analyst knows what is best suited and that he or she is equally comfortable using each theory and can move from one to the other like changing gloves. Analysts, however, are more comfortable with some theories than with others. Indeed, some are fiercely committed to their favorite theory. Analysts differ in more than just style and form (Wallerstein, 1990); they differ in values (Aron, 1999) that influence how the analyst views what is important and unimportant, what is good and bad, what is healthy and unhealthy.

Although analysts have access to multiple theories, there are numerous limitations on the resolution of choice of theory for a particular intervention; the analyst may have difficulty accessing his or her own unconscious factors that are influencing that choice. We should recognize that in any single, particular clinical instant the analyst cannot alternate between conflicting models; a dialectic is not possible. The analyst cannot at the same instant be both deliberate and spontaneous, or even somewhere in between the two. Although the analyst has access to multiple theories, they are hierarchically organized, and it is in a clinical instant, when one theory must be selected, that the analyst's value-based, idiosyncratic, preferred theory is likely to emerge, rather than a standard theory. This provides a conceptual framework for Mitchell's self-reflective responsiveness, which is a theory of technique compatible with the concept of Habitual Relationship Patterns.

Guidelines for Analytic Treatment

I have been arguing for focusing primarily on patient–analyst interaction in the here and now (Yalom, 1980), rather than exploring for hidden traumatic childhood memories. What guidelines should be utilized to direct the examination of Habitual Relationship Patterns? Mitchell (1997) believes there is a need for a fundamentally different model of psychoanalytic treatment and offers an alternative guideline, namely,

> a self-reflective responsiveness of a particular (psychoanalytic) sort, not a striving for a particular state of mind, but an engagement in a process. . . . I find that aspiring to states of mind like "evenly hovering attention" (Freud), the "analytic attitude" (Schafer), and "reverie" (Bion) foreclose other possibilities, other kinds of responsiveness to my patients. There are times when it seems useful for my attention to be highly focused, not evenly hovering; there are times when I feel that my patients need a more genuine response from me, not an attitude; there are times when concerted, careful reasoning seems more fruitful than reverie. . . . We are always committing ourselves to one or another form of responsiveness and participation and foreclosing others. At any particular moment, we might choose to be even-handed or explicitly partisan; sympathetic or self-expressive; dogged or yielding. I believe that each clinician maintains an implicit model of rich, particularly analytic experience, and that implicit model serves as a kind of preconscious compass, guiding the perpetual choices that constitute analytic participation. *The compass used by each analyst is unique.* There is in psychoanalysis, unlike in navigating the earth, no objective, singular electromagnetic field and generic compasses. Each analyst's clinical judgment is shaped by his or her per-

sonal integration of psychoanalytic models and concepts, sea-
soned with his or her personal dynamics, character, and life
experience [pp. 193–195; italics added].

Thus, each clinician's "implicit model" refers to each analyst's covert,
personal, idiosyncratic theory about technique and psychopathology.
Mitchell eschews the use of a standard theory, such as traditional psychoanalytic theory, as does Yalom (1980), who urges the therapist to
"listen without the presuppositions that distort understanding" (p. 17).

Attention to the analyst's feelings as an essential guide is also urged
by Bromberg (1994), Coen (1994), and Aron (1999). Lachmann and
Beebe (1995), however, counsel that "the dangers of ascribing the analyst's experience to the intent of the patient cannot be overestimated"
(p. 380). Aron elaborates, "What I am advocating is that the analyst
adopt a maximally self-reflexive strategy—a goal similar to the goal
we set for patients" (p. 25). Pizer (1999), commenting about Aron's
position, discusses the importance of the analyst's "internalized institutional legacy" (p. 63) as an additional element in shaping the analyst's feelings and reactions. For Pizer, as for Aron, there are always
supervisors under the couch.

Böhm (1999) notes that one can object that freedom from a program is also a program. He argues nonetheless that this program (freedom from a program) is worth following because "it has become a
clinically convincing experience as seen from both the couch and the
analyst's chair" (p. 503).

The essence of self-reflective responsiveness is, I believe, best illus-
trated by the following beautiful analogy from Pizer (1999).

If you have seen [Yo Yo] Ma in a live chamber concert, playing
the classical repertoire with Emmanuel Ax or an improvisation
riff with Bobby McFerrin, you will have noticed that Ma's technique feels like the absence of technique. The ease and tenderness with which he holds the cello, the unstrenuous flow of
strength, the transparency of sound, combine with Ma's vital
connectedness to the other musicians. In his duets (or trios, or
quartets) is an eye contact and a sense that the musicians, while
executing their own virtuosity, are really playing intimately for
each other. It is this state of love in the act of producing music
that, when achieved, transports us in the audience. Where do
we locate Ma's musicality? In his discipline? In his bowing or
fingering technique? In his spontaneity? In his seamless bridg-
ing of these multiple components, held in each moment's act

> of inseparability and simultaneity? Are we ever distractingly aware of Ma's "musical Third"? Is he? . . . How do we learn to use our own *analytic* instruments? [p. 62].

The approach of self-reflective responsiveness, which seems to urge that the analyst "fly by the seat of his or her emotional pants," is less radical than it might appear. Renik (1996) asserts "that *elements of effective analytic technique are necessarily outside the analyst's conscious control*, that many of the best things we do, we do for reasons of which we *cannot* be aware at the time" (p. 392). To the degree that Renik is correct, analysts who for many years have consciously shaped their technique on traditional principles have, unbeknown to themselves, necessarily been "flying by the seat of their pants" because much of their treatment behavior actually was outside of conscious control. Although countertransference has long been described, it has taken analysts a great deal of time to acknowledge fully the role of their own unconscious in treatment in each analyst's decision whether to invoke abstinence or to proffer an interpretation, or in the myriad small details of everyday practice.

The compass of self-reflective responsiveness appears untrustworthy and unreliable when compared with that clear, explicit guide to explore for hidden, traumatic childhood memories. It does, however, avoid the inevitable complications accompanying the tailoring of an explicit system to fit to a particular dyad, or vice versa. It now seems less plausible that the Procrustean bed of standard technique, in which the patient lies on a couch four or five times per week and "free associates" in order to recover traumatic childhood experiences/fantasies, is likely to be optimally helpful for all dyads. Also, self-reflective responsiveness provides the patient with a model of a person, the therapist, who trusts his or her own thoughts and feelings and risks spontaneity. Perhaps *who* the analyst is as a person, or that the analyst *is* a person, is as important or possibly even more important than what the analyst *says*. Such a view would help explain why analysts of varied persuasions help so many of their patients. We have accepted that patients may identify with the analyst's analyzing function. Beyond that, child analysts, particularly, grapple with identification with the analyst as an individual, "a new object" whose own Habitual Relationship Patterns are experienced by patients in multiple interactions. Isn't the child's identification with attributes of the parents, both fact and fantasy, a central mechanism of the child's development? Why wouldn't that also play a role in the adult's development?

The dearth of rules may provide optimal conditions for the analyst to deal with his or her own issues of ethics and responsibility in the relationship with the patient. Explicit regulations provide standard ethical answers, but the security they afford may minimize the analyst's awareness of the need for exploration and development of the integrated personal ethics and responsibility specific to the particular therapeutic dyad. George Eliot (1860) has eloquently made the same point:

> Moral judgments must remain false and hollow, unless they are checked and enlightened by a perpetual reference to the special circumstances that mark the individual lot. . . . And the man of maxims is the popular representative of the minds that are guided in their moral judgment solely by general rules, thinking that these will lead them to justice by a ready-made patent method, without the trouble of exerting patience, discrimination, impartiality—without any care to assure themselves whether they have the insight that comes from a hardly-earned estimate of temptation, or from a life vivid and intense enough to have created a wide fellow-feeling with all that is human [p. 435].

Miller (1998) argues for that point by using neighborhoods as a metaphor. The essence of the neighborhood, he writes, is the significant lack of order when compared to institutions like the family and the state, in which order is created by hosts of rules and regulations.

> The neighborhood is a place of transition and transience. Neighbors casually pass through it. . . . They remain in a special way strangers to each other. . . . Perhaps only in a neighborhood of healthy chaos are humans faced with the task, without knowing it, of learning ethics and responsibility. . . . Perhaps only as neighbors do people learn, untutored, undirected, to live with each other, well or badly, without absolute guidelines telling them what to do. (As if there could be guidelines?) [pp. 80–86].

To the degree that less reliance is placed on guidelines and regulations, there is likely to be less order in the treatment process. This, indeed, will move the treatment situation toward disorder. "The turn toward disorder," Nowotny (1998) observes, "seems the hallmark of postmodernism" (p. 92). But, to borrow from Miller, let us observe that the disorder we seek in treatment need not be anarchic; it can and ought to be "neighborly."

Self-reflective responsiveness, to be sure, is not without its problems. Its idiosyncratic nature almost assuredly means that reliability, in the sense of agreement between different analysts, will not be demonstrable. Regarding analytic treatment, because of its idiosyncratic, nonreplicable characteristic, as an art rather than a science, makes that failure to find agreement of little moment, though critics who search for comparability disagree. Aron (1999) is troubled by the problem inherent in his own position of relying on the analyst's feelings.

> Those who have been critical of fundamentalist assumptions have been left with nothing but an appeal to the analyst's authenticity, spontaneity, moral scrupulousness, and ongoing self-reflection. . . . The downside of this approach is that, at the extreme, it may lead to an anything-goes strategy in which there is no basis for determining when an intervention is or is not within a psychoanalytic framework—that is, whether it leads to a deepening of the psychoanalytic process [p. 18].

Cooper (1999) escalates the critique above and beyond Aron's own: "I think he is exposing us to wild analysis" (p. 38). Cooper also responds to Aron's worried agnosticism as to whether an intervention is psychoanalytic by declaring his own standard: "The best interventions help to produce more material, more questions, more riddles" (p. 38).

Friedman (1999), in a similar vein, expresses comparable concerns about Hoffman's (1996) dialectical constructivism. He fears that by abandoning fundamentalist assumptions, Hoffman's approach could break from its therapeutic moorings: "Without rules to stretch for and models to superimpose, Hoffman's favored ironic attitude would give over to nihilistic cynicism" (p. 897). Although Friedman acknowledges that he does not find such in Hoffman's practice, his caveat echoes Cooper's: "It wouldn't tell us what we should do with a patient" (p. 898).

I argue that no theory of technique will tell us "what we should do with a patient," because no theory *can* tell us what we should do. In this respect, traditional "transference" theory is no more adequate as a guide to treatment than other theories of technique. No theory of technique can encompass the idiosyncratic personality and values of each particular patient, the idiosyncratic personality and values of the particular analyst, or the complex emotional forces operating in the patient-analyst interaction in the here and now—forces that would be termed "vectors" in a field-theory conception of the psychoanalytic situation. Pizer (2000), when discussing the clinical issue of presenting and publishing patients' stories, concludes, "Surely, there is no once-and-for-all answer. There is no single rule, or formula, or substitute for clinical judgment and responsibility" (pp. 257–258). True, as Hoffman points out, there are many "right" actions—not just one—and as Sass (1999) notes, many "wrong" actions as well. But, in addition, whether an action will be "right" or "wrong" cannot be foretold; we cannot predict the effect of any action. For that reason we can't know what "we should do with a patient." Retrospectively, however, we can try to assess the impact of an action, its "rightness" or "wrongness." To practice analysis we must constantly be looking back over our shoulder to try to understand what we have done, to try to understand where we have come from, while, at the same time, interacting with the emotional forces operating in the here and now.

Brown (2001), a writer, eloquently makes a similar point about readers' expectations of her novels. One reader complained that the author's book "didn't tell me how I should live *my* life." Brown comments:

> The innocence of her disappointment fascinated me. I myself, as creator of that book, had thought I had been addressing such tangles as the primordial relation between mother and daughter; one particular view of history and another; the difference between accident and intention; the question of where responsibility and blame might lie for the satisfactions of a life, especially as a mother and daughter might feel that responsibility. . . . We do not . . . expect a novel to be a kind of AAA strip map to guide us safely through the uncharted territory of the psyche [p. B1].

She concludes, tellingly, "To be reminded of the difficulty of things— to be taught the inescapable complexity of the world—frequently makes one unfit to be a smiling moral arbiter" (p. B2).

In today's analysis, where so much in the way of rules is being overthrown or powerfully relativized against invocations of their opposites, when the emphasis is lately so much on spontaneity and openness to encounter, the felt need for rules will likely be enhanced at a deeper level. I agree with Hoffman (1999) that many of the routines and rules in every analytic treatment are implicit rather than explicit, and, indeed, that routines and rules do play important roles. To return to my previous argument, however, I don't think that guidelines or rules prevent wild analysis, or even egregious ethical breaches, such as sexual liaisons between analyst and patient, despite the explicit prohibitions of professional associations and licensing boards. I think most analysts resist the temptation to sexual involvement with a patient because internally they are convinced it is wrong and would be damaging to the patient. When Aron says we "have been left with nothing but an appeal to the analyst's authenticity, spontaneity, moral scrupulousness and on-going self-reflection," I think he is quite right. That is what we always have relied on, whatever we believed was guiding us. And that is all we can rely on. True, that is not entirely satisfactory. But life is not entirely satisfactory—so the poets long have told us.

Emotionally charged patient-analyst interactions are so complex and idiosyncratic that relatively simple, uniform rules and regulations hardly apply. On this, we find agreement from both Aron's (1999) "I do not believe we serve them [supervisees] best by answering with the rules of analytic technique, the basic or standard model" (p. 26) and Cooper's (1999) "the inherent indeterminacy of any actions of the analyst prevents any rigid technique" (p. 36). Further, uniform rules and regulations have the additional disadvantage that they tend to interfere with the analyst's spontaneity, which plays an important role in fostering an emotional presence in the patient-analyst interaction. Genuine warmth can be communicated only spontaneously; preprogramed, deliberate expressions of warmth cannot have the same impact. Deliberate manipulations of the "transference" have rightly been long criticized in the literature. By contrast, an indication, at least in part, of the importance of spontaneity is that when former patients are asked what stood out in their analysis they are apt to recall some spontaneous interaction rather than an interpretation.

Regression and the Logic of "Deep" Analysis

Will my recommendation to focus on current unconscious feelings and fantasies in exploring Habitual Relationship Patterns produce a "superficial defense analysis" rather than a "deeper analysis"? No one has defined depth of analysis. Munder Ross (1999) notes pointedly: "Properly practised, defense analysis, lending depth to the surface (Erikson, 1954) is no less than a supreme act of empathy" (p. 110)— hardly superficial.

Since "deeper" may also refer to the patient's regression, however, this complex subject must be considered. The place of regression in analytic work is one of the tasks Freud left us to carry out, observes Winnicott (1955) and Jackson and Haley (1963). Calder (Panel, 1958), reporting on a panel discussion of the problems of either too little or too much regression, summarized the question: Why didn't patients regress enough for optimum psychoanalytic work? Macalpine (1973) pointed out that regression, for Freud, referred to recapitulation, in reverse order, of earlier stages of mental or sexual development to more primitive levels, a very precise usage, but hardly to be heard nowadays. Sandler and Sandler (1994) note that we still do not have a very precise definition of the concept. Inderbitzin and Levy (2000) discuss the multiplicity of meanings of the term regression, explore its problematic aspects, and focus on the mistaken belief "that the analyst's main technical task is to promote regression" (p. 207). They comment that "the regression epithet has pejorative connotations that tend to obscure the adaptive aspects of all the ego's responses and the importance of acknowledging them in the analytic situation" and they "favor abandoning the concept" (pp. 220–221).

The term *regression* is currently used to refer both to exacerbation of symptoms and infantile behavior, as well as to increased tolerance for unconscious, infantile feelings and fantasy, the latter also called regression in the service of the ego. I will refer to the former as *inhibitory regression*, because it inhibits more mature modes of feeling and functioning, and the latter as *facilitatory regression*. Inderbitzin and Levy (2000) describe the latter as follows:

> There is increasing freedom to associate to these emerging mental products as interferences to self-revelation diminish. Primary process mentation manifests itself more clearly. These phenomena are often mistakenly referred to as "regressions;" they are in fact progressions toward an important psychoanalytic goal: to free analysands to become aware of the fullest possible range of their thoughts, wishes and feelings [p. 209].

Gill (1994) and others have questioned whether inhibitory regression is desirable or even appropriate during analytic treatment (p. 75). Inhibitory regression typically occurs when a person is confronted with a conflict situation he or she cannot master (Alexander, 1956). Macalpine (1950) suggests that the analytic patient's inhibitory regression is primarily iatrogenic and that the analytic situation is inherently infantilizing: "With this unexpected environment [the analytic setting] the patient—if he has any adaptability—has to come to terms, and he can do so only by regression" (p. 526). Characteristics of the analytic setting that she regards as infantilizing include the analyst's neutrality, the analyst's authority, frustration of every gratification, diminished personal responsibility, free association, not receiving replies from the

analyst, curtailment of external stimuli, and interpretation on an infantile level. She notes with historical acuity that these residues in Freud's
technique derive from hypnotic therapy, and so an initial aim of analysis, she comments, is to induce regression.

Jackson and Haley (1963), without referring to Macalpine's paper,
make precisely the same point:

> The patient is in a situation where he cannot behave in an adult
> way and when he does not the analyst points out to him that
> his childlike behavior is evidence of a point of view carried
> over from childhood. . . . The analyst induces a kind of behav-
> ior which he then treats. However, this behavior need not nec-
> essarily mirror the infantile neurosis experienced by the patient
> in his early years. The patient's responses to the analytic situ-
> ation are not necessarily a duplicate of moments in his early
> life history. He may respond idiosyncratically, but still his
> responses might be similar to those anyone would make who
> sought out this situation and cooperated with it. Under cer-
> tain stressful circumstances the individual will exhibit unusual
> behavior which is related to his human biological possibilities
> as well as his experiential history. But his response is not nec-
> essarily *repetitive* of his life history. The adult patient who
> "regresses" in psychoanalysis does not behave as he did
> when he was a child, he behaves like an adult being child-
> like [pp. 368–369].

Inderbitzin and Levy (2000) concur: "It is our belief that the iatrogenic
effects of an overly austere [application of abstinence] approach can
result in unnecessary suffering and an unproductive exaggeration of
psychopathology in the analysand" (p. 208).

Freud did not distinguish between inhibitory regression and
facilitatory regression (regression in the service of the ego). He was
convinced that the impact of childhood experiences caused adult psychopathology; thus he counted it a plus for his treatment if it engaged
the patient's childhood experiences. In order for the patient to rework
and resolve the unconscious conflicts and fantasies from childhood,
he believed, the patient had to relive them in relation to the analyst,
and in this vein he recognized that the analytic situation induces regression: "the patient's falling in love is induced by the analytic situation"
(Freud, 1915, pp. 160–161), and the analyst "has evoked this love by
instituting analytic treatment in order to cure the neurosis" (p. 169).
Freud regarded the "suggestion" of hypnotic treatment as quite closely

related to "transference," indeed, derived from it, and I suspect that he recognized that just as suggestion could induce a hypnotic state, so the characteristics of the analytic situation could induce an inhibitory regression, reflected in the exacerbation of symptoms and infantile behavior.

Freud (1900) noted that when the patient in analytic treatment is asked to suspend his critical faculty and free associate, the patient moves into a psychical state that "bears some analogy to the state before falling asleep—and, no doubt, also to hypnosis" (p. 102), resulting in a widening of the scope of consciousness. If this was the route also intended to induce the patient to reexperience the putative etiological infantile feelings and fantasies, then it was appropriate to shape the conditions of analytic treatment in order to optimize induction of inhibitory regression (infantile behavior) in the patient. The entire treatment focused on exploring for and reliving these infantile feelings and fantasies. Freud (1912a) noted that "it is precisely that they [the phenomena of transference] do us the inestimable service of making the patient's hidden and forgotten erotic impulses immediate and manifest" (p. 108). Regression was seen as the only means for the patient to reexperience these hidden and forgotten impulses and to rework them.

Given a formidable rationale such as the foregoing, it is not out of place to record and to second Cooper's (1987) impression that "there is an implied demand on Freud's part for submission to him by his male patients—in fact by all his patients" (p. 142). Noteworthy confirmatory evidence is Freud's rejection of Jung's recommendation that he, Freud, undertake a personal analysis—an invitation Freud refused lest he risk his authority (Kerr, 1994). Presumably, at least in part, Freud's concern was that his professional authority would be eroded by undergoing inhibitory regression in the presence of another.

But what if Freud was wrong in his conviction about the etiology of adult psychopathology? What if he was wrong that reworking infantile feelings and fantasies from the past in the "transference" is the only way to help patients? As Grandfather in Prokofiev's "Peter and the Wolf" said to Peter, if he had not caught the wolf, "*what then*?" If Freud was wrong, then analysis loses its rationale for inducing inhibitory regression as well as the rationale for structuring treatment to explore for infantile feelings and fantasies from the past. Indeed, deliberately structuring the analytic situation to induce regression is so unusual and so unnatural that it parallels F. Alexander's structuring the treatment situation to provide a "corrective emotional experience." Alexander deliberately shaped the analyst's behavior in order to help the patient more expeditiously to resolve conflicts with significant others. Alexander was fiercely criticized for "manipulating the transference." Today we can ask, isn't deliberately shaping the analyst's behavior in order to induce regression and help the patient more expeditiously resolve conflicts with significant others no less a "manipulation of the transference?"

Of course, traditional analysts such as Blum (1999) believe that Freud was correct and that it is necessary to structure treatment as he recommended: "An ahistorical purely 'here and now' treatment, and a narrative constructed in the present, evade childhood conflicts and avoid a patient's infantile traits and trends" (p. 1137). Blum could not be more explicit about the necessity of examining the past to understand the present: "The transference cannot actually be understood or resolved without genetic interpretation within a framework of reconstruction" (p. 1133).

I believe that a more natural, customary style of relating between analyst and patient will, as in marriage, result in sufficient situations of conflict, anxiety, and anger for episodes of inhibitory regression to occur spontaneously. Deliberately inducing inhibitory regression is neither necessary nor desirable. To the degree the analyst's contrived behaviors in creating and maintaining the traditional psychoanalytic setting create negative feelings in the patient, they will interfere with the positive feelings associated with the therapeutic alliance, feelings that appear to be central in the internalization of the analyst by the patient and thus among the best predictors of therapeutic benefit. Further ruptures in the alliance may be the very cause of the regression. Miller (Panel, 1995c), in a discussion of Kohut's ideas on treatment, warns that the "production of more primitive material by a patient may signal a rupture of the self-object bond in narcissistic patients. Fragmentation occurs leading to regression and there is a breaking up of the representation of the self and the analyst" (p. 190).

Another dichotomy that parallels the previous "superficial" versus "deep" analysis antinomy is the dimension of intellectual versus emotional analysis. Freud (1905) early recognized the danger of intellectualization in traditional analytic treatment, and he linked the analysis of the "transference" with the need to surmount it.

> This happens . . . to be by far the hardest part of the whole task. . . . It is easy to learn how to interpret dreams, to extract from the patient's associations his unconscious thoughts and memories and to practice similar explanatory arts. . . . Transference is the one thing the presence of which has to be detected without assistance and with only the slightest clues

> to go upon . . . and . . . it is only after the transference has been
> resolved that a patient arrives at a sense of conviction of the
> validity of the connections which have been constructed dur-
> ing the analysis [pp. 116–117].

Bird (1972) expresses similar concerns about interpretations becoming explanatory and thereby intellectual that, "as an act of [the analyst's] self defense, handling of the transference has been steadily
attenuated until analysis has finally become, in a great many hands at
least, an explanatory art" (p. 280). Joseph (1985) cautioned about
another concern: there is an issue as to when and how to interpret the
relation to the past, when to reconstruct.

> It is important not to make these links if the linking disrupts
> what is going on in the session and leads to a kind of explana-
> tory discussion or exercise, but rather to wait until the heat is
> no longer on and the patient has sufficient contact with him-
> self and the situation to want to understand and to help to
> make links. Even this, of course, can be used in a defensive
> way [p. 452].

Rogers (1989) opts to quote Frieda Fromm-Reichmann on this subject:
the "patient needs an *experience* not an explanation" (p. 235).

Exploring the patient's Habitual Relationship Patterns favors a primary—but not exclusive—focus on the patient's current feelings and
fantasies toward the analyst. The patient can picture the analyst as
playing any of a broad spectrum of roles, and therefore the patient's
Habitual Relationship Patterns toward each of these roles can be examined. If the analyst's perceived gender, age, or other attributes are used
by the patient to impose constraints on picturing the analyst in certain
roles, this constriction then becomes the focus of analysis, but not to
the exclusion of examining the patient's Habitual Relationship Patterns
in relation to extraanalytic relationships.

Mutative Effects of Analytic Treatment

What enables a patient successfully to modify entrenched Habitual
Relationship Patterns? Rogers (1989) emphasizes the therapist's gen-
uineness or authenticity, his or her positive regard for the patient, and
his or her empathic understanding. Without agreement about the muta-

tive elements in analytic treatment, other factors are also generally and widely credited with effects. For example, insight may help the patient to recognize and even to anticipate a stereotyped pattern, thus providing an opportunity to modify or prevent its expression. Similarly, the analyst's commitment, reliability, support, affirmation, and relatively nonjudgmental stance may enhance the patient's feelings of being a likable and worthwhile person. Early therapeutic alliance is the best predictor of psychotherapeutic benefit (Luborsky, 2000), so it may well be that as a consequence of an alliance felt to be positive, self-esteem is bolstered and feelings of hopelessness and helplessness are mitigated. The same threat that in the past would have produced an uncontrollable or less well-controlled emotional reaction, triggering a longstanding defensive pattern, now will seem less overwhelming. When the intensity of the emotional reaction is decreased, the patient has an opportunity to modify the pattern of response. Identification with the analyst, no longer viewed through the lens of the old pattern, may also provide new mechanisms of adaptation.

The recommendation to discard historical "transference" interpretations propels us to consider further the multiple factors that contribute to the mutative effects of treatment. Davies (1998) and Fonagy (1998) each present poignant reports of the treatment of severely traumatized adults and agree that historical "transference" interpretations have no place in the treatment of these patients. What was helpful were interpretations about how the patient viewed, thought about, and felt about the patient-analyst interactions in the here and now. The role of historical interpretations in the treatment of less than severely traumatized patients is discussed later by Fisher and Greenberg (1996).

Diverse strategies of treatment can be and are associated with mutative effects. Wallerstein (1986), based on the Menninger study, and Gedo and Goldberg (1973) and Holinger (1989), from clinical observation, report that noninterpretive interventions that are affirmative and supportive produce substantial therapeutic benefits, comparable to those of interpretive interventions. These interventions increase the patient's psychological stature, that is, self-esteem, and again, by reducing the patient's feelings of hopelessness and helplessness, make threats and anxieties less overwhelming and enable the patient to modify defensive responses and to enhance facilitatory regression.

Fisher and Greenberg's (1996) review of nearly 2500 studies of psychotherapy supports Wallerstein's conclusion. They note that their conclusions are based on studies that largely ignore the issue of whether the interpretations are accurate or off the mark. They observe that these studies "have consistently failed to support an association between higher frequencies of transference interpretations and better therapy outcomes" (p. 232). They note, on one hand, that treatment potency increases when therapists can weave patient productions into consistent explanatory stories, and on the other hand, they conclude that interpretive techniques have been shown to be generally useful and often related to positive outcome across many types of psychotherapy; but their singular contribution to positive outcome in psychodynamic psychotherapy has not been clearly established. They raised the concern that transference interpretations can be detrimental if they are delivered with high frequency, and added, "Interestingly, the negative impact of an overreliance on transference interpretations may be particularly apparent in patients who are more adept at relating to others" (p. 236). Evidence for a direct association between insight attainment and outcome continues to be sparse. They concluded, "Finally, our review of the evidence highlights that an approach strongly emphasizing interpretations may not be best for everyone, even when interpretations are accurate" (p. 250).

Because evidence supports a variant of the Dodo bird's judgment in *Alice In Wonderland*—all psychotherapy systems are prizeworthy— Fisher and Greenberg note that there is growing acknowledgment that common factors in different treatments should be regarded more as "signal" than "noise" when searching for effective treatment ingredients.

Evaluation of historical "transference" interpretations, considered by many to be centrally important therapeutically, led Wallerstein (1986) to conclude: "What this adds up to has been, in overall perspective, a tendency to overestimate the necessity of the expressive-analytic mode, and of its central operation via conflict resolution based on interpretation, insight, and working through, to achieve therapeutically desired change" (p. 723). Wallerstein's study suggests that one common element in successful therapies is the use of supportive techniques:

> Across the whole spectrum of treatment courses in the 42 patients—ranging from the most analytic-expressive through the inextricably blended to the most single-mindedly supportive—in almost every instance (the psychoanalyses included), the treatment carried more supportive elements than originally intended, and these supportive elements accounted for more of the changes achieved than had been originally anticipated [p. 730].

Wallerstein emphasizes that supportive modes are indistinguishable from analytic interpretations in their therapeutic effectiveness in both their extensiveness—character traits, personality, and lifestyle—and stability. Gedo and Goldberg (1973), building on the work of Kohut, conceptualize some noninterpretive interventions, not as "supportive" in a conventional sense, but as nonetheless noninterpretive and still therapeutic, for example, the use of optimal disillusionment for patients with narcissistic personality disorder. Holinger (1989) asserts that patients with primitive, archaic personality organization, in which self-object differentiation has not been achieved, require these interventions in preparation for subsequent analytic "transference" interpretations.

Additionally, I regard the analyst's empathy, his or her perception of a valuable core to the patient, and his or her regard for the patient as basically a good and worthwhile person as helpful to many patients. When patients find such positive regard troublesome, analytic work with this difficulty is often very rewarding. The analyst's understanding and usually nonretaliatory position when Habitual Relationship Patterns ordinarily provoke and irritate may enlighten and then mitigate a vicious cycle that the patient evokes with other people. In addition, if the analyst seems healthily self-assured and unafraid, this new object of identification for the patient may become internalized in a way that promotes flexibility and growth. Wampold (2001), who reviewed studies of the efficacy of psychotherapy, concluded, "Dramatically more variance is due to therapists within treatments than to [different] treatments" (p. 226), and added that "clearly, the person of the therapist is a critical factor in the success of therapy" (p. 202).

Other analysts would modify this list of mutative factors, weighting them differently and adding others, making it clear that there is no consensus about how analytic treatment helps patients. Further, it seems likely that different patients are helped in different manners. It may even be that interpretation is what the patient and analyst talk about while the patient is getting better. Jackson and Haley suggest that self-understanding provides a subject for patient and analyst discussion, a *modus operandi* for dealing with each other, while Yalom (1980) asserts that "the search for insight, the task of excavating the past are all interesting, seemingly profitable ventures that engage the attention of patient and therapist while the real agent of change, their relationship, is germinating" (pp. 404–405). As Loewald (1986) put it, "Observing and understanding the patient analytically and conveying this understanding to him by interpretive interventions, *is* the analyst's enactment of his caring for another person" (p. 286). It seems accurate to conclude that although analysts have a variety of ideas about the mutative elements of treatment, in truth, we do not *know* how patients are helped.

Why Don't We Know Why Analytic Treatment Works?

Why don't we *know*, after 100 years, how psychoanalytic treatment helps patients? Perhaps we are not viewing analytic work from the right perspective. A visit to an exhibition of Chuck Close's paintings at the Museum of Modern Art provides a heuristic metaphor. Close paints very large individual portraits, each comprised of thousands of small ovals of colored paint each within a small square. His technique involves drawing a grid on a portrait photograph of the person and then superimposing and enlarging the grid on his canvas. His early paintings utilize a grid of one-quarter-inch squares that often contain two or more colors within the oval. Pelli (1999), a professor of psychology and neural science, experimentally determined that in order for a viewer to perceive the painting as a face, he or she must stand at a distance more than 200 times the size of the squares in the painting, that is, 50 inches away, in order to perceive the features in the portrait. The specific element Pelli tested was the distance at which the nose was visualized. Optimally, for these one-quarter-inch-grid paintings, the viewer has to be 50 inches away; at closer range the viewer perceives a meaningless array of flat multicolored squares filled with colored ovals. Alternately, if the viewer is too far away, the individuality of the portrait is compromised. Interestingly, the exact distance at which the nose actualized and the shape of the face was perceived varied among the viewers.

This experiment, demonstrating the need for a specific, appropriate distance in order to achieve meaningful perception, may serve as a metaphor for the appraisal of an analytic treatment situation. What is the optimal psychological distance for viewing the analytic dyad? Analytic treatment includes thousands of sentences and tens of thousands of words. Microscopic examination of the sentences and the words may not be the best psychological distance from which to elucidate meaningful large-scale patterns. Alternatively, some analysts prefer to examine the construct termed "analytic process," a high-level inference about the meaningfulness of the data, yet as Weinshel and Renik (1991) have noted proponents of the concept of "analytic process" do not agree as to its definition. Vaughan et al. (1997), whose study of analytic process found that analysts could not judge analytic process reliably, concluded that "analytic process" might not be a viable concept or a useful approach to extract meaning from the analytic situation. Five years of deliberation by a Committee on Psychoanalytic Education study group failed to produce agreement on a definition of "analytic process." This suggests that this high level inference, "analytic process," may be too far removed, and not at an optimal psychological distance to elucidate meaningful patterns in the data.

Our failure to find the optimal psychological distance from which to view the patient-analyst interactions may prevent us from seeing the patterns that would give the most meaning to the enterprise. If Pelli's study is an appropriate analogy, then individual analysts may perceive meaning at different psychological distances, making achieving reliability very difficult. Further, not only is there a question of psychological distance, but also of the choice of focus. Perhaps finding a way to view and characterize, not specific treatment events (foreground), but the ambience of the relationship (background) would facilitate our search for meanings in the analytic situation.

What Criteria Determine If a Treatment Is Psychoanalytic?

How can we judge if an intervention is both psychoanalytic and fruitful? Cooper's (1999) criterion, that it produces "more material, more questions," is, I think, a residue of the one-person model of psychoanalytic treatment when "free association" provided the essential material for the treatment. In those terms, useful interventions yield fresh, new associations. In the postmodern period of intersubjectivity there is less concern about "free association" and more concern about patient-analyst interaction and relationship. Providing new associations per se is of less interest; their significance is a function of their meaning in the context of the analytic relationship.

What then determines whether an intervention is psychoanalytic? Here, again, I agree with Aron (1999) that in discussions of a well-analyzed, successful, psychoanalytic case:

> There is typically substantial disagreement not only about the particulars of the analyst's approach, theory, or technique but even considerable disagreement as to whether the patient substantially improved. My point is that we disagree about far more than our metapsychologies and about far more than just our clinical approaches to patients. We disagree with one

another to the core because psychoanalysis is so thoroughly value laden. We cannot agree on what a success is, on what our goals are, or on what constitutes a true psychoanalytic process because many of us . . . maintain quite different sets of personal and professional values and ideals [p. 7].

Whereas these views of the analytic situation, the dearth of rules, and the inability to determine if an intervention is psychoanalytic seem to bring us to the verge of chaos, alternatively, the traditional view of a structured, well-ordered situation that proceeded through a predictable series of phases appears to have been a Potemkin Village that yielded to deconstruction. I prefer the postmodern view we now discern despite, or, more accurately, because it falls on the fringe of chaos. If you're not living on the edge, you're taking up space.

Without guidelines and regulations, what identifies a treatment situation as distinctively psychoanalytic? I do not agree with Kernberg (1999) that the three essential features of the psychoanalytic method are interpretation, historical "transference" analysis, and technical neutrality. Interpretation is not exclusive to psychoanalytic treatment, "transference" analysis incorporates the theory of childhood etiology, and neutrality is inconsistent with both the analyst's idiosyncratic system of values and the ubiquitous influences of the analyst's unconscious. In contrast, dealing with the power of unconscious forces, Freud's fundamental contribution, is the significant identifier of psychoanalytic treatment, and this alone defines the nature and goals of patient-analyst interaction in analytic treatment. Horney (1939) asserted that the "doctrine of unconscious motivations" (p. 18) deserved first place among Freud's most fundamental and most significant findings, and 60 years later Westen (1999) has further described and empirically validated this contribution:

Taken together, the studies described here lead to a single conclusion: Freud was right in his central hypothesis that much of mental life, including thought, feeling and emotion is unconscious. The findings of these studies are so robust, and taken from so many unrelated areas of psychological research, that the hypothesis of the existence and importance of unconscious processes is probably as close as any hypothesis in the history of psychology to being able to claim the status of fact [p. 1094].

The treatment proposed here keeps the focus on the many influences of unconscious thoughts and feelings in both patient and analyst and this supports its characterization as psychoanalytic. I know of no other method of treatment that is devoted to the examination of the unconscious of both patient and analyst.

Summary

A theory of technique is both necessary and useful, and at the same time, constraining. Mitchell proposes, as a guideline for the analyst's conduct, "a self-reflective responsiveness of a particular (psychoanalytic) sort." He eschews relying on a standard theory, such as traditional psychoanalytic theory, and proposes, alternatively, that each analyst utilize his or her own personal, value-based, covert, idiosyncratic theory, in part because doing so is actually unavoidable. This recommendation is less radical than it appears, if we agree that all of the analyst's interventions are inevitably influenced by unconscious factors outside the analyst's awareness. The analyst cannot readily switch from one theory to another, as if all were equally congenial. And in a particular clinical instant the analyst cannot use conflicting theories, but must select one.

The resulting dearth of rules facilitates more spontaneous reactions by the analyst, renders interactions more affect-laden, and provides them with greater presence. Although this may seem a less certain compass for the analyst to steer by than the structure of traditional theory, it avoids the complications of fitting a structured system to a particular dyad, and energizes the analyst to deal with ethical issues specific to the dyad. The relative absence of rules does mean there is likely to be less order in the treatment process, perhaps extending to the fringe of disorder, which, a postmodern view asserts, is the proper state for treatment. What identifies such a treatment situation as psychoanalytic is that it is based on Freud's fundamental contribution, that of identifying the power of unconscious forces. No other method of treatment examines the unconscious both of patient and analyst.

11

A Psychoanalytic Treatment Without "Transference"

I begin to think we can only get healthy by having people about us who raise good feelings.

—George Eliot, *Daniel Deronda*

I use as a clinical illustration a psychoanalytic treatment that did *not* employ the traditional concept of "transference." In this report, my self-reflective appraisal of my own conscious and unconscious responsiveness and the interaction of these feelings with the patient's conscious and unconscious responsiveness are examined and hypotheses about their current meanings developed. In turn, these current meanings are extrapolated to formulate hypotheses about the meaning of the patient's feelings in historically earlier relationships—rather than vice versa, as hypothesized by the traditional theory of "transference." A conceptualization of this approach to treatment is formulated, and a justification for characterizing it as psychoanalytic is presented.

My Psychoanalytic Treatment of Pat

Pat is a very successful, wealthy professional man in his 50s, approximately 20 years my junior, who essentially no longer works. Background material will be limited in the interest of protecting confidentiality. He came for treatment five years earlier at the urging of his then wife because their marriage was in serious jeopardy. It became clear that he wanted to end this very unsatisfying marriage, and he accomplished his goal by covertly provoking his wife to divorce him. During analysis he remarried and has had a very happy second marriage. His previous, long-term analysis featured the couch, but at the start of this treatment he elected to sit face to face. He acknowledged drinking too much alcohol. At the start I urged him to end or reduce the drinking, which I said I thought would interfere with analytic work. He refused; I accepted his decision, and we proceeded on the basis of four sessions per week. He traveled with some frequency, and we agreed he would be financially responsible for four sessions per week, some of which could be conducted on the telephone. I charged him my full fee. He has given permission for publication of this material. I invited him to write about his treatment experience for possible inclusion in this book, but he declined to do so.

His analytic treatment has helped him to have better access to his feelings, to regulate his angry feelings much more effectively, and to reduce his intense self-criticism substantially. Treatment termination was imposed by my retirement, leaving him with several residual problems: (1) although a talented, avid golfer, he has had great difficulty with his golf game; (2) he is unable substantially either to modify or discontinue drinking six to nine ounces of alcohol every night; (3) some residue of self-criticism remains. We like and respect each other and feel we worked well together. I think he still idealizes me and at the same time deprecates and has contempt and pity for me. On occasions he became quite angry with me. I changed my style by acceding to his request that I not take notes during the session because he felt it diminished my talking to him. The data of all the sessions thus derive from notes I made after the sessions, except for telephone sessions when I made notes during the sessions. My reports are condensations of the sessions rather than full reporting of all the details in my notes. I will start with session 729, which gives a sense of the ambience of our relationship as well as an example of my self-reflective responsiveness.

Session 729

Pat reported playing golf very well. It was the best ball-striking he's done in the 1990s. His partner was taken aback by how much further Pat's drives were than his own. Before the session, while sitting in the waiting room, he did the *New York Times* crossword puzzle, though he didn't quite finish it. The puzzle involved Yogi Berra sayings, including, when his team lost the world series, "We made the wrong mistakes." In the past, he hadn't been able to do the *New York Times* puzzle. Thinking he had taught himself to do this, I responded with the comment that I had been reading Socrates, and Socrates emphasized that a person has to learn things for himself; he, Socrates, couldn't teach anyone. Pat reacted, "Don't tell me you're reading Greek!" He then thought that I probably couldn't read Greek, and his thinking that I was reading Greek was a form of self-deprecation.

In thinking about my spontaneous comment about reading Socrates, I realized that I wasn't at all sure that *I* could do the *New York Times* crossword puzzle, and his comment about his doing so made me feel this was something he could do better than I could. I became defensive and tried to assert my superiority by referring to my reading Socrates; I explained this to him. He said he might have had some sense that his comment about doing the puzzle would put me down a bit. I said I thought he had reenacted in the session the competitive feelings he had experienced with his golf partner, whom he had bested. He felt guilty at sensing that he had also put me down, and, seeing me become defensive, he reacted with guilt and consequently with self-deprecation by elevating me through the fantasy that I could read Greek. He did acknowledge that hitting a "longer" ball than his partner, which he characterized as "a real castrating event," made him feel guilty. That's probably why he beats up on himself about all the things he "should" do.

Session 732

The theory of "transference" utilizes memories of earlier experiences to explain the meaning of the patient's current feelings and fantasies about the analyst. In session 732 this theory is turned upside down and the understanding of the patient's current feelings about the analyst is used to develop hypotheses about earlier relationships with others.

Pat began the session, as he usually does, by reporting a dream: His golf partner moved Pat's golf ball, which disqualified Pat and made him angry. Then he had to play against another man (someone who doesn't like him), and the man's wife said that Pat's wife was Jewish, thereby slandering her. Pat knows my wife and I are Jewish.

He went on to recall that when he was an adolescent, his father had unexpectedly shown up to watch him play in a very important golf tournament, and this had unnerved him. He lost by one stroke. I com-

mented that as he continues to play golf well in reality, the dream suggests that he needs to picture that someone is interfering with his golf.
Further, I thought the fact that Jewishness is used as a slander suggests he feels that I, like the man who got him disqualified, oppose his
golf success. He replied he had seen his father as an adversary who
didn't want him to do well at golf, and now he transferred those feelings on to me. (Pat is psychologically sophisticated and quite familiar
with the traditional theory of "transference.")

I remarked, "I don't think I actually do oppose your success in golf,
so your feeling that I do suggests that you need to believe that—the
belief serves some function." I added, "*if* that is the case, it suggests
that when you were an adolescent and viewed your father as being
opposed to your success in golf, you may have needed to believe that,
as well, rather than that your father himself had actually opposed your
golf success." Pat wondered why he might have seen his father as an
opposing force. Maybe his father had been afraid that Pat might try to
become a golf pro. He had been really good at golf and not good at
academics, so that golf was awfully appealing to him. He had had some
feelings of wanting to pursue golf and other feelings of not wanting to
do so. I thought he may have dealt with an internal conflict about
whether to pursue golf as a career by projecting the opposition onto
his father, transforming an uncomfortable inner conflict into a more
manageable external conflict.

Does his belief that I oppose his golf success mean he is externalizing a current internal conflict? That is, does he have conflicting feelings about devoting his present life to the game of golf, rather than to
other presumably more "worthwhile" activities? Does he actually have
such an internal conflict, or is my conception of such a conflict an
expression of my value system, my own subjectivity? I still don't know.

Session 739

This session further illustrates the ambience of our relationship and
demonstrates Pat's willingness to risk getting angry at me, which is
important insofar as modulation of his anger ranks high among the
goals of treatment.

I told Pat I had been asked to give Grand Rounds at one of the
Pittsburgh hospitals and asked his permission to present some material from our work together. (I feel it is an ethical imperative to obtain
a patient's permission to present material about his or her treatment,

no matter how disguised or where presented.) He had previously refused to allow me to audiotape our sessions as part of a research project, so I was not concerned he would respond with obligatory compliance. His response was, "Sure, but I'm not sure I'll give you much today to help you with your presentation. I can't remember any dreams, and I think this session will be a waste of time."

He then reported that he had been drinking less. He had automatically been entered in an upcoming golf tournament in which he had already decided not to participate. Although he had not received the notice of this tournament, which would have allowed him to decline participating, he wasn't aware of any reaction to the man who had failed to send him the notice. He was, however, angry at his golf partner, because it would have been much easier for his partner to cancel their participation rather than having him do so. This reminds him of past anger at his mother who would react either with stony silence or with a clear message that she didn't give a shit about him. He was curious about what I would say at Grand Rounds, but he was reluctant to ask me; he didn't think I'd give him much of an explanation. He thinks maybe he wants to avoid getting angry about not being given an explanation. But he would like to know. I explained that I was going to discuss reversing the concept of "transference" and using understanding about the patient's current relationship with the analyst to understand earlier relationships rather than vice versa, as in the traditional theory of "transference."

He said, "Like my perception of what my father's attitude was." He appreciated my telling him what I was going to talk about. The ideas sounded so clear when I described them, but he found it difficult to rephrase them. I commented that I thought that he had been wrong at the beginning of the session when he said he wouldn't give me much to help me with the presentation. He laughed and said he now thinks he was giving me material, but didn't know it then.

Review of the session suggests that after my request for permission to present material from our work, his discussion of his anger at others reflected that he was angered by my request. He recalled the disturbing consequences of having been angry at his mother, presumably reflecting his concern about the consequences of being angry at me. Despite that concern, he was able to risk more open anger at me by asking what I was going to present because he thought I probably would not answer. He dealt with his anger at my request and risked open expression of these feelings without making the session nonproductive or becoming self-recriminatory.

Session 758

Approximately one month later, in session 757, he reported a long, complex dream, which, uncharacteristically, we were unable to understand. The day residue included playing in a tournament with a partner who was an outstanding amateur golfer; they had won. When he drove the golf ball well, he drove it significantly further than everyone else, including the outstanding amateur. In the next session, 758, which he knew was two days before I presented at Grand Rounds (I had told him the date of my presentation because it conflicted with his regular session time), he reported a nightmare, also exceedingly unusual for him. Perhaps he was still ambivalent about my presenting material about him. During the course of the analysis he had had many dreams of being in situations that would be expected to be quite frightening, but, paradoxically, he had never experienced any fear in those dreams.

Session 758 was conducted by telephone from another state. He began by saying he might have to quit the session five minutes early. I said, "Let me know when you want to stop the session." He replied, "As soon as I say something brilliant," and then went on. "A dream woke me up: I was in a room, trying to solve some kind of mystery that had to do with me. There was a sense that someone else was with me because I was discussing something with them. On the wall of the room was a very small mirror, like six inches by six inches. Stuck in the mirror were four spears of asparagus. The mirror suddenly twisted rapidly. I think I said something like, 'How could that have happened? There is no one in the apartment.' I ran quickly and opened the door and looked out. How frightening! There were two large figures in long cloaklike clothes moving as though gliding in air. The one in front, who seemed to be the leader, was in whiteface. I am assuming the one in front represented a woman. There was a cold rush of air. The one in whiteface turned to look at me with very evil, bloodshot eyes. I may have found the mystery, but I better not pursue it! The feeling was terrifying!"

The four spears of asparagus were lying flat on the mirror, as though lying on it with a rubber band around them. Green vegetables—except for a few—are like medicine to him. He eats them first to get them out of the way. When the asparagus were pointing toward the ground, like four fingers, it was like a catcher giving a signal to a pitcher. The figure in front makes him think of *Star Wars*. Darth Vader fought his son and was unmasked. His eyes remind him of the eyes in the dream. Darth Vader had saved his son, turned back from evil to good.

I asked what came to mind about the two large figures? Pat replied "Kabuki"; then he laughed and said he thought of another word, "Karaoke," when people in a bar get up and sing rock and roll—people pretending to be what they're not. He hasn't played golf for several days; hasn't felt well. Next he talked about the extremely successful people who own homes in the winter real-estate development he had recently joined. Pat had gotten stock from his father and feels he hadn't been really successful on his own. The Kabuki-like figure in his dream may have been a reference to pretending to be something he wasn't; he sure wouldn't want to fool with her!

I reminded him that in my office, on the wall facing where he customarily sat, were two sets of Japanese woodblock prints of Kabuki actors; one included a male actor playing the role of a woman in white face with white hair—a frightening looking image. He remembered that earlier in the analysis he had had a dream about one of those Kabuki actors in the prints, a man, with a significant looking sword in his hand (one of my other prints has that image). I suggested that the current dream was an expression of his feelings about having driven further than the outstanding amateur golfer with whom he had played. The Kabuki figures were representations of me threatening to do something terrible to him for what he had done, for having defeated a powerful opponent. In the dream he was trying to solve a mystery, which may have represented understanding the nature of the fear that continued to inhibit his golf performance. This was the first time in his five years of analysis that he had allowed himself to experience that terror.

The four spears of asparagus, which were not intrinsic to the mirror but were "as though lying on it with a rubber band around them," perhaps symbolize his genitals, as suggested by his association that it was like a catcher signaling to a pitcher, which the catcher does by extending several of his fingers pointing downward in front of his genitals. Yogi Berra, the subject of the *New York Times* crossword puzzle he had discussed some weeks before, was a catcher. His associations to Darth Vader and to his own prior dream of a Kabuki actor "with a significant sword in his hand" suggest that the punishment anticipated with terror was castration. As Rangell (1978) has noted, despite the fact that castration anxiety is central to the theory of oedipal anxiety, it relatively rarely appears clinically during the course of an analysis. Its appearance in this analysis, in which the traditional view of "transference" was eschewed and few attempts at historical reconstruction were made, indicates the depths and affective availability that can be achieved.

The patient's golf game continued to improve. In session 791 I informed him that I was planning to retire in a little more than a year. He was surprised because I seemed to enjoy my work. The idea of missing me made him feel sad. He asked my age and plans after retirement, and I answered his questions. The next session he had little to talk about and I suggested he was reverting to an earlier pattern: when faced with a really tough problem, such as dealing with my retirement, he removes himself in order to work it out on his own. What emerged was his feeling of relief that he would be able to leave the analysis, and that made him uncomfortable. It was like the relief he had experienced in relation to his father's terminal illness and death, which he felt had released him. At the same time there was anger at me for leaving.

His golf game continued to improve, but he remained unable to handle his persistent drinking and smoking. In session 811 he reported two dreams. He got a call from "Dick Little"—(he joked about the obvious phallic implications of the name, interpolating "that was a dream for a graduate student, not for you") who wanted to ask him for a favor. He got annoyed at Dick Little for taking so long to get to it, hung up on him, and felt a little guilty. In the second dream, a big man with white hair wearing a blue blazer had barged into his hotel bathroom, was smoking and urinating; Pat was furious with him.

I suggested that Dick Little was a part of himself that he kept helpless and impotent in that he did not allow himself to do anything about his undesirable drinking and smoking. I added that perhaps he needed to keep himself impotent to undo the reality of his power and stature in the real world. When he was younger, before he had developed his present power and stature, he had been able to deal with an undesirable characteristic, being overweight, by losing pounds without difficulty. Now, dealing with his drinking and smoking seemed beyond him. These comments brought to his mind the image of the edge of a cliff with a few boards over a dark abyss—if he dealt with the drinking and smoking, it would be like the boards giving way.

Session 813

This session gives some indication of how unconsciously he uses his feelings about the analyst in relation to his feelings about his exercise of power.

Pat reported three dreams. In the first he was in a large conference room where there was a meeting. He had some interest in what was going on, but knew it wouldn't affect him. In the second he is an adult in his parents' bedroom. His father is doing something and is in his way, preventing him from doing what he wants to do. His father looks larger than he really is. He'll just wait till his father finishes and then he'll be able to do what he wants. In the third dream, the Queen was giving a dinner party at Windsor Castle. There were a few people eating at a large table, and additional tables were set up in the fire station. There was a lovely tree-lined promenade leading to the castle, but on each side it was lined with boxes containing cartons of Coke or Pepsi and some British soft drink as advertising. It really cheapened the scene. (He had frequently seen me drink Coke in sessions.)

He talked about extending a trip to a foreign country in September. (I would be on vacation in August and back at work in September.) He got a call yesterday from a man who had been fired from a job that he, Pat, controlled. Despite the temptation to restore the job, he resisted, because if he had done so, he'd really be angry with himself. After the phone call he had fleeting thoughts that this man might come to his house and create trouble. He recalled the realization that he had long felt that his father was taller than his actual height. He felt, similarly, that the analyst is taller than he is; actually, we are really the same height.

I commented that his waiting till his father finished to be able to do what he wanted sounded like another expression of a feeling he had reported earlier: he could wait until I retired and then go on with his drinking and smoking. (Later material suggested it may also have included a reversal; he has only a short time to get his life in order before his treatment ends.) I added that I thought unconsciously part of him feared retribution for his exercise of power, having the man fired, which in reality had hurt someone. He externalized the feared retribution first in the fantasy that the victim might cause trouble and second in the dream of a paternal figure (the analyst), pictured as large and powerful, who could either prevent him from exercising his power, or would criticize and punish him for doing so. Although there was no confrontation with the paternal figure, he was disturbed by his fear of the external control, and so, in the third dream, he proceeded to cheapen and thereby deprecate the image of the analyst (Queen = King).

Session 814

This session revealed additional feelings about my retirement.

A dream: he's in jail, not for a very long sentence, maybe three weeks, and he has another seven or eight days to go. He's innocent, has done something immoral, but not illegal. He is allowed to go home temporarily. He has a ragged little dog in jail with him. He hopes someone will care for it while he is away; there's nothing more he can do about it. He goes home and is reading in his study by the light of just one lamp; he doesn't turn on the other lights.

He was going to play in a golf tournament yesterday, but when he saw with whom he would be playing, he decided not to play. Since he wasn't going to play, he could have tried to schedule an analytic session, but he didn't want to. He had somewhat less to drink last night. He decided not to attend a professional meeting tonight because it would be in a setting in which he would be exposed to drinking, and he wanted to be at home where he would have a better opportunity to regulate his drinking. He mentioned he was still having the physical problem created when he had tried to improve himself physically. Someone tried to increase his flexibility by stretching him, and this fellow had ended up hurting him. He wondered whether that refers to his analysis as well? He doesn't know, but thinks being in jail refers to going to analysis. I agreed, and suggested that one of the reasons he came for treatment was that he had difficulty "owning" his own feelings; in contrast to that difficuly, I added, that he had just reported several instances of acknowledging what his feelings were and acting on them. I speculated that not being able to care for the little dog himself may represent a residue of helplessness about owning and acting on his own feelings about drinking and smoking. If he does deal with the drinking and smoking, I thought he will be better off, will have "more," and not turning on the other lights in the study may represent having "more." I suggested that leaving the constraints of analysis may also reflect a sense of having "more." At the same time, I added, I thought he felt that because analysis would end soon, he had better learn to access and act on his own feelings. He replied that when he learned I was going to retire, he decided he didn't want additional treatment with anyone else. The first thing he did was to discontinue taking the antidepressant medication I had prescribed for him, because he didn't want to be dependent on anyone else to give it to him.

Session 815

Pat reported two dreams, but couldn't remember the order in which he had them. In one he was at a party when three women with whom he previously had been involved were present. One of them said he really looked funny in those glasses. In the other dream, which occurred after I had written my earlier comments about whether my value system might result in my being critical of his focusing his life on golf, I said to him that he should be doing something more significant with his life than playing golf. In the dream, although he had a somewhat prestigious position, he had a large stack of mail and a pile of papers he had not read.

In reality, Pat isn't satisfied with the glasses he wears when he plays golf. He's going to see if there is a better pair he can use. He doesn't think the professional position he had in the dream is such a big deal. He doesn't have respect for people who take that position, which involves sitting and listening a lot, and that's not what he wants to do. He added that he thought the idea that he should be doing something more significant than playing golf is coming from a part of him, rather than from me. Although he thought I probably oppose his drinking and smoking, he also thought I probably felt if he wants to play golf, it's his life. It was amazing to him how well he and his wife reconciled after a really intense fight the other night.

Pat thought that after yesterday's session he felt guilty about going away in September. He had arranged most of the trip before he knew about my retirement. Recently, though, he did extend the trip because there is one other city he enjoys visiting; it is something he wants to do. He felt guilty because he felt he was supposed to come for sessions, despite our arrangement that he pays for four sessions per week even if he is unable to use them.

I thought that in the dream about doing something more significant than playing golf he tried to deal with his self-criticism for missing additional sessions by externalizing it onto me. Deprecating the prestigious position, which involved doing things I do—sitting and listening a lot—probably deprecated me in the service of reducing the shame evoked by my criticism. Although this was not discussed, I wonder if his not being available for certain sessions in September was retaliatory, both for my lack of availability to him in August and for my plan for retirement. That retaliatory aspect would have evoked the self-criticism with which he was trying to deal.

Having externalized the criticism to me, however, did not inhibit the expression of angry, retaliatory impulses. These are expressed in the dream in his failure to read his pile of mail or tend to his pile of papers. Here, too, the meaning of his current behavior with me can provide a hypothesis about his past behavior with his father. To understand his current feelings about me, it is useful to elaborate how important I believe my caring for him is. Although he is happily married to a loving wife, he feels the lion's share of the responsibility for caring in that relationship falls to him. He has no family, and although he does have friends, I think he feels that few care about him as deeply as I do. Why wouldn't he be hurt and angry at my leaving him for August, especially when I am also planning to leave him permanently by retiring? The hurt and anger are probably expressed by his leaving me for additional days in September, thereby depriving himself of what he wants most.

This suggests a hypothesis about his childhood and adolescent behavior. Why did this bright child and adolescent do poorly in school year after year, thereby hurting himself? His mother was a deeply troubled woman who at one time required psychiatric hospitalization. His father, his sole source of caring for many years, aside from an affectionate housekeeper during early childhood, spent the entire week in a distant city, ostensibly for professional reasons, and came home only on weekends. Pat felt that his father wanted as little contact as possible with his difficult wife, and therefore burdened him with his emotionally disturbed mother. I hypothesized that his hurt and anger toward his father were expressed in his self-damaging sabotage of his schoolwork, which was very upsetting to his father. No matter how many hours his father confined him to his bedroom to do his schoolwork, the work never got done. Much later, when he chose to be successful academically in his professional work, he achieved an outstanding record. Thus, by extrapolating backward from his current feelings and defenses about my August vacation and subsequent retirement, it is possible to develop a personal narrative.

Session 819

In session 817 he had shown me pictures of his golf swing to illustrate what his golf problem was. In session 818 I remarked he had shown me the pictures so quickly that I had really not understood them, and asked if he would bring them in again to show them to me so that I would be able to understand them. Thus, at the start of session 819 he again showed me the pictures of his golf swing, and I was able to understand what the problem with the swing was.

He reported a dream that was total golf frustration, though he couldn't recall the details. A neighboring couple from his winter home are coming to visit him for the next two days. He doesn't want to go to the airport to pick them up, but his wife says he must. I remarked that I did think that was protocol. During the next 48 hours of their visit he won't be in control of all the planning, and this annoys him.

I commented that perhaps his irritation at not being in control might also refer to my August vacation; the total golf frustration in the dream may reflect turning the irritation back upon himself. Pat responded that it was a question of his reaction to the August vacation and probably more importantly to my retirement. He hadn't said this before, but he had been looking for a way to end the sessions and hadn't known how. He had had a similar difficulty knowing how to end his prior marriage. Pat went on to mention that when the friend who was going to be staying with him mentioned that he was going to be playing golf with a mutual friend, Pat had a flash of a reaction—why wasn't he invited? Actually, he didn't want to play on that particular golf course because it would be bad for his hip. I said that his flash of hurt feeling at not being invited to join them in golf was consistent with the idea that even though he had wanted to end the sessions, the fact that I was ending them and he was not in control may have bothered him.

Pat added that although he wants to end the sessions he doesn't want to end our relationship, and he doesn't know how to preserve it. He doesn't want a relationship between couples, including our wives, because that would be a very different situation from the relationship he and I have.

Has Pat Been Helped Therapeutically?

Pat and I both believe he has. He has much better access to his unconscious feelings and defenses, far better regulation of his anger (earlier he had kicked a piece of furniture so hard he had broken his toe), a great deal less self-criticism, and has increasing sense of agency (ownership of his feelings and behavior), as well as a very happy marriage and a wonderfully improved golf game. These gains were made despite the absence of some markers of traditional psychoanalytic technique or of historical reconstruction. Although there was some development of a personal narrative, it was not very comprehensive. His therapeutic benefits are in no way surprising; analysts of many different theoretical persuasions—traditionalists, intersubjectivists, object-relationists, Kleinians, self psychologists, Lacanians, and neo-Freudians such as Jungians, Adlerians, and Sullivanians—all presumably help many of their patients.

What is perhaps distinctive about the benefit in Pat's treatment is that it was achieved *without the concept of historical "transference,"* which is utilized by most and probably all of the above groups of analysts. Indeed, the central organizing concept in Pat's treatment was the *reverse* of "transference": understanding the patient's feelings about the analyst became the basis for hypotheses about the patient's feelings in historically earlier relationships. It demonstrates that knowledge of the etiology of the patient's disorder is unnecessary for therapeutic benefit. Impressively, the patient experienced intense castration anxiety, reported to be rarely expressed in analyses in which the traditional concept of "transference" is utilized. Such intense anxiety belies the possibility that this was a superficial treatment.

Field Theory as a Precursor to the Present Unconscious

Let me present a formulation that provides a conceptual context for a theory of technique focused on examining the patient's Habitual Relationship Patterns in the here and now. In the late 1930s and the early 1940s, a well-developed theoretical formulation, that of Lewin's (1935) field theory, had a wide currency. Lewin's social psychological theory is so similar to Sandler and Sandler's subsequent conception of the present unconscious that it is worth summarizing, although at the time it was ignored by psychoanalysis, which was deeply rooted in the historical approach. Lewin emphasized psychological explanation for psychological events; he did not evoke physical or neurophysiological factors to develop psychological laws. He dealt with psychological processes, emphasizing the perception of the external event, not the event itself, but its *psychological* existence. He never equated this psychological existence with consciousness; he realized that many important psychological influences operate unconsciously. The concepts and methods of psychology had to be intersubjective and, therefore, psychological processes in another person could only be apprehended from externally observable data: Psychological processes are *"always to be derived from the relation of the concrete individual to the concrete situation. . . .* It is meaningless to speak of behavior without reference to both the person and his environment. . . . Psychological events . . . have to be explained in terms of the properties of the field which exist *at the time* when the events occur" (p. 41).

The application of this concept to Pat's treatment is reflected in my concern about and attention to the ambience, the quality of our relationship, which is the context of our work. As one element enhancing this quality and fostering mutuality I developed a practice of making coffee for both of us, which I brought into the office at the start of our session. Our sharing this felt congenial. We examined the meanings and feelings about this for each of us, at times joked about it, and continued to enjoy it.

In his explication of Lewin's theory, Deutsch (1954) explains further that

> this is not to deny the significance of the past in indirectly affecting behavior. However, even though a past event can create a certain condition which carries over into the present, it is, nevertheless, the *present* condition that is influential in the present. Strictly considered, linking behavior with a past event is an extremely difficult undertaking; it presupposes that one knows sufficiently how the past event affected the psychological field at that time, and whether or not in the meantime other events have again modified the field. While the notion that only the present is influential in the present is an obvious concept, one can still find [in 1954] in abnormal psychology textbook accounts of how an event in childhood "caused" a neurosis. A more adequate explanation would have to describe the "neurotic trends" resulting from the childhood event, the vicissitudes of these trends during the period between the event and the neurosis, and the interactive nature of the present situation and neurotic trends which "result" in the neurotic symptoms [pp. 183–186].

Lewin also differentiated conflict situations into those between two positive valences, between two negative valences, and between a positive and negative valence. Lewin thereby clearly presaged Kris's (1985) formulation of convergent and divergent conflicts.

A unique series of intraindividual studies of symptom formation reveal the utility and power of the field-theory approach to the investigation of psychopathology. Luborsky (1996) studied individuals' symptoms not retrospectively, but as they arose in the present. The "context" of the symptom is temporally defined as a period before, during, and after the symptom appears. A within-subjects baseline is established by examining "control contexts" in which symptoms do not appear. He examined symptoms such as forgetting, shifts in depressed mood, and phobic behavior. *He made no attempt to hypothesize about the etiology of these symptoms in historical terms,* but found that the most commonly observed antecedents for all of the symptoms were a sharp rise in feelings of hopelessness, lack of control, anxiety, being blocked, and helplessness. Symptom onset was closely related to the central interpersonal conflicts of the patients as they were expressed in the interactions with the therapist. Eells (1997) noted, in a review of Luborsky's book, "It is distinctive in its focus on contemporary interpersonal relationships" (p. 316). The impact of patient-therapist interaction was the critical variable that was predictive of symptom formation.

Postmodern psychoanalysis extends our attention to the context—or field—in which the analytic dyad functions. It is congenial for field theory to consider that there are more than two dimensions to the field of the analytic dyad. Aron (1999) illustrates this by describing the importance of an analytic Third quite different than Ogden's "analytic third," which is jointly created by the analytic pair: "Our identities as psychoanalysts are established through our relationships to psychoanalytic theory and to the psychoanalytic community—and to the values and ideals established by this society and embodied in its theories and practices" (p. 4). He considers the psychoanalytic relationship as always existing within the context of both the psychoanalytic community and the broader culture, which constitutes an analytic Third. Thus, there is a patient-analyst-Third triangle, with several charged, shifting vectors of relations among them (Greenberg, 1997; Spezzano, 1998).

Cooper (1999), commenting on Aron's paper, remarks that the professional community on which analysts fall back for affirmation and reassurance "may be a more fragile reed" (p. 32) than Aron believes. Translating this into field theory, this suggests, if Cooper himself relies little on the analytic community, then the influence of the analytic community on Cooper's analytic work would be described by a weak vector, whereas for Aron it would be quite a strong vector.

Knoblauch (1999), in his discussion of Aron's paper, comments about the Third "as potentially embedding the dyad in many fields, including professional, ethnic, economic and political. Here the calculus metaphor suggests a fourth, fifth and so on to the nth [field]" (p. 47). This extension of the field or context beyond the Third to multiple dimensions that vary from time 1 to time 2 is quite congenial to field theory.

Ogden (1994) has conceived of the patient and analyst as interdependent subject and object who come together to form a "third object," the jointly created analytic third. In this separate space both patient and analyst can invent and practice a creative, spontaneous relating. Analyst as well as patient are free to express feelings, creating "positive" forms of enactment. Hinshelwood (1999) notes that this "appears to offer the patient an equal partnership in a process that restores a normal mutuality in the 'affective response' of one to the other'"(p. 807). Hinshelwood adds: "The increasing (perhaps democratizing) pressures of society towards an equality in the relationship between patient and analyst have influenced the conception of a mutuality between the partners" (p. 811).

An additional dimension of the ambience of the dyad, one constituting a vector in the field, is that of either a hierarchical or relatively egalitarian, mutual patient-analyst relationship. Several factors influence this quality. Renik (1999) relates the analyst's self-disclosure to mutuality in the dyad.

> *The benefit of an analyst's willingness to self-disclose is that it establishes the analyst's fallible view of his or her own participation in the analysis as an appropriate subject for collaborative investigation—something analyst and patient can and should talk about explicitly together.* . . . A willingness to self-disclose on the analyst's part facilitates self-disclosure by the patient, and therefore productive dialectical interchange between patient and analyst is maximized. [An analyst's willingness to self-disclose makes for] a more truly, collaborative, mutually candid interchange between analyst and patient about the treatment relationship than can take place when the analyst pursues a policy of even relative analytic anonymity [pp. 529–530].

Aron emphasizes the influence of the analyst's values:

> The affirmative postmodern sensibility that has so shaped contemporary relational and intersubjective psychoanalysis leads to the recognition that analysts must accept responsibility for the fact that it is their own personality, their own subjectivity, that underlies their values and beliefs, infuses their theoretical convictions, and forms the basis for their technical interventions and clinical judgments. . . . Our understanding is always value laden, and in turn, our values are always personal [pp. 22–23].

In field theory terms, the analyst's values constitute vectors in the field that influence patient-analyst interaction.

The conception of an analytic Third, my self-disclosure, and the influence of values each played a role in Pat's treatment. My analytic identity is that of a wannabe innovator, which makes me questioning and critical of psychoanalytic theory, psychoanalytic organizations, and psychoanalytic training. Consequently, I have moved to peripheral positions in these domains. This clearly influences my technique; my orientation is to differentiate myself from the standard, rather than to rely on it. Furthermore, my agreement with Renik that self-disclosure by the analyst fosters mutuality, has led me to be quite open with Pat about my analytic positions and beliefs. These are important elements of the field or context in which his treatment was being conducted.

Pat and I differ substantially in our values, and I have felt that being open about the differences was the best approach to dealing with the influences of these differences. Pat's conception of making a contribution in his professional life is quite different from my own conception. I have struggled to understand how my values may shape my attitude toward his devoting his life primarily to the game of golf. It is clear, too, that we have very different political attitudes, and on occasion we have had political discussions. We have agreed to disagree.

The Theory of the Present Unconscious

Sandler and Sandler's (1987) creative conception of the present unconscious provides a formulation consistent with field theory for focusing upon current emotional interactions between patient and analyst, rather than on exploration for hidden childhood traumas in the patient.

> We can conceive of the present unconscious, of this here-and-now adaptive aspect of the person as an *area* of the mind having conceptual links with the preconscious system of the topographical theory and the unconscious ego of the structural model. It has, as a major function, the updating and modifying of *current* wishful (and conflict-arousing) fantasies arising in the deeper part of the *present unconscious*. . . . The present unconscious can be thought of as bringing about the necessary modifications of the "child-like" unconscious fantasy by the use of mechanisms of defense, including, among

others, those which can be subsumed under the broad heading of projective identification. The objects involved in the fantasies arising in the present unconscious represent objects as perceived and imagined *in the present* (most strikingly the analyst in the transference), but the content of the wishful fantasies reflects the early childhood fantasies *we can never really know but which we attribute to the past unconscious*. . . . As a consequence of the adaptive, defensive and other modifying processes which have been applied to them in the present unconscious, they are usually very different from the fantasies of early childhood of the past unconscious. We can say that because the wishes and impulses arising in the deeper layers of the present unconscious *are a threat to the individual's current equilibrium,* the present unconscious has to do something to deal with the anxieties, feelings of guilt and other painful affects (or affect signals) involved, and *it does so by making defensive transformations in fantasy.* The technique which is associated with these formulations places great emphasis on making the central contents of the patient's present unconscious as accessible and tolerable to him as possible. We have put forward the view that in order to achieve the aim of the analytic work we need in various ways to bring the patient to the point where he can tolerate, in a safer way than before, the previously unacceptable aspects of himself. To do this he will need to gain insight in an emotionally convincing manner, not only into the content of his unconscious fantasies but also into the nature of his "inner world," his unconscious relation to his introjects, with whom he can be regarded as having a continual internal dialogue reflected in the unconscious fantasies *of the present unconscious* [pp. 335–337].

Several of Pat's present unconscious fantasies that were troublesome to him and reflected Habitual Relationship Patterns to which we devoted considerable attention were that accepting help would make him intolerably vulnerable to being humiliated, that his winning in a competitive situation would be severely punished, and that his aggressive feelings and impulses were lethal in their destructiveness.

Both field theory and the conception of the present unconscious draw attention so clearly to examination of the here and now that it is worth underscoring the traditional reluctance to engage in such examination. Indeed, one of the early differences that shaped Jung's separation from Freud was Freud's insistence that treatment focus on the exploration of the patient's past, and Jung's belief that the proper conduct of analysis entails directing the patient back to the current life conflict (Kerr, 1994). Bauer (1993) has described numerous factors that shape an analyst's reluctance to work with the patient's feelings and fantasies about him or her in the here and now.

> The therapist faces the potential discomfort and anxiety of offering himself as a target for feelings, fantasies, and perceptions that may threaten his own self-esteem and self-image. A patient's perception of the therapist may be insightful and penetrating. The therapist who can't tolerate close scrutiny of themselves may find here-and-now work difficult, especially when the patient chances upon real foibles. The therapist may have a hard time listening to things that wound his ego. . . . It is often more comfortable for the therapist to make a genetic connection than to focus on the here-and-now manifestations of transference. Flight away from the transference and to the past can be a relief to both patient and therapist. . . . Therapists may resist here-and-now work because they are not sure they can help. . . . This requires the therapist to have some measure of confidence in his ability to effect changes in the manner in which patient and therapist relate to each other. An underlying belief, for instance, in the inherent rigidity of character structure may prompt the therapist to provide more support, advice, and encouragement than an analysis of transference behavior. . . . Therapists with problems tolerating negative affect slowly accumulate a caseload of primarily grateful patients [pp. 69–74].

Resistance and Defenses

The subject of resistance and defense is discussed because those concepts necessarily are involved in analyzing Habitual Relationship Patterns. When Freud (1910b) first acknowledged the influence on analytic treatment of "countertransference," he let the camel's nose into the tent. Initially, there was a one-person model of treatment, and one of the early constructs was that of resistance, which involved two different, though related mechanisms. One was the patient's opposition to cooperating with the analyst, expressed by not freely associating and by not becoming relieved of symptoms and distress. The other was the patient's opposition to accessing unconscious feelings and fantasies that aroused discomfort. Freud used the metaphor of a battle to describe analytic treatment. Schafer (Panel, 1995) hypothesizes that Freud's inference about the patient's adversarial attitude toward the analyst, which is based on a one-person model of treatment, can be understood as Freud's own "countertransference," primarily a reflection of his own impatience and frustration at being unable to cure the patient. Freud's honest acknowledgment that the analyst's feelings and fantasies influenced the treatment process began the long, difficult journey in the history of psychoanalysis from its origin as a one-person model, derived from his self-analysis, to an increasingly two-person model.

Many patients try within their capacities to cooperate with the analyst in their treatment. It is not necessary to assume they are motivated to oppose the analyst's efforts. The patient's opposition to accessing disturbing unconscious feelings and fantasies can be understood as a defense, without hypothesizing a motivation to frustrate the analyst. Brenner (1991) describes the function of a defense is to reduce unpleasure. Of course, evidence may accumulate that the patient has developed oppositional motivation toward the analyst. These feelings should be examined and analyzed in the same manner as other feelings toward the analyst. Schafer argues that modern analytic treatment does not emphasize resistance per se, but rather is characterized as the analysis of "transference," defense, and, increasingly, "countertransference." Michels (Panel, 1995c), in his discussion of the issue, notes that Schafer's proposal implies that resistance, referring to opposition to the analyst, could be treated as a clinical phenomenon without assuming an abstract concept of resistance. Schafer's parsimonious conception seems useful to me, and directs the analyst's attention to the operation of his or her own feelings of frustration in the treatment situation. My treatment of Pat, who was appropriately cooperative, concentrated on examining and analyzing his defenses, with attention to the impact on our interactions of my own feelings and values.

A colleague who read this material describing Pat's treatment suggested, perhaps as a result of some defense of my own, that I may have overlooked a significant concern of Pat's. My colleague thought that several dream symbols, such as the frightening witchlike figure and the Queen, as well as Pat's preference that our wives not be involved in any posttermination contacts, may have been associated with his

seriously disturbed mother. Pat may have feared that winning in com-
petition would result in the loss of a protective paternal figure and
leave him exposed to dealing with the very frightening maternal figure. His dream of the frightening witch preceded my retirement
announcement. But who is the representation of that dreaded maternal figure? It does not seem to be his current wife. One possibility is
that I was a representation of that maternal figure as well as of the
protective paternal figure, and that I failed to perceive any manifestation of the former in our here-and-now interactions. Another possibility is that the representation was an introject of the disturbed mother,
whom he would have to deal with on his own after treatment termination. If so, is that an instance in which more attention to historical
experiences with the disturbed mother might have exposed his introject and modified his "transference" to me? I hope there is sufficient
material for the reader to reach his or her own judgment.

Is Pat's Treatment Psychoanalytic?

Currently there are many conceptions of psychoanalytic treatment, but
the definition should be based upon Freud's fundamental discovery,
the identification of the power of unconscious forces. Freud (1925)
recalled that visiting Bernheim in 1889, and observing his astonishing
experiments, gave him "the profoundest impression of the possibility
that there could be powerful mental processes which nevertheless
remained hidden from the consciousness of man" (pp. 29–30).
Psychoanalytic treatment, therefore, is treatment that analyzes unconscious feelings and fantasies—of both patient and analyst. Historically,
in the one-person model of treatment, it was the patient's unconscious
that was analyzed; the analyst's feelings and fantasies about the patient
were regarded as relatively minor impediments. Hinshelwood considers that it was Heimann (1950) who transformed "countertransference"
into a principal tool: "the analyst's emotional response to his patient
within the analytic situation represents one of the most important tools
for his work. The analyst's counter-transference is an instrument of
research into the patient's unconscious" (p. 81). Hinshelwood (1999)
notes "that alteration is based upon understanding the psychoanalytic
setting as a relationship" (p. 798). He adds, the analyst's "feelings are
an important factor (maybe *the* important factor) in creating a therapeutic ambience to the setting" (p. 807).

Wallerstein (1999b), emphasizing the common ground to the

various schools of psychoanalysis, concludes in his review of plenary clinical presentations from three regions of worldwide psychoanalytic activity:

> They have each addressed in quite comparable fashion the phenomena of conflict and compromise, of impulse and defense, of inner and outer object world, of reality and fantasy, of uncovering interpretation and of necessary supportive intervention, i.e., all the interactions within the transference-countertransference matrix that occupy the domain designated by the Sandlers as the "present unconscious" [p. 392].

My treatment of Pat conforms to Wallerstein's characterization of the common ground of psychoanalysis, which mentions neither etiology nor the exploration of childhood trauma.

Pat's analysis is psychoanalytic in that there is the attempt at non-manipulative scrutiny of *both* my present unconscious as well as his, and of the interaction between them, in order to help him modify his Habitual Relationship Patterns, including his defenses and his troublesome unconscious feelings and fantasies. That mutual examination shapes the treatment situation into an authentic joint psychoanalytic enterprise.

12

"Transference" and the Posttermination Relationship

We do not have a satisfactory explanation for Mr. K's psychosis, though not for want of trying. However, isn't it preferable to know and acknowledge what we don't know than to apply to a situation a familiar term which masquerades as an explanation but is fundamentally flawed?

—Lawrence Inderbitzin and Stephen Levy,
"Regression and Psychoanalytic Technique"

Why is discussion of the posttermination patient-analyst relationship included in a book about "transference"? Because I believe that conceptions of the posttermination patient-analyst relationship expose most vividly the conception of the fundamental nature of the patient-analyst relationship during treatment. Freud's concept of "transference" is intrinsically connected with a particular perspective on the patient-analyst relationship; it originated in the context of a one-person model of psychoanalytic treatment and extended that notion into the period after termination. Viewing the analyst as a professional who provides a service to a sick person—one metaphor was that of analyst as surgeon—leads inevitably to the conclusion that once the sick person is cured, there is no reason for further contact between the cured person and the professional. "Transference" was an expression of the sick person's distorted feelings and fantasies about the professional, and Freud assumed that the patient's "transference" would be the same no matter which person played the role of professional. Neither the sick person nor the treating professional were dimensional, real persons; each was playing a designated role. Oddly enough, there was not even provision for a follow-up visit to check on the completeness and persistence of the cure.

The concept of posttermination meetings and the possibility of a nonanalytic posttermination relationship directly contravenes that traditional conception. While this book challenges the traditional conception within the context of analytic treatment, heuristically the disagreement and distinction is most vividly manifest and magnified in relation to those assumptions underlying posttermination patient-analyst meetings.

It is true that traditional analysts have modified their technique of treatment and abstinence, and neutrality and anonymity are no longer so rigidly adhered to. Yet, until very recently, there has been no indication that the attitude of traditional theory toward posttermination patient-analyst contact has altered. Consequently, the differences between the two models are magnified in relation to this subject. The two-person model, which conceives of two real persons working mutually to help a troubled person, makes understandable that both might be interested in posttermination meetings and the possibility of extending their real relationship beyond the termination of treatment.

As explicated in chapter 10, rather than focusing on the childhood origins of the patient's psychopathology, treatment should be aimed at helping the patient learn, from examining the interactions between the troubled person and the treating person, how best to modify conscious and unconscious defenses that contribute to his or her distress.

In the analytic treatment situation, in the office, the analyst is in a greatly advantaged position, defining the rules and judging how well the patient cooperates with them and utilizes them. Most important, it is primarily the patient's psychopathology that is examined and exposed. Traditional treatment focuses on "transference" and "countertransference," concepts which themselves reflect a significant difference in the stature of patient and analyst, because the patient is troubled by "transference" and the analyst by "countertransference," the latter carrying the implication of *less serious*, reactive difficulties. The analyst is assumed to be an emotionally healthier person.

Traditional analysts argue that because the patient's "transference" persists after termination, they are obliged to remain in the analyst role for the duration of the former patient's life in order to remain available qua analyst for future treatment. The former patient is thus unilaterally consigned to remain in the patient role—that is, the less advantaged position—though no longer a patient in treatment. The traditional analyst's attitude, no matter how sincerely conceived, thereby perpetuates the analyst's advantaged position at the moment of parting.

"Transference" does persist after termination. If, however, the historical concept of "transference" is replaced, as recommended here, by the concept Habitual Relationship Pattern, it becomes clear that what persists after termination are patterns of conscious and unconscious defenses for dealing with unconscious conflicts. Those patterns had existed before analysis, were worked on during the analysis, and will continue to exist after analysis, presumably modulated and mitigated so that the former patient can deal with them much more expeditiously. Development and growth should not be undermined by denying the former patient a responsible, autonomous role in relation to the analyst in negotiating whether there will be posttermination patient-analyst meetings, and how they will be structured. Further, since the term Habitual Relationship Pattern applies to the analyst as well as to the patient, the term provides no implication that the patient's now modified Habitual Relationship Patterns are any more psychopathological than the analyst's Habitual Relationship Patterns.

Buckley (1989) cites Anna Freud (1954) who notes trenchantly that "we should leave room somewhere for the realization that analyst and patient are also two real people of equal adult status, in a real personal relationship to each other" (pp. 616–617). Interestingly, Buckley failed to include her acknowledgment that "these are technically subversive thoughts and ought to be labeled 'handle with care'" (p. 617). Her remark was necessitated by her observation that during traditional treatment, patient and analyst, instead of appearing as real people of equal adult status, appear, in a sense, in effigie, in that they each play a role, one as patient and the other as analyst. A posttermination relationship outside the treatment situation may provide the first opportunity to minimize, if not to discard, those effigies, thereby enabling exploration of aspects of their interaction that were difficult and perhaps impossible to do during treatment.

Traditional psychoanalytic theory long postulated that posttermination meetings that enabled the patient to view the analyst as a real person interfered with the patient doing appropriate posttermination analytic work (Panel, 1969), whereas now such contacts are seen as fostering posttermination analytic work (Schachter et al., 1997). It may be that in the posttermination relationship, when the analyst has significantly relinquished his or her advantaged position as therapist, the prior impact of the analyst's authority during treatment, with its attendant ambiance of suggestion, can be freshly examined. Further, the patient's idealization of the analyst, based at least in part upon the authority of the analyst in his or her advantaged role as therapist, may be understood more fully during the posttermination relationship than was possible during treatment.

Anna Freud (1954) provides dramatic examples of how the patient's viewing the analyst in the context of reality can undermine the patient's "transferential" belief in the analyst's omnipotence. "This 'magical' transference of certain patients dropped to zero when Hitler seized power. Being ourselves victims of the regime had rendered us unfit for the role of powerful, God-like beings which they had cast for us." During the London Blitz, one of her patients "continued his attendance, undisturbed by the bombing, and resisted all temptations to leave London until one night, when a bomb was dropped at the entrance to my street. This shattered not only the house on which it fell but also his belief in my omnipotence" (pp. 616–617).

If analyst and patient are conceived as comparable human beings, rather than the analyst being viewed as operating at a healthier emotional equilibrium, then it should be possible that analyst and former patient may, during the posttermination period, develop a mutually satisfying nonanalytic relationship. Despite risks and the complex issues inherent in such a development, the conception of the *possibility* of forming such a nonanalytic relationship is a critical indicator of the fundamental nature of how the patient-analyst relationship is conceived.

Historical Roots of Attitudes Toward Posttermination Meetings

I am unaware that Freud wrote anything about posttermination meetings with former patients, other than to mention inadvertent contact with former patients. Principally, he was interested in follow-up data that might confirm his views. Thus, in the Dora case, he is pleased to pass on a report he heard of her life after treatment. Similarly, he was thrilled that Little Hans grew up to be a splendid youth when he met him years later, because this seemed to confirm the efficacy of his "analysis." To be sure, Freud was capable of enjoying the friendship of colleagues whom he had analyzed and some close friendships developed this way (see "Freud's Friendships" later in this chapter); but this was an extratheoretical indulgence, without theoretical significance.

Ferenczi and Rank (1923) describe one root of Freud's lack of interest in posttermination meetings with patients: Freud (1914c) believed that reconstruction and insight cured the patient's transference neurosis. There was no reason, therefore, ever to see the patient again unless new problems arose; the "ideal case" was never seen again. If a "case" did develop subsequent problems, it was, indeed, less than ideal.

Because analysts accepted Freud's mistaken conception that patients could be cured, posttermination contact was considered an indication that the patient had not been cured, and the resulting inference was that the analyst had not done a very good job in his or her treatment of the patient. Any posttermination contact with a former patient would necessarily expose the analyst to the recognition that the analytic work was incomplete, and might raise a question about the adequacy of the treatment. This makes it understandable that at termination, analysts may covertly communicate to the patient that he or she would probably not ever need to contact them again, while still holding themselves available if there is need. The impression is that after long, intensive, and intimate analyses, only approximately 50 percent of patients ever again contact their analyst (Panel, 1969, Norman).

Persistence of "Transference" after Satisfactory Analysis

Bergmann (1988) comments that when Freud (1912b) first referred to resolution of the transference, the German word he used was *Lösung*, "which implies solution, the way a riddle is solved" (p. 143), which is less strong than "resolution." Bergmann notes that Annie Reich (1958) was the first to articulate that "transference" may not always be resolvable, and Pfeffer (1959) was the first to present evidence that residues of "transference" persisted after completion of analysis. Pfeffer (1961) replicated this finding, using five detailed follow-up interviews of another analyst's patient who, four years earlier, had terminated a satisfactory analysis. Additional studies have confirmed the finding that "transference" persists after completion of analysis (Pfeffer, 1963; Oremland, Blacker, and Norman, 1975; Norman et al., 1976; Schlessinger and Robbins, 1983).

What is the nature of the patient's behavior on follow-up that is considered evidence for the persistence of "transference"? A patient Pfeffer (1961) interviewed commented, during the second follow-up interview, that she realized during the first interview she had been talking to him as if he knew all about her, despite the fact she knew from her former analyst that the analyst would not communicate with Pfeffer until after the follow-up study. She added that she thought she connected Pfeffer with her former analyst unconsciously. She noted that during her analysis she used to put her coat in a closet outside the office, and because of that, when she came to Pfeffer's office, she did not know where to put her coat. She laughed and said she certainly wasn't going to put it on the couch. In the fourth interview she said she must have had some sort of fantasy about being a patient here. Prior to the fifth and final interview she reported that she had felt a little queasy, nauseous, and shaky, which she spontaneously connected with the termination of the follow-up study; she had talked earlier about her uncertainty at the time of termination of her analysis as to whether or not she could get along on her own. In a subsequent letter to Pfeffer she mentioned she developed an acute attack of anxiety the morning following that last interview, such as she had experienced many times during analysis. She concluded she had had a reactivation of the feelings she had when the termination of her analysis was imminent.

Pfeffer characterized the patient's feelings and reactions as a residue of her neurosis, "a remnant of the neurosis for which analysis first had been sought and now reappears in the form of a residue of the analytic transference" (p. 714). He noted further, "The residual analytic transference [was] . . . manifested by a further displacement onto the follow-up analyst" (p. 718). It seems convincing that the patient did indeed have parallel feelings about her analyst and about Pfeffer. If, however, as Pfeffer stated, there was *displacement* (of libido) of her feelings about the analyst, then, as Anna Freud pointed out (see Sandler, Kennedy, and Tyson, 1980) there should have been a decrease in her feelings about her analyst. There was no indication that that was the case. Inasmuch as the feelings about Pfeffer were similar to those about her analyst, there is an association, a correlation, but we cannot say if her feelings about her analyst were the *cause* of her feelings about Pfeffer, that is, that her feelings about Pfeffer were derived from, displaced from, her earlier feelings about her analyst. If her feelings about Pfeffer had been derived from her feelings about her analyst, then it would follow theoretically that if she had never seen her former analyst, she would not have had these feelings about Pfeffer. That, of course, cannot be tested. Perhaps if she had never been in analysis, but had come to Pfeffer for the possibility of analysis, she would have had the same feelings about him that she reported about him during the follow-up interviews. Of course, it is not possible to test that either.

She might have similar feelings toward any male physician she consulted, perhaps toward any male authority figure, or perhaps toward any person to whom she turned for support and nurturance. These feelings represent what I have characterized as a Habitual Relationship Pattern.

It is difficult to say what Pfeffer's data prove, if anything, about the earlier treatment, save that it was still on the patient's mind (as indeed it might be, since she was contacted specifically to talk about it). Which is to say that Pfeffer's findings scarcely add up to a validation of the historical notion of "transference."

While at this date we are not surprised to discover that what was termed "transference" persists after termination of successful analysis, at the time, the finding appeared surprising because analysts had accepted Freud's earlier, mistaken belief that analysis by historical interpretation could resolve the "transference" and cure the patient. Habitual Relationship Patterns and their underlying unconscious conflicts are present before analysis as well as after analysis; one hopes that after treatment they are modified so that they cause less constriction and distress in the patient's life.

Conceptions of Patient-Analyst Relationship After Termination

This distinction between Freud's concept of "transference" and the concept of Habitual Relationship Pattern is significant because the presence of "transference" after completion of analysis is the core of Rothstein's (Panel, 1995a) argument, and that of others, that after termination the analyst must always remain in the analyst role in relationship to the patient. The only appropriate posttermination contact between former patient and analyst is for further treatment. Indeed, for Rothstein, former patient-analyst contact for any purpose other than further treatment, such as analyst and former patient writing a paper together, is inappropriate, a boundary violation, and unethical.

Rothstein's (Panel, 1995a) view derives from a one-person model of psychoanalytic treatment in which a neutral, abstinent, and anonymous analyst interprets the patient's "transference." Since "transference" persists after termination, the analyst must maintain the analytic role to be available if the patient needs additional treatment. He creates a straw man by erroneously attributing to those analysts who leave open the possibility of nontherapeutic posttermination contact a belief that "transference" is resolvable during treatment. Parenthetically, if a patient needs further treatment, the option and desirability of consulting another analyst seems not to enter into these considerations.

Rothstein's view represents traditional psychoanalytic theory, which for almost a century interpreted Freud's attitude as imposing a powerful taboo on posttermination patient-analyst contact for any purpose other than further treatment (Schachter, 1990). The taboo was so effective that analysts rarely had any nontherapeutic contact with former patients. Despite the absence of experience with nontherapeutic contact with former patients, analysts continued to believe and teach that such contacts would be deleterious, creating regression and anxiety—a hypothetical conviction. Now it seems quite unnatural that after working intimately and intensively for years with another person, there would be no further contact between them after termination. Analysts ignored their own inevitable experiences of professional and social contacts with their own former candidate analysands within institutes and societies, which were not characterized as problematic. It was recognized that posttermination contact, especially if outside the office setting, would make it difficult to maintain the anonymity that was an element in the idealization of the analyst. Several analysts have commented that it is understandable if analysts are loath to relinquish the flattering, advantaged position that is intrinsic to the treatment situation (Buxbaum, 1950; Lampl-de Groot, 1954; Watillon, 1998; Orgel, 2000).

The widespread shift to a two-person model of treatment has important implications for both the treatment and the posttreatment relationship. Treatment focuses on examination of interaction between patient and analyst, including subjective and unconscious forces that influence analyst as well as patient. Treatment is less the shadowy, mysterious, unnatural relationship often projected in the one-person model, and more a familiar, customary human relationship. There is far more to analytic treatment than "transference" and "countertransference," the focus of the one-person model. There is consideration, flexibility, affirmation, caring, concern, empathy, authenticity, and generativity, as well as conflict, misunderstanding, evasion, and incompatibility. The possibility of a posttermination, nonanalytic relationship, in which these attributes would be important, may well sensitize the dyad to them during the treatment phase. The analytic relationship is a long-term, specialized, intense, intimate relationship between two persons. In that context, why wouldn't it be natural and appropriate for both mutually caring persons in such a relationship to be interested in meeting again after termination of treatment?

Posttermination meetings enable the former patient to evaluate the prior treatment and subsequent course, and to reinforce the sense of the analyst's caring, which provides a reference point for additional therapeutic work. They also provide the therapist with an advantaged view of the prior treatment compared to the view that was possible at termination. The opportunity to learn how the former patient has fared is an appropriate expression of the analyst's continued caring and concern for the patient. Although the patient's interest in posttermination contact may be a defense against feelings of loss, it may not be only that, or it may not be that at all. Conversely, the patient's lack of interest in posttermination contact may also reflect a defense against feelings of loss.

For the patient, meeting the analyst after termination may be considered analogous to a person's contact with an icon, in this case a living icon. Many of the world's religions have for thousands of years utilized icons to enhance people's feelings of connection to a religious institution and its deity. Posttermination contact, similarly, is likely to enhance the former patient's feeling of connection to the analyst by enhancing the patient's internal representation of the analyst. Perhaps, as a consequence, some patients find that such contact mobilizes feelings of loss and facilitates mourning.

Posttermination meetings may well enhance the patient's internal representations of the analyst, both identifications and introjections, which enables the former patient to continue the work of treatment after termination. Wzontek, Geller, and Farber (1995) studied the dimensions and consequences of former patients' thoughts and feelings following termination of psychotherapy. They distinguished the patient's introjective representations of the therapist, and of the dialogue between them, from identificatory self-representations modeled after the therapist. They concluded, "Former patients who tended to evoke representations of the therapist that serve the function of 'continuing the therapeutic dialogue' engaged in afterwork more frequently and perceived their therapy as more successful" (p. 406). Schachter and Brauer (2001) report a related finding, that those analysts, as former patients, who think more frequently about their own former analyst are more likely to feel their analysis helped them. Schachter and Brauer also found a powerful, positive association between the degree to which the analyst reported thinking about his or her former analyst and the likelihood that former patients of that analyst contacted that analyst within the prior six months. That is, analysts who think more about their own former analyst are more open to posttermination contact by their own former patients.

Wzontek, Geller, and Farber (1995) conclude that "both constructive identifications with the therapist's abilities and functions (e.g., his or her knowledge and decision making) and introjections that enable individuals to evoke conversations with their therapists, enable former patients to sustain the work of therapy in the absence of their therapists" (p. 407). They noted also that "patients whose representations tend to reflect the theme of 'mourning' are more likely to feel they have benefited from therapy" (p. 408). They referred to Loewald's (1962) observation that one of the most important aspects of termination is the work of mourning, a process that includes not only the gradual relinquishment of a cherished relationship, but the internalization of the relationship as well.

Brickman (2000) has developed a conception that provides an intriguing formulation of the role of internal representations and post-termination meetings in terms of neural networks. He developed "the acronym CARD—Contingent Affect-imbued Relational Dispositions" (p. 19) that are expressions of persistently active underlying neural networks. The mutative effects of analytic treatment, he conceives, reflect altered neural innervation patterns. He does wonder what the fate is of earlier, maladaptive neural networks after analytic gains:

> Neurobiologically speaking, neural network selection explanations would tend to leave moot the question of whether habitual but maladaptive innervated patterns of interactivity would need to be extinguished as a result of mutative experience in the transference. The likely absence of total extinction of these innervated patterns would help to account for the widely observed clinical fact that even the most successful analyses often fall short of complete "cure" [p. 34].

I propose an alternative hypothesis regarding the posttreatment fate of these earlier habitual but maladaptive neural networks. Luborsky (Panel, 1989) has reported that following psychotherapy, some patients exhibit gradual vitiation of their therapeutic gains. He noted, however, that those patients who had posttermination meetings with their former therapists did not show this diminution in therapeutic improvements over time. Presumably, these posttermination meetings with the former therapist reinvigorate internal representations in the patient of the therapist, and this serves to reinforce the activity of the newly developed, more adaptive neural networks. It seems plausible that in addition, positive feedback from the behavioral consequences of the new, adaptive neural network itself would provide an additional source of reinforcement.

If, however, these two sources of reinforcement combined of the newer, more adaptive neural networks gradually degrade over time—involving the internal representations of the therapist—the old, still available, maladaptive neural networks will increasingly become reestablished as the default neural system. That is, continual reinforcement is necessary for the maintenance of therapeutic benefits. In the absence of sufficient reinforcement, old defenses would gradually again become more automatic and more intense.

While recognizing that there may be contraindications to posttermination meetings for certain dyads, the option to have such meetings is recommended for most dyads. Meetings consisting of occasional single or a brief series of contacts from time to time, in the analyst's office or outside, have been found to be beneficial to the patients involved and supported facilitation of mourning (Schachter et al., 1997).

During the last five years, questionnaire data (Schachter and Brauer, 2001) indicate that lately a significantly increased proportion of analysts suggest some form of posttermination contact, not designed to provide further treatment. Parenthetically, although analytic candidates know they will have posttermination contact with their training analyst, there is no evidence that this knowledge minimizes their feelings of loss compared to patients who do not anticipate posttermination contact with their analyst. Geller (personal communication, 2000) has the same impression regarding treatment of psychotherapists who know they will have posttermination contact with their own therapist; there does not seem to be a diminution in the feelings of loss. Expectation of posttermination contact does not seem to interfere with the mourning response, and the contact itself seems to facilitate it at least for some.

What of the much-bruited risk that posttermination meetings of any nature may start the dyad down the "slippery slope" to patient-analyst sexual involvement? There is no answer. I have had difficulty finding analysts to report such experiences to my clinical discussion group (most said they had heard of none) but those few analysts who *did* report deleterious posttermination experiences described serious, unresolved patient-analyst problems that prevailed during the prior treatment. Posttermination difficulties did not seem to develop following completion of reasonably satisfactory treatment. We can assume that in rare instances, posttermination meetings do develop into a patient-analyst sexual relationship, but just as we do not recommend that patients avoid analytic treatment itself because of the risk of sexual involvement with the analyst, so we should not recommend that patients avoid posttermination contact with the analyst because of the same risk. As I mentioned earlier, we must rely on the integrity and emotional health of the analyst to prevent patient-analyst sexual involvement during and after treatment.

Structure of Patient-Analyst Relationship after Treatment

A new approach to defining the posttermination relationship may be based on a review of the development of the treatment relationship itself. The patient-analyst relationship is initially hierarchical, but its first consequential act is to negotiate a consensually agreed contract for treatment, which includes such items as session frequency and fee. The contract does not include any statement by the analyst that he or she will remain the patient's analyst for life; on the contrary, every treatment contract carries a clear implication that the treatment will have some limited duration, an end. *The initial contract is not for a life-long treatment relationship.* When treatment ends, the contract is completed.

Paralleling the development of the initial structure of treatment, the discussion of termination should include the patient's fantasies, anxieties, and wishes regarding the possibility of posttermination meetings. If the patient has not raised these issues, the analyst should explore why they have not come up. This may then lead to the development of *a consensually agreed new contract for determining whether there will be a posttermination relationship, and its nature.* At the conclusion of a reasonably successful analytic treatment the patient, now presumably more assured and autonomous, should be far better equipped to negotiate a new contract than at the start of treatment, and these negotiations would be less hierarchical and more mutual than the initial negotiation. The relevance of Habitual Relationship Patterns of both patient and analyst to future contact should be considered because, in this frame of reference, the patient is not still dealing with childhood "transferences." Instead, at termination, the patient who has modulated his or her Habitual Relationship Patterns deserves the analyst's respect for both feelings and judgments.

It is both an undesirable extension of the patient's investiture of authority in the analyst and an exercise in arrogance for the analyst to decide *unilaterally* that he or she knows what is best for the patient for the rest of the patient's life, that is, that the relationship of former patient and analyst must remain unmodified. In doing so, the analyst arbitrarily extends the initial treatment contract for the rest of the patient's life. This unilateral position is entrenched in our language. When a person walks into an analyst's office for professional help we have a term for such a person—a *patient*. When, after completing treatment, the person walks out of the analyst's office, the only term we have is a "former patient."

Conceptions of Friendship

A wide range of relationships is possible in the posttermination period between the former patient and the analyst. These would include the kind of casual connection that often characterizes our relationship with our neighbors. It could also include the closer, more intense association of friendship. Having these possibilities in mind during the treatment is likely to sharpen the exploration by both patient and analyst of the realistic attributes of the other person. After termination, would they really want the other person as neighbor, or friend?

Germane to a discussion of this possibility of friendship is a discussion of the concept of friendship itself. There are as many definitions of friendship as there are social scientists studying the topic (Fehr, 1996). Friendship, Rubin (1981) notes, is "without institutional form, without a clearly defined set of norms for behavior or an agreed-upon set of reciprocal rights and obligations" (p. 106). Kurth (1970) defined friendship as an intimate interpersonal relationship involving each individual as a personal entity. Friendship ordinarily includes such features as intimacy, loyalty, honesty, trust, and enjoyment in one another's company (Fehr, 1996). Rawlins (1992) describes a close friend as "somebody to talk to, to depend on and rely on for help, support and caring, to have fun and enjoy doing things with" (p. 271). Duck (1983) observes that friendships provide "the provision of personality support—that is, the bolstering and propping up of our beliefs and opinions. Friends help to cushion our personalities and reassure us about our value as people" (p. 31). Fleming (1972) writes, "We are never completely independent of the need that a trusted person exists and could be called if necessary" (p. 35). Fromm (1941), describing the value of friendship, comments that while it may not be a resolution to personal isolation and insecurity and questions about the meaning of life, "along with music, science, art and many of the other creations of our life . . . friendship, as some kind of more immediate personal answer to our questions, comes close" (pp. 368–369). Whatever our definition, as early as fourth century B.C. Greece, Aristotle expressed the view that friendship had gone downhill since his grandfather's day (Duck, 1983).

Boswell (1980) asserts the arbitrariness of distinctions between "friendship" and "love," and how it is "not easy to conceive of an experiment which might be performed to determine whether one person's love for another was friendly or erotic. From a phenomenological point of view, it seems likely that 'friendship' and 'love' are simply different points on a scale measuring a constellation of psychological and physiological responses to other humans" (p. 46).

Freud (1922) differentiated friendship as follows:

> The social instincts belong to a class of instinctual impulses which need not be described as sublimated, though they are closely related to these. They have not abandoned their directly sexual aims, but they are held back by internal resistances from attaining them; they rest content with certain approximations to satisfaction and for that very reason lead to especially firm and permanent attachments between human beings [including friendship] [p. 258].

Sullivan is credited in the psychoanalytic literature with separating out friendship as a specific developmental line in analytic theory (Gerson, 1993). Bowlby (1973) discussed the significance of friendship in adulthood, noting, in almost the same words as Fleming, that people are most productive when they are "confident that, standing behind them, there are one or more trusted persons who will come to their aid should difficulties arise" (p. 359).

Rangell (1963), author of the only traditional psychoanalytic paper on the subject, notes that friendship "has been left mostly to the philosophers, novelists and poets, in whose domains, indeed, it has been far from neglected" (p. 4). He believes friendship takes root, flourishes, and becomes a center of activity during adolescence. Friends are "used for instinctual discharge . . . libidinal as well as aggressive by means of sublimation and aim inhibition"(p. 19). "Introjected objects . . . are now, during the still formative stages [adolescence], reprojected and extrojected onto external objects, from which supplies are then reobtained and reintegrated. . . . Such external sources serve as reservoirs, for narcissistic supplies into which we can dip as necessary" (p. 21).

Ruptures of friendship, Rangell adds, "can be traced quite regularly to a threat of a return of the repressed, more specifically to a threatened break-through of the original homosexual strivings with their original oedipal and sibling matrix" (pp. 42–43).

Freud's Friendships

Freud's life, itself, demonstrates the value of friendship. Erikson (1980) quotes Jones (1953), who calls Freud's relationship with Fliess "the only really extraordinary experience in Freud's life" (p. 287). Freud (Bonapart, Freud, and Kris, 1954) wrote to Fliess, "There can be no substitute for the close friendship which a particular, almost feminine side of me calls for" (Letter no. 318). Erikson noted that Freud's friendship with Fliess "coincided with his most creative period and with his self-analysis" (p. 47), and added, "this friendship may have provided for Freud the one truly playful and intimate communication of ideas" (p. 46). "The mutual support of such further development [of continued identity renewal] is the main psycho-social function of friendship. It permits a reciprocal narcissistic mirroring which allocates to each partner the self-love necessary for creative activity and yet also, by intimate critique, keeps it within necessary limits" (p. 48).

Freud's best-known friendship with a former patient was with Ferenczi, who had several sporadic analytical contacts followed by three weeks of intensive analysis with Freud in June 1916 (Grubrich-Simitis, 1986). In 1917, Freud responded negatively to Ferenczi's request to continue the analysis, but they sustained a rich, mutual correspondence, and made trips and visits to each other in Vienna and Budapest. All his life, Ferenczi seems to have looked for a strong father-figure (Dupont, 1994). Differences of opinion between Freud and Ferenczi began with the 1924 publication of a book by Ferenczi and Rank (Grubrich-Simitis, 1987), which Freud perceived leading away from psychoanalysis. By 1931, Freud sharply criticized Ferenczi's technique of "mother tenderness," which he feared could lead to the degeneration of psychoanalysis. Fogel (1993), however, attests to the importance of the relationship: Ferenczi's "papers ring with clinical authenticity—the need and wish to facilitate and demonstrate the experiential and relational aspects of psychoanalysis, to create and validate theory with actual clinical experience every time he did an analytic treatment. . . . Ferenczi's key role and powerful influence on Freud is beyond question" (p. 597). Ferenczi reproached Freud for ignoring and

failing to analyze his negative transference; it seems likely that Freud
also ignored his own negative countertransference (Dupont, 1994).
Grubrich-Simitis noted that "Freud looked back with a certain wist-
fulness on their long friendship and called it 'an intimate sharing of
life, spirit and interests'" (p. 259). Freud's (1937b) famous statement,
"not every good relation between analyst and his subject was to be
regarded as transference: there were also friendly relations which were
based on reality and which proved to be viable" (p. 222), referred to
his friendship with Ferenczi.

Freud went on to develop friendships with numerous analysands.
Lampl-de Groot (1976), for one, refers to her subsequent warm friendship with Freud and his family. Bergmann (1988) provides additional
evidence: "One would have to say that at least in the case of some
patients the analysis was transformed into an abiding friendship" (p. 144).
But to repeat what was said earlier, Freud seemed to view these friendships as utterly outside his normal therapeutic rationale for work with
patients, and lacking any theoretical consequences.

The Possibility of Posttermination Patient-Analyst Friendship

Contemporary views of posttermination patient-analyst friendship are
polarized. At one extreme is the view that, except for the purpose of
additional treatment, *any* posttermination contact is a boundary violation (Rothstein, in Panel, 1995a), while counterposed is the belief
that a posttermination patient-analyst friendship may be the natural
and healthy outcome of a long-term, intimate, mutually caring treatment relationship (Schachter, 1992). Ganzarin (1991) seems to share
this latter view, which was Freud's view, that friendly relations were
possible by observing, without criticism, "After treatment some analysts befriend their former patients" (p. 137). Gabbard and Lester
(1995), referring not to friendship in particular, but to posttermination
contact generally, move to a middle ground so far as analytic candidates are concerned: "Some of those [postanalytic] contacts may facilitate the candidate's psychological growth. Others may be more
problematic and compromise the candidate's autonomy" (p. 164).

Whereas some characteristics of a patient-analyst relationship are
consistent with friendship, two attributes of friendship that distinguish
it from a therapeutic relationship are that it is an egalitarian relationship (Matthews, 1986) and that mutual intimate self-disclosure is a hallmark (Fehr, 1996). The mutual caring and concern that is likely to have

developed by the end of a successful treatment relationship would facilitate development of friendship, whereas the hierarchical nature of the relationship and the fact that self-disclosure has not been mutual are not consistent with the development of friendship. These latter attributes of the patient-analyst relationship have to undergo change for friendship to develop. Even with traditional attempts at neutrality and relatively limited explicit self-disclosure by the analyst, however, the curious, uninhibited analytic patient observes and infers from the analyst's behavior, clothes, office, books, car, etc. as well as from outside sources, a fairly accurate appraisal of many of the analyst's characteristics and attitudes. The impact of the current trend toward increasing self-disclosure by the analyst, culminating in Renik's (1999) rationale for full disclosure, has sensitized analytic awareness to the patient's appropriate interest in the analyst's humaneness.

The analyst's own conception of friendship must have a profound influence on the probability of friendship developing. If one is confined to the traditional psychoanalytic view that friends are used for instinctual discharge by means of sublimation and aim inhibition of sexual, especially homosexual, and aggressive drives, and for necessary narcissistic supplies, there is an implication, because no other factors are mentioned, that all friendship can be reduced to sublimation of sexual and aggressive drives. There is doubtless some validity to these hypotheses, if we don't make them absolute; probing and exploring motivation for friendship will provide reasonably convincing evidence that dealing with sexual and aggressive impulses plays a role. Character traits as well as many socially accepted goals and activities similarly are hypothesized to have developed by sublimation of sexual and aggressive drives.

Reducing friendship to desexualization of psychic energy, however, implies that friendship is a substitute, and in that sense, second best, for something originally desired. While not explicitly psychopathological, neither is there much that is particularly healthy or positive about this conception. The aspects of intimacy, loyalty, honesty, trust, support, mutual enjoyment, and generativity, the flesh and blood of friendship, are nowhere mentioned.

This unfortunate reductionism of traditional theory fails to appreciate Hartmann's (1939) theoretical contribution of primary and secondary autonomy of motives. He postulated that attributes such as speech, perception, and thinking developed relatively independently of the sexual and aggressive drives (primary autonomy). Other behaviors, such as friendship, originating as defenses against instinctual drives, might become free of such influence in the course of development, and develop secondary autonomy. It is this important role of secondary autonomy in friendship that traditional theory overlooks. Isn't this critique of reductionism out of date? Haven't many traditional analysts modified their views? Perhaps, but it is my impression that virtually all traditional analysts are horrified at crossing the Rubicon and developing a friendship with a former patient.

Development of Patient-Analyst Friendship After Termination

There are at least three patterns by which friendship between patient and analyst might develop subsequent to treatment termination. One is a gradual development, based on adventitious social contacts in a small community. Another is the gradual transformation of posttermination patient-analyst meetings into those with more social characteristics, so that friendship begins to develop. A newer possibility is consensual agreement during termination that there will be no further professional or therapeutic contacts after treatment ends, but that social engagements would be explored that might develop into friendship.

Development of friendship by any route requires changes in both patient and analyst. The patient must relinquish the comforting, benign, invested authority of the therapist, and perceive the therapist as he or she actually is, complete with emotional limitations and problems. The patient must expand his or her curiosity about the therapist's private concerns and anticipate and tolerate increased self-disclosure by the former therapist. The analyst, in turn, must relinquish the narcissistic gratification provided by the aforesaid investiture with benign authority and omniscience, as well as the related fantasy of anonymity, and become increasingly self-disclosing about himself or herself, as well as about family and friends. These substantial, even profound changes are required both for patient and analyst, and therefore, both patient and analyst would have to value such friendship quite highly. Even absent the taboo against posttermination patient-therapist friendship, given the inherent difficulties involved in the change, the development of such relationships is likely to remain relatively rare, though the application of the two-person model with more self-disclosure by the analyst and greater emphasis on mutuality may gradually support a more widespread development of former patient-analyst friendships. After all, few relationships overall end in true friendship.

As rewarding as the benefits of such a friendship may be, the risk for the former patient is that the friendship may founder and leave the former patient with unanalyzed negative feelings. The patient then loses both his or her fantasied friend and his or her analyst. Indeed, the patient's negative feelings may undermine some of the therapeutic gains. On the other hand, the analyst may learn that when the investiture of benign authority and omniscience is replaced by increased self-disclosure of what the therapist is like as a person, the patient may lose interest in him or her and the friendship may falter. Incompletely analyzed aspects of the relationship may cause the analyst to lose both the friendship and the former patient.

At its best, however, the friendship could be of extraordinary value to both parties. Genuine, long-term intimate friendships are relatively rare for most people; such friendship may be more gratifying, supportive, and generative than most other relationships can be. We need to respect the priorities of a former patient who may responsibly choose to give more weight to the possibility of developing a friendship, while recognizing that this choice involves abandoning the possibility of further treatment with the former analyst. If further therapeutic help is needed, other analysts are available.

Examples of Posttermination Former Patient-Analyst Friendships

A patient-analyst friendship of more than 20 years developed adventitiously. In medium and small-sized cities, the frequency of posttermination contact between the analyst and former patients with similar interests is relatively high, much like the frequency of contact between a candidate and former training analyst. In this case, the female analyst and the female former patient, each with a like-aged offspring in the same school, had frequent contacts and gradually developed a friendship. The analyst had urged the former patient, a mental health professional, to enter private practice. One example of the generativity operative during the analysis is that the patient still recalls a comment of the analyst that she found reassuring and encouraging: "Although you'll find patients who are brighter than you, patients who are wealthier than you, patients who are more attractive than you and patients who are more sophisticated then you, you are capable of being helpful to them all." As the intimacy between them grew it involved their families as well. The former patient has never felt the need of additional therapeutic help. Neither can identify any problems that have arisen as a function of this friendship; both consider it to be mutually rewarding as individuals and as families.

An example of cross-gender friendship is one that developed adventitiously within the "small city" of an analytic organization. An analyst and former training analyst were appointed to the same committee and began working together. The increased collegial contact gradually began to include social meetings, and these flowered into a close relationship that involved both families. Since the termination of the training analysis, the analyst had no interest in further treatment. Neither the analyst nor the former training analyst report any problems associated with their friendship of more than 20 years' duration.

Summary

Freud's concept of "transference" is intrinsically connected to a particular conception of the patient-analyst relationship, the one-person model of psychoanalytic treatment. The concept of posttermination patient-analyst meetings and the possibility of a nonanalytic posttermination relationship contravenes this traditional conception of the patient-analyst relationship and most vividly manifests the difference between them in the fundamental conception of patient and analyst that prevailed throughout treatment. In the traditional conception, the patient is a sick person and the analyst a professional who provides a service. Curing the sick person is the only basis for the relationship. In that sense, neither are real persons; rather, each is an individual playing a role. When the sick individual has been cured, there is no reason for any further contact with the professional individual. In the two-person model, two real persons are working mutually to help the designated troubled person. It is understandable that both may be interested in posttermination meetings and the possibility of extending their real relationship beyond the termination of treatment.

The growing shift to a two-person model of psychoanalytic treatment recognizes the importance for patient and analyst of consideration, flexibility, affirmation, caring, concern, empathy, authenticity, and generativity, in addition to analysis of "transference" and "countertransference." Taken together, these qualities would make it seem natural and appropriate to have posttermination meetings out of mutual interest. The nature of the posttermination patient-analyst relationship should be discussed in the light of the patient's fantasies, wishes, and anxieties, and a new contract consensually agreed upon during the termination period about such a possibility. Such meetings, or adventitious meetings, are likely to be mutually beneficial. If the patient chooses the possibility of friendship over maintaining the analyst's availability for possible future treatment, the patient's choice should be respectfully considered, along with the analyst's feelings.

Posttermination meetings, it might reasonably be supposed, will rarely develop into a friendship, and when this occurs it requires major changes of both patient and analyst. The patient must abandon the comforting investiture of the analyst with benign authority and omniscience, and the analyst must relinquish the gratification of this investiture and become much more self-disclosing. These changes are of such magnitude that even if the taboo about developing such friendship diminishes or disappears, it seems likely that development of such a friendship will be a relatively rare event. Developing such a friendship will probably always mean traversing a rocky path—as do many other journeys that we value.

13
Conclusion

Life is short, and the Art is long; the occasion fleeting; expe-rience delusive; judgment difficult.

—Hippocrates, the first aphorism

Freud's fascination with neurosis as an opening into large vistas was captured by Sulloway (1979, p. 497) who quotes Freud's (1941, p. 299) late remark: "With neurosis it is as though we were in a prehistoric landscape—for instance, in the Jurassic. The great saurians are still running about; the horsetails grow as high as palms."

Freud's goal was to discover the cause of neurosis, and his treat-ment of patients was in the service of that goal—as well as to enable him to earn a living. His theory of "transference" hypothesized that childhood experience or fantasy was the *cause* of the adult patient's untoward feelings about the analyst as well as the predisposing cause of neurosis. This etiological theory of "transference" has never been validated, and I have argued that it is not possible to validate it. Of course, failure to validate does not mean that it may not be true—only that we don't know. Freud believed that uncovering the predisposing cause was necessary for the successful treatment of neurotic patients. He was wrong. A great many medical disorders that are effectively treated are disorders whose cause is unknown. Patients are helped by analytic treatment without elucidating the cause. To what degree dis-covering the putative childhood cause of the patient's feelings and fan-tasies about the analyst or of the patient's neurosis *is* therapeutic remains controversial.

Indeed, Meehl (2001), in a recent letter to Grünbaum, expresses skepticism that interpreting the putative cause has much therapeutic efficacy:

> We might further decide, as a matter of technology, that uncovering them [the putative causes] is not the prime efficient cause of symptomatic improvement. . . . I think any honest clinician who is not totally dogmatic becomes aware of the imperfect correlation—not zero, but certainly small—between the clarity with which an unconscious regnant process [cause] is elucidated with symptomatic benefit [Grünbaum, personal communication, 2001].

Consider *hypothetically* that the dearth of maternal nurturing during childhood is actually, in some way, conclusively demonstrated to be the cause in an individual patient of some particular adult psychopathology. Does the specific identification of that childhood cause so inform the analyst's interventions that the therapeutic benefit is significantly greater than if the cause had not been identified? More specifically, is it necessary to interpret the significance of childhood cause to the patient vis-à-vis the patient's attitude toward the analyst? To me, it is not self-evident that it would be. It is not obvious that the patient would be better able to make the current changes via the analytic relationship necessary to reduce or relieve the psychopathology than he or she would if the childhood cause had not been identified. Thus, whether knowledge of the childhood cause improves therapeutic benefit is itself an additional *hypothesis* which needs to be tested empirically. Treatment benefit would have to be examined in comparable samples of patients, comparing those in whom a cause had been identified with those in whom no cause had been identified. No such study has been reported, and, given the methodological and human complexities involved, it is unlikely such a study will be conducted. Therefore, we arrive again at the specific conclusion that the hypothesis that identification of a childhood cause enhances the therapeutic benefit of analytic treatment can neither be empirically tested nor validated.

Let us be clear that uncovering the predisposing cause and analyzing the "transference" are connected: Freud's concept of "transference" embodies the goal of finding—and confronting *in situ*—the cause of neurosis. For a century, Freud's understanding has structured and focused analytic treatment on the patient's feelings toward the physician as part of the exploration for the childhood origins of adult psychopathology. Recently, while some analysts have moved from the traditional, historical concept of "transference" to new ideas and techniques—usually without coining a new term for the new conception—this shift away from reconstruction toward analyzing current "transference" has occurred without explicitly discarding Freud's theory of "transference." In the history of psychoanalysis there have been three designated shibboleths: the Oedipus complex, the interpretation of dreams, and now the theory of "transference" (Person, 1993). I assert that all three have lost their salience; the latter arguably has become less a shibboleth and more an albatross.

In this book I have proposed abandoning Freud's overarching goal of discovering the cause of neurosis, giving up the search for the *caput Nili* and the pursuit of the Holy Grail. Rather, we should substitute the more modest goal of understanding how better to help patients, deliberately choosing to concentrate on psychoanalytic therapy rather than developing further traditional psychoanalytic theory. My position contrasts with Rangell's decrying of a separate "clinical theory" and an "abstract theory." Whereas Rangell proposes a unified, composite theory of the science of psychoanalysis based on the analyst's empirical observations and incorporating the metaphors of economic, topographical, and structural theory, I suggest that the intrinsic complexity of the dyad limits the validity of many of the analyst's observations as a basis for scientific generalizations. For the art of psychoanalytic treatment, the analyst's idiosyncratic theory and personal emotional reactions to the patient offer a sounder guide. One by one, the value of Freud's critical theories has been questioned. His theory of the death instinct was never well accepted (Cooper, 1987). Economic (libido) theory (Kardiner, Karush, and Ovesey 1959), topographic theory (Arlow and Brenner, 1964), structural theory (Brenner, 1994, 1998), and the theory of regression (Inderbitzin and Levy, 2000) have been questioned, and now the theory of "transference" as well.

If psychoanalysts decide to put aside traditional psychoanalytic theory in favor of a truly revised understanding of psychoanalytic treatment, who is to say that that treatment is or is not psychoanalysis? We should attempt to focus on treatment in accord with the views of G. Klein and Gill, without any standard theory of mind, relying only on the personal, covert, idiosyncratic theory of each analyst, which, to be sure, is inescapable. I disagree with Crews (2000) who, like Grünbaum, faults Freud for not being appropriately scientific, and then adds, therefore his work is of limited value: "A Freud whose ideas cannot be considered within their intended domain of psychological theory is no Freud at all" (p. 101).

In the treatment domain, Freud's descriptions of the interactions of unconscious dynamic mechanisms such as defenses greatly facilitate understanding the patient's feelings and meanings. Freud's characterizations of defenses are independent of postulating any distal, childhood cause, even though defenses may play a proximal, causative role in the here and now.

The therapeutic goal, in Cooper's (1987) terms, is to enable "a sufficient reorganization of ego capacities . . . so that there is a greater coherence of conscious and unconscious elements" (p. 146). Arlow's (1987) characterization of the therapeutic goal is "the successful resolution of conflict, rather than the recovery of repressed memory" (p. 76). Our conduct should be guided by Mitchell's (1997) recommendation that the analyst rely on "self-reflective responsiveness," supplemented by a pragmatic set of clinical procedures, such as those suggested by Ehrenberg (1992), which include monitoring the affectivity of both participants and giving priority to analyst-patient interactions in the here and now. Gedo (1999) notes that Ehrenberg deals with clinical psychoanalysis as an art rather than as applied science, as do I. Gedo's opinion is that her approach scarcely adds up to a psychoanalytic theory: "It is at best a more or less coherent list of pragmatic guidelines for conducting the treatment in a humane atmosphere and hoping for the best" (p. 209). Precisely so.

I do think clinical psychoanalysis is not science but art, in the sense that each psychoanalytic treatment is a function of the idiosyncratic values, feelings and fantasies, conscious and unconscious, of each member of the dyad and therefore is not replicable. Kantrowitz (1993) argues that "the quality of each patient-analyst match creates a unique, non-replicable treatment experience" (p. 894), and adds that "Differences between what emerges in one treatment and what might have emerged from another can never really be tested" (p. 902). Psychoanalysis as an art is difficult to learn, and almost impossible to teach. Kerr (1994), too, considering the failure to generate homogeneous results in the early history of the psychoanalytic movement, soberly concludes, "Whatever it is, psychoanalysis is not a science" (p. 509). Green (2000a) also concurs that "the specificities of its practice and of its mode of thinking were not compatible with the ordinary requirements of scientific evidence" (p. 22). He adds (2000c) that the so-called scientific method seems very unscientific "because of its irrelevance to the object of psychoanalysis" (p. 66). Fairfield (2001) makes the same point: "For postmodernists, then, an epistemology in which an objectively real external phenomenon can be observed in an unmediated fashion by a neutral researcher is not suitable when it comes to the psyche" (p. 234).

Conceiving of psychoanalytic treatment as art isn't inappropriate once we recognize—and accept—that each analyst's treatment is influenced by his or her own values and personality (Kantrowitz, 1995; Aron, 1999). "The art of psychoanalytic technique," write Westen and Gabbard (2001), "lies as much as anything in the art of selecting, from among the thousands of points of entry in any given hour, material that is likely to go *somewhere*, that is, to have some import more broadly for the patient's life" (p. 29). Canestri (1994) believes "that the activity of the analyst is very close to that of the artist" (p. 1079). He quotes Freud (1911) as characterizing the artist as a person who turns away from reality to fantasy, but finds the way back to reality "by making use of special gifts to mould his fantasies into truths of a new kind, which are valued by men as precious reflections of reality" (p. 224). But can this not also be said of analytic reflection, with the result being new understandings of the patient? Sandell et al. (2000) noted in an outcome study that therapists who considered psychotherapy as "more a work of art than a craft or science" (p. 933) had better patient outcomes.

Nor is it surprising that we have not agreed which elements of treatment are mutative, since they probably vary with each dyad. The best predictor of favorable outcome (Luborsky, 2000) is the early therapeutic alliance, marked by the patient's positive feelings about the therapist. Moreover, supportive, noninterpretive interventions, plus "transference" interpretations, varying in content with different psychoanalytic schools, *all* seem helpful. Although plausible historical interpretations and narrative constructions may appear to produce impressive, even dramatic therapeutic reactions, I believe the role of suggestion and of placebo effects cannot be ruled out in the impact of those experiences.

Strikingly, Freud notes that "the patient's conviction of the truth of the reconstruction achieves the same therapeutic result as a recaptured memory" (1937a, p. 266)! I believe that psychoanalysis has not demonstrated that its help has been delivered through anything other than a nonspecific effect—nor has any other therapeutic technique. Wampold (2001), who has examined the results of thousands of psychotherapy by means of metaanalysis, concludes that "decades of psychotherapy research have failed to find a scintilla of evidence that any specific ingredient is necessary for therapeutic change (p. 204). Delineation of mutative factors remains a major challenge. Examining and understanding nonspecific effects, rather than not attending to them, may well enhance our therapeutic effectiveness.

Green (2000b) does raise a question whether, if one's point of view about psychoanalysis "is not scientific then one has to be—whether one likes it or not—a hermeneuticist" (p. 46). Though Green's comment has merit, let me leave that aside and grant that my proposal puts me in bed with the hermeneuticists, even though I am a natural scientist at heart, having spent years engaged in quantitative, biological research. Traditional psychoanalytic theory is criticized for attempting causal explanations unsuccessfully; hermeneutics is criticized for not attempting causal explanations. Grünbaum (1990) strongly endorses Freud's search for causal explanations, which, in their turn, become the main target of Grünbaum's critique. Eagle (1986) joins Grünbaum in faulting analysts for failing to meet this imposing theoretical goal, "to think clearly and fruitfully about how human behavior can be meaningfully explained" (p. 232). Eagle adds, "The programmatic aim of hermeneuticians seems to be nothing less than to render human behavior exempt from causal accounts and scientific explanation" (p. 231).

The problem with regard to causal explanations is similar to that in relation to inherited biological predispositions. As Peskin (2000) points out, the necessary quest for integration with neighboring sciences leads us "to a reconfrontation with the old ghosts of biological disposition and instincts . . . which still roam, unburied, in the labyrinthine halls of mind for the sound reason that they are not dead" (pp. 230–231). Although these biologic predispositions influence the patient's behavior, they are impossible to delineate at this time, and must be held in abeyance for lack of clinical relevance, though some day they will be important in research into etiology. Medication aside, I know of nothing in natural science that can inform the choice of interventions in a clinical analytic situation.

Psychoanalytic hermeneutics does eschew all causal explanations, not in any attempt to oppose the unity of natural and human sciences (Grünbaum, 1999), and not because there are neither facts nor causes in relation to psychoanalysis, but because they are unascertainable. Eagle (1986) again supports Grünbaum's telling critique of psychoanalysis for failing to be accountable for assessing the efficacy of analytic treatment. Whether analytic treatment is more effective than other forms of treatment can be determined only by scientific testing, but there are daunting, perhaps insurmountable human and methodological difficulties in doing such testing (Edelson, 1986).

No satisfactory controlled study, as called for in principle by Grünbaum and Eagle, of the effectiveness of analytic treatment in comparison to other treatments and to no treatment has ever been conducted. How could persons be assigned randomly to psychoanalytic treatment, to no treatment, and to a placebo, and their participation assured for a number of years? How do you manualize psychoanalytic treatment? In addition, how well can you measure a fantasy, or self-esteem? I agree with Mitchell (1993), Wolff (1998), Wallerstein (1999b), Green (2000b), Mosher (2000), and Sandell and colleagues (2000) that it is not possible to conduct such a controlled study in the foreseeable future. How is a patient to select a therapist if psychoanalysis has not validated its effectiveness? Perhaps in the same way a person would select a portrait painter, or an architect. Although outcome research has been informative, it has been unable to address the fundamental questions that require a truly controlled study. Psychoanalytic research has been fruitful. Indeed, certain questions can be answered only by empirical study. But I believe psychoanalytic research cannot address etiological problems; how well it will elucidate the mutative factors in analytic treatment remains to be seen.

I am not troubled that hermeneutics adopts an ahistorical attitude toward the patient. Grünbaum (2000), himself, proposes a resolution. Theoretically, the person's history can be eliminated "by encapsulating its cumulative effects in a sufficiently complex state-description of the human organism at one time" (p. 341). That is, only those registrations of past experience that are currently accessible, consciously or unconsciously, to the patient are relevant to the current situation; the vast remainder of registrations of the patient's history, since not accessible or available, are irrelevant to the here-and-now situation. Grünbaum's conception is congruent both with Lewin's field theory and with Sandler and Sandler's present unconscious.

Once the analytic practitioner focuses on helping the patient, developing theories of causality of human behavior—though haply such may occur—will manifestly be seen to be of lesser clinical utility. The development of theory, like the search for happiness, may only come to pass as a byproduct. Freud wrote, more elegantly than I can, in a letter to Ferenczi in 1915 (quoted by Gribinski, 1994), "I consider that one should not make theories. They should arrive unexpectedly in your house, like a stranger one hasn't invited" (see Grubrich-Simitis, 1985, p. 113). Samuel Butler (1882) had made the same point: "He did not yet know that the very worst way of getting hold of ideas is to go hunting expressly after them" (p. 193). As Friedman (2000) observes, the effectiveness of analytic treatment "reveals *something* about the nature of the mind" (p. 257).

Analytic practitioners are left with only one pragmatic option at this time, to cobble together what I will designate as "hermeneutics," for want of an alternate term, in which uncertainty colors all attempts to assess treatment effectiveness as well as all attempts to identify the causes of "transference," or of psychopathology. The uncontrolled, idiosyncratic, complex nature of the dyadic situation makes validating causes impossible. The analytic situation can be studied by scientists, but the difficulties inherent in such an effort, including the inability to measure subjectivity, to evaluate the influence of chance, or to assess the role of inherited biological factors in the individual, are likely to limit the fruitfulness of the results.

My impression is that analysts long have helped patients while hypothesizing causes that were not and could not be validated. The patient's reasons and meanings can become causes. What is useful about a hypothesized cause in treatment is not the question of its validity, but how we can understand whether it has a therapeutic impact, or, in Arlow's (1987) terms, "What is important is the dynamic effect of the interpretation" (p. 84). My pragmatic adoption of a hermeneutic framework does not mean that I privilege narrative development among mutative effects.

What is left to guide analytic treatment if the *theory* of "transference" and its associated principles of technique are discarded? I think that many analysts, without explicitly disavowing the theory of "transference," or articulating a rationale, have gradually modified their focus on putative childhood causes in favor of examining patient-analyst interaction in the here and now. It is my impression, however, that this shift is mainly theoretical and only partial, and intermittently they reinvoke childhood experiences and fantasies as the origins of adult characteristics. Such explorations may not only divert the treatment from dealing with emotionally charged patient-analyst interactions in the here and now, but blunt those critical moments.

"Transference" is so integrally connected to etiology that I have proposed an alternate concept, Habitual Relationship Patterns, which eschews any futile search for childhood causes. Habitual Relationship Patterns refers to persistent feelings and fantasies, conscious and unconscious, that shape our customary ways of relating to others. Analytic treatment examines the functions and meanings of those

Patterns and especially the resistances that interfere with changing them to improve the person's ways of relating to others, especially to the analyst.

In examining these patterns, the analyst is guided by what Mitchell has described as the analyst's "self-reflective responsiveness," rather than by a standard theory. Essentially, this is all the analyst can do since the unavoidability of the influences of the analyst's idiosyncratic values and unconscious feelings and fantasies on all interpretations and interactions is recognized. Consistently maintaining the focus on the affective patient-analyst interactions in the here and now, about which the analyst as participant observer is uniquely informed, provides hope of enhancing the efficacy of analytic treatment.

The analyst interacts with the patient as sensitively, as empathically, as humanely as possible, substantially influenced by his or her own unconscious feelings and fantasies, while continually looking back, trying to understand prior interactions—knowing full well that causes can never be identified with certainty. Without establishing verifiable causes, patients are nonetheless helped to modify conscious and unconscious defenses. That is the art of psychoanalytic treatment. That art, like that of other artists, utilizes intuition and creativity, often originating in the accessible unconscious. The analyst, as artist, is as entitled to a fee for his or her services as other artists in our society. Granted, insurance companies are unlikely to reimburse for such services, but that is already largely the case.

Parenthetically, art and aesthetics are not as foreign to science as often they are conceived to be. Stone (2000) observes that "art and beauty have always been about finding the universal in the particular" (p. 51), and that universal is the stuff from which theories emerge.

The pragmatic, hermeneutic "solution" to the epistemological problems of psychoanalysis seems workable, though it is neither elegant nor scientifically satisfying. Neither is life. Lewis (2001), in an obituary for Nobel laureate Herbert A. Simon, describes the latter's view of human decision making as "satisficing," looking for a course of action that is satisfactory or "good enough."

Does discarding the traditional *theory* of "transference" and its integral treatment goals undermine psychoanalysis, or, instead, constitute the beginning of an invigorating paradigm shift? Makari (2000) asserts that "changes in psychoanalytic theory can be read as adaptive ways for psychoanalysis to remain meaningful to a changing culture. . . . for the most part as history moves, it is the dog, and psychoanalytic theory the tail being wagged" (p. 259).

   If the credibility of psychoanalysis rests on its theoretical under-pinning—a theory increasingly acknowledged to be indefensible—abandoning the *theory* of "transference" might seem destructive. To the contrary, I think the credibility of psychoanalysis, both of the individual practitioner and of the profession as a whole, is based on its therapeutic efficacy. Those analysts who have successful, full practices are those skillful at helping patients, not those learned about psychoanalytic theory. Patients, the locus of credibility of psychoanalysis, have little interest in theory; they are concerned about being helped. Although the structure of theory may, as Spence (1994) has noted, reassure some analysts, I assert that nothing can enhance the credibility of psychoanalysis as emphatically as increased therapeutic efficacy.

   Mosher (2001, personal communication), who read an earlier version of this "Conclusion," found its implications were quite frightening: "It becomes more and more difficult to say what psychoanalysis is about. . . . What is left of psychoanalysis other than a bunch of opinions about what is helpful from a disparate group of literate individuals?" But that is exactly where the current analytic treatment situation is. And that, I argue, represents a positive development in psychoanalysis. Limitations of knowledge require us to acknowledge that no extant, standard psychological theory uniformly applied to all patients is likely to be optimally helpful. Psychoanalysis is acknowledging that treatment is an art, best approached idiosyncratically.

   Despite the fact that psychoanalysis cannot claim any specific distinguishing therapeutic effects, it can claim to employ a distinguishing technique, namely, the intensive examination of conscious and unconscious feelings and fantasies of *both* patient and analyst that underlie their Habitual Relationship Patterns. I know of no other approach that utilizes such a technique. That technique, I propose, not the theory of "transference," is the current shibboleth of psychoanalysis.

   No single quotation can epitomize a person as multifaceted as Freud. One commentary by Stoppard, although not referring to Freud, I thought was remarkably apropos of one aspect of Freud:

> He trusts to his felicity of instinct. When that fails him, no one
> can defend more stubbornly a plain corruption, or advocate more
> confidently an incredible conjecture, and to these defects he
> adds a calamitous propensity to reckless assertion [1997, p. 34].

   Nonetheless, Freud was one of the towering geniuses of the twentieth century. Kardiner (1977) epitomized his accomplishments: Freud created a new conception of human nature by delineating the intrapsychic, complex, dynamic unconscious forces in the human mind. Macalpine (1973) adds: "Today it is as impossible to think of psychiatry without the dynamic unconscious as it is to think of medicine without the circulation of blood" (p. 137).

In closing I quote two verses from Auden's (1967) poem, "In Memory of Sigmund Freud." The last phrase has become a commonplace, but the lines that precede it also deserve our attention and assent.

> *If some traces of the autocratic pose,*
> *The paternal strictness he distrusted, still*
> > *Clung to his utterances and features,*
> *It was a protective coloration*
>
> *For one who'd lived among enemies so long:*
> *If often he was wrong and, at times absurd,*
> > *To us he is no more a person*
> *Now but a whole climate of opinion.*

From the heady vantage point of Freud's contributions, we have the challenging opportunity to apply the understanding Freud provided us of the dynamic mechanisms of the unconscious mind to enhance our capability to treat and help emotionally troubled persons. This goal, more modest than the one Freud chose, enhances rather than constrains the psychoanalytic enterprise. In Stephen J. Gould's (2000) words, "The deflation of hubris is blessedly positive, not cynically disabling" (p. A15). It is we who determine how surprising and exciting the development of psychoanalysis proves to be.

REFERENCES

Abend, S. M. (1993). An inquiry into the fate of the transference in psycho-analysis. *J. Amer. Psychoanal. Assn.*, 41:627–651.

Adler, N. E., Boyce, T., Chesney, M. A., Cohen, S., Folkman, S., Kahn, R. L. & Syme, L. (1994). Socioeconomic status and health. *Amer. Psychol.*, 49:15–24.

Akhtar, S. (2000). From schisms through synthesis to informed oscillation: An attempt at integrating some diverse aspects of psychoanalytic technique. *Psychoanal. Quart.*, 59:265–288.

Alexander, F. (1956). Two forms of regression and their therapeutic implications. *Psychoanal. Quart.*, 25:178–196.

Allport, G. W. (1937). *Pattern and Growth in Personality*. New York: Holt, Rinehart & Winston, 1961.

Andersson, O. (1979). A supplement to Freud's case history of "Frau Emmy v. N." in *Studies on Hysteria* (1895). *Scand. Psychoanal. Rev.*, 2:5–16.

Anzieu, D. (1986). *Freud's Self-Analysis*, ed. S. C. B. Yorke (trans. P. Graham). London: Hogarth Press.

Arlow, J. (1969). Unconscious fantasy and disturbances of conscious experience. *Psychoanal. Quart.*, 35:1–27.

——— (1987). Perspectives on Freud's "Analysis Terminable and Interminable." In: *On Freud's "Analysis Terminable and Interminable,"* ed. J. Sandler. International Psychoanalytical Association Educational Monographs, pp. 73–88.

——— (1981). Theories of pathogenesis. In: *Psychoanalysis: Clinical Theory and Practice*. Madison, CT: International Universities Press, pp. 327–346.

——— (1995). The concept of psychic reality—how useful? Presented August 1 at 39th Congress of the International Psychoanalytic Association, San Francisco, CA.

——— (1998). Analysts at work with patients whose lives are characterized by the traumas of everyday life. Symposium of the Journals of the CD ROM, February 28–March 1, New York.

——— & Brenner, C. (1964). *Psychoanalytic Concepts and the Structural Theory*. Madison, CT: International Universities Press.

Aron, L. (1999). Clinical choices and the relational matrix. *Psychoanal. Dial.*, 9:1–29.

Auden, W. H. (1967). *Collected Shorter Poems, 1927–1957.* New York: Random House.

Bachrach, H. M., Galatzer-Levy, R., Skolnikoff, A. Z. & Waldron, S., Jr. (1991). On the efficacy of psychoanalysis. *J. Amer. Psychoanal. Assn.*, 39:871–916.

Bachant, J. & Richards, A. (1993). Review essay of S. Mitchell's *Relational Concepts in Psychoanalysis. Psychoanal. Dial.*, 3:431–460.

———— & Adler, E. (1998). Transference: Co-constructed or brought to the interaction? *J. Amer. Psychoanal. Assn.*, 45:1097–1120.

Balaban, E. (1998). Exploring the Innate. Psychoanalysis, Neurobiology and Therapeutic Change. A Conference in Celebration of the 65th Anniversary of The Institute for Psychoanalysis. Chicago, March 21.

Baranger, M., Baranger, W. & Mom, J. (1983). Process and nonprocess in analytic work. *Internat. J. Psychoanal.*, 64:1–15.

Barratt, B. B. (1996). Commentary on the irrelevance of infant observations for psychoanalysis. *J. Amer. Psychoanal. Assn.*, 44:396–404.

Bauer, G. P. (1993). *Analysis of the Transference in the Here and Now.* Northvale, NJ: Aronson.

Belsky, J. (1999). Interactional and contextual determinants of attachment security. In: *Handbook of Attachment: Theory, Research, and Clinical Applications*, ed. J. Cassidy & P. R. Shaver. New York: Guilford Press, pp. 249–264.

Bergmann, M. S. (1988). On the fate of the intrapsychic image of the psychoanalyst after termination of the analysis. *The Psychoanalytic Study of the Child*, 43:137–153. New Haven, CT: Yale University Press.

———— (1997). The historical roots of psychoanalytic orthodoxy. *Internat. J. Psychoanal.*, 78:69–86.

Bird, B. (1972). Notes on transference: Universal phenomenon and hardest part of analysis. *J. Amer. Psychoanal. Assn.*, 20:267–301.

Block, J. (1993). Studying personality the long way. In: *Studying Lives Through Time: Personality and Development*, ed. D. C. Funder, R. D. Parke, C. Tomlinson-Keasey & K. Widaman. Washington, DC: American Psychological Association.

Blum, H. P. (1996). Seduction trauma: Representation, deferred action, and pathogenic development. *J. Amer. Psychoanal. Assn.*, 44:1147–1164.

———— (1999). The reconstruction of reminiscence. *J. Amer. Psychoanal. Assn.*, 47:1125–1135.

Böhm, T. (1999). The difficult freedom from a plan. *Internat. J. Psychoanal.*, 80:493–505.

———— (1988). *A Secure Base.* New York: Basic Books.

Bollas, C. (1989). *Forces of Destiny: Psychoanalysis and Human Idiom.* London: Free Association Books.

Bonaparte, M., Freud, A. & Kris, E. (1954). *The Origins of Psychoanalysis: Letters to Wilhelm Fliess, Drafts and Notes, 1887–1902*. New York: Basic Books.

Boswell, J. (1980). *Christianity, Social Tolerance, and Homosexuality: Gay People in Western Europe from the Beginning of the Christian Era to the Fourteenth Century*. Chicago: University of Chicago Press.

Bowlby, J. (1969). *Attachment and Loss: Vol. 1*. London: Hogarth Press.

——— (1973). *Attachment and Loss: Vol. 2*. London: Hogarth Press.

——— (1980). *Attachment and Loss: Vol. 3*. New York: Basic Books.

——— (1988a). *A Secure Base*. New York: Basic Books.

——— (1988b). Developmental psychiatry comes of age. *Amer. J. Psychiat.*, 145:1–10.

Brenner, C. (1991). A psychoanalytic perspective on depression. *J. Amer. Psychoanal. Assn.*, 39:25–43.

——— (1994). The mind as conflict and compromise formation. *J. Clin. Psychoanal.*, 3:473–488.

——— (1996). The nature of knowledge and the limits of authority in psychoanalysis. *Psychoanal. Quart.*, 65:21–31.

——— (1998). Beyond the ego and the id revisited. *J. Clin. Psychoanal.*, 7:165–180.

Breuer, J. & Freud, S. (1893–1895). Studies on hysteria. *Standard Edition*, 2. London: Hogarth Press, 1955.

Brickman, H. R. (2000). Revisiting Freud's "Bedrock": Evolution and the neurobiological turn in psychoanalysis. Presented at the Meeting of the American Psychoanalytic Association, New York, December 15.

Briere, J. (1984). The long-term effects of childhood sexual abuse: Defining a post-sexual syndrome. Paper presented at the Third National Conference on Sexual Victimization of Children, Washington, DC.

Britton, R. & Steiner, J. (1994). Interpretation: Selected factor or overvalued idea? *Internat. J. Psychoanal.*, 75:1069–1078.

Bromberg, P. M. (1994). "Speak! That I may see you": Some reflections on dissociation, reality, and psychoanalytic listening. *Psychoanal. Dial.*, 4:517–548.

Bronstein, H. (1998). Time-schemes, order and chaos: Periodization and ideology. In: *Time, Order, Chaos: The Study of Time IX*, ed. J. T. Fraser, M. P. Soulsky & A. J. Argyros. Madison, CT: International Universities Press, pp. 33–49.

Brooks Brenneis, C. (1999). The analytic present in psychoanalytic reconstructions of the historical past. *J. Amer. Psychoanal. Assn.*, 47:187–201.

Brown, R. (2001). Characters' weaknesses build fiction's strengths. *The New York Times*, January 1, pp. B1,B2.

Browne, A. & Finkelhor, D. (1986). Impact of child sexual abuse: A review of the research. *Psychol. Bull.*, 99:66–77.

Buckley, P. (1989). Fifty years after Freud: Dora, the Rat Man, and the Wolf Man. *Amer. J. Psychiat.*, 146:1394–1403.

Bukerton, D., Hall, R. & Williams, A. L. (1991). Women's experience of sexual abuse in childhood. *Public Health*, 105:447–453.

Butler, S. (1882). *The Way of All Flesh*. Roslyn, NY: Walter J. Black.

Buxbaum, E. (1950). Technique of terminating analysis. *Internat. J. Psychoanal.*, 31:184–190.

Calkins, S. D. & Fox, N. A. (1992). The relations among infant temperament, security of attachment, and behavioral inhibition at twenty-four months. *Child Develop.*, 63:1456–1472.

Campbell, R. (1999). On blubbering. *The New York Times Book Review*, September 12, pp. 13, 14.

Canestri, J. (1994). Transformations. *Internat. J. Psychoanal.*, 75:1079–1092.

Carter, K. C. (1980). Germ theory, hysteria and Freud's early work on psychopathology. *Med. History*, 24:259–274.

Caspi, A. (2000). The child is father of the man: Personality continuities from childhood to adulthood. *J. Personality & Soc. Psychol.*, 78:158–172.

Cassidy, J. (1999). The nature of the child's ties. In: *Handbook of Attachment: Theory, Research, and Clinical Applications*, ed. J. Cassidy & P. R. Shaver. New York: Guilford Press, pp. 3–20.

———— (2000). Attachment patterns across the life span. Presentation to the Pittsburgh Psychoanalytic Society and Institute, April 8, Pittsburgh, PA.

Caston, J. & Martin, E. (1993). Can analysts agree? The problems of consensus and the psychoanalytic mannequin, II: Empirical tests. *J. Amer. Psychoanal. Assn.*, 41:513–548.

Chess, S. & Thomas, A. (1990). The New York Longitudinal Study: The young adult periods. *Canad. J. Psychiat.*, 35:557–561.

Chodorow, N. J. (1996). Reflections on the authority of the past in psychoanalytic thinking. *Psychoanal. Quart.*, 65:32–51.

Chu, J. A. & Dill, D. L. (1990). Dissociative symptoms in relation to childhood physical and sexual abuse. *Amer. J. Psychiat.*, 149:887–892.

Cioffi, F. (1986). Did Freud rely on the tally argument to meet the argument from suggestibility? Commentary/Grünbaum: *Foundations of Psychoanalysis. Behavioral & Brain Sci.*, 9:230–231.

Coen, S. J. (1994). Barriers to love between patient and analyst. *J. Amer. Psychoanal. Assn.*, 42:1107–1135.

Cohler, B. J. & Galatzer-Levy, R. M. (2000). *The Course of Gay and Lesbian Lives: Social and Psychoanalytic Perspectives*. Chicago: University of Chicago Press.

Cooper, A. M. (1987). Changes in psychoanalytic ideas: Transference interpretation. *J. Amer. Psychoanal. Assn.*, 35:77–98.

———— (1994). Formulations to the patient: Explicit and implicit. *Internat. J. Psychoanal.*, 75:1107–1120.

———— (1999). Psychoanalytic technique: Diversity or chaos? Commentary on paper by L. Aron. *Psychoanal. Dial.*, 9:31–39.

Craige, H. (in press). Mourning analysis: The post-termination phase. *J. Amer. Psychoanal. Assn.*

Crews, F. (2000). Letter to the Editor regarding Daniel Mendelsohn's review of Israel Rosenfeld's novel *Freud's Megalomania*. *The New York Review of Books*, 47(20):100–101.

Crittenden, P. M. (1995). Attachment and psychopathology. In: *Attachment Theory: Social, Developmental, and Clinical Perspectives*, ed. S. Goldberg, R. Muir, & J. Kerr. Hillsdale, NJ: The Analytic Press, pp. 367–406.

Davies, J. (1998). Analysts at work with severely traumatized patients. Symposium of the Journals of the CD ROM. February 28–March 1, New York.

——— & Frawley, M. G. (1991). Dissociative processes and transference-countertransference paradigms in the psychoanalytically oriented treatment of adult survivors of childhood sexual abuse. *Psychoanal. Dial.*, 2:5–36.

DeBellis, M. (2000). Developmental traumatology: Biological stress systems and brain development in maltreated children with posttraumatic stress disorder. Holiday Inn Select, University Center, 100 Lytton Avenue, Pittsburgh, March 31.

Dennett, D. (1991). *Consciousness Explained*. Boston: Little, Brown.

Deutsch, M. (1954). Field theory in social psychology. In: *Handbook of Social Psychology, Vol. 1: Theory and Method*. Cambridge, MA: Addison-Wesley.

DeWitt, K. N., Kaltreider, N., Weiss, D. S. & Horowitz, M. J. (1983). Judging change in psychotherapy: Reliability of clinical formulations. *Arch. Gen. Psychiat.*, 40:1121–1128.

De Wolff, M. & van IJzendoorn, M. H. (1997). Sensitivity and attachment: A meta-analysis on parental antecedents of infant attachment. *Child Development*, 68:571–591.

Doidge, N., Simon, B., Gillies, L. A. & Ruskin, R. (1994). Characteristics of psychoanalytic patients under a nationalized health plan: DSM-III-R diagnoses, previous treatment, and childhood trauma. *Amer. J. Psychiat.*, 151:586–590.

Dorpat, T. L. & Miller, M. L. (1992). *Clinical Interaction and the Analysis of Meaning: A New Psychoanalytic Theory*. Hillsdale, NJ: The Analytic Press.

Downey, J. I. & Friedman, R. C. (1995). Biology and the Oedipus complex. *Psychoanal. Quart.*, 64:234–264.

Dozier, M., Stovall, K. C. & Albus, K. E. (1999). Attachment and psychopathology in adulthood. In: *Handbook of Attachment: Theory, Research, and Clinical Applications*, ed. J. Cassidy & P. R. Shaver. New York: Guilford Press, pp. 497–519.

Duck, S. (1983). *Friends for Life: The Psychology of Close Relationships*. New York: St. Martin's Press.

Dupont, J. (1994). Freud's analysis of Ferenczi as revealed by their correspondence. *Internat. J. Psychoanal.*, 75:301–320.

Eagle, M. N. (1986). Psychoanalysis as hermeneutics. Commentary/Grünbaum: *Foundations of Psychoanalysis. Behavioral & Brain Sci.*, 9:231–232.

—— (1993). The dynamics of theory change in psychoanalysis. In: *Philosophical Problems of the Internal and External Worlds: Essays on the Philosophy of Adolph Grünbaum*, ed. J. Earman, A. Janis, G. Massey & N. Rescher. Pittsburgh: University of Pittsburgh Press.

—— (1995). The developmental perspectives of attachment and psychoanalytic theory. In *Attachment Theory: Social, Developmental, and Clinical Perspectives*, ed. S. Goldberg, R. Muir & J. Kerr. Hillsdale, NJ: The Analytic Press.

Earman, J. (1986). *A Primer on Determinism*. Dordrecht: D. Reidel.

Eddington, A. S. (1958). *The Nature of the Physical World*. Ann Arbor: University of Michigan Press.

Edelman, G. (1989). *The Remembered Present: A Biological Theory of Consciousness*. New York: Basic Books.

—— (1992). *Bright Air, Brilliant Fire*. New York: Basic Books.

Edelson, M. (1986). Psychoanalysis as hermeneutics. Commentary/Grünbaum: *Foundations of Psychoanalysis. Behavioral & Brain Sci.*, 9:232–234.

Eells, T. D. (1997). Book Review: *The Symptom-Context Method: Opportunities in Psychotherapy* by L. Luborsky. Washington, DC: American Psychological Association.

Ehrenberg, D. (1992). *The Intimate Edge*. New York: Norton.

Eliot, G. (1860). *The Mill on the Floss*. Boston: Houghton Mifflin, 1961.

Ellenberger, H. (1972). The story of "Anna O.": A critical review with new data. *J. Hist. Behav. Sci.*, 8:267–279.

Emde, R. (1981). Changing models of infancy and the nature of early development: Remodeling the foundation. *J. Amer. Psychoanal. Assn.*, 29:179–220.

—— (1988). Development terminable and interminable. I. Innate and motivational factors from infancy. *Internat. J. Psychoanal.*, 69:23–42.

Erikson, E. H. (1954). The dream specimen in psychoanalysis. *J. Amer. Psychoanal. Assn.*, 2:5–56.

—— (1956). The problem of ego identity. *J. Amer. Psychoanal. Assn.*, 4:56–121.

—— (1959). Identity and the life cycle. *Psychol. Issues*, 1:1–171.

—— (1968). *Identity: Youth and Crisis*. New York: Norton.

—— (1980). Themes of adulthood in the Freud-Jung correspondence. In: *Themes of Work and Love in Adulthood*, ed. N. J. Smelser & E. H. Erikson. Cambridge: Harvard University Press, pp. 43–74.

Erle, J. B. (1979). An approach to the study of analyzability and analysis: The course of forty consecutive cases selected for supervised analysis. *Psychoanal. Quart.*, 48:198–228.

—— & Goldberg, D. (1979). Problems in the assessment of analyzability. *Psychoanal. Quart.*, 48:48–84.

—— & —— (1984). Observations on the assessment of analyzability by experienced analysts. *J. Amer. Psychoanal. Assn.*, 32:715–737.

Esterson, A. (1999). "Getting in on the act": The hysterical solution. Letters to the editor. *Internat. J. Psychoanal.*, 80:1237–1239.

——— (2000a). "Freud under analysis": An exchange. *The New York Review of Books*, 47(3):47.

Fairbairn, W. R. D. (1944). Endopsychic structure considered in terms of object-relationships. In: *Psychoanalytic Studies of the Personality*. London: Routledge & Kegan Paul, 1952, pp. 82–136.

Fairfield, S. (2001). Analyzing multiplicity: A postmodern perspective on some current psychoanalytic theories of subjectivity. *Psychoanal. Dial.*, 11:221–251.

Fehr, B. A. (1996). *Friendship Processes*. Thousand Oaks, CA: Sage.

Ferenczi, S. & Rank, O. (1923). *The Development of Psychoanalysis*, trans. C. Newton. Madison, CT: International Universities Press.

Feynman, R. P. (1986). *"Surely You're Joking, Mr. Feynman!" Adventures of a Curious Character*. New York: Bantam.

Fischer-Homberger, E. (1975). *Die Traumatische Neurose: Vom Somatischen Zum Sozialen Leiden*. Berne: Hiber.

Fisher, S. & Greenberg, R. P. (1996). *Freud Scientifically Appraised: Testing the Theories and Therapy*. New York: Wiley.

Fleming, J. (1972). Early object deprivation and transference phenomena. *Psychoanal. Quart.*, 41:23–49.

Fogel, G. I. (1993). A transitional phase in our understanding of the psychoanalytic process: A new look at Ferenczi and Rank. *J. Amer. Psychoanal. Assn.*, 41:585–602.

Fonagy, P. (1998). Analysts at work with severely traumatized patients. Symposium of the Journals of the CD ROM, February 28–March 1, New York.

——— (1999a). Points of contact and divergence between psychoanalytic and attachment theories: Is psychoanalytic theory truly different? *Psychoanal. Inq.*, 19:448–480.

——— (1999b). Memory and the therapeutic action of psychoanalysis. *Internat. J. Psychoanal.*, 80:215–223.

——— (2000). Response to P. Mollon's letter. *Internat. J. Psychoanal.*, 81:169.

——— Leigh, T., Steele, M. Kennedy, R., Mattoon, G., Target, M. & Gerber, A. (1996). The relation of attachment status, psychiatric classification, and response to psychotherapy. *J. Consult. & Clin. Psychol.*, 64:22–31.

Fosshage, J. L. (1994). Toward reconceptualizing transference: Theoretical and clinical considerations. *Internat. J. Psychoanal.*, 75:3–17.

Fraser, J. T. (1998). From chaos to conflict. In *Time, Order, Chaos: The Study of Time IX*, ed. J. T. Fraser, M. P. Soulsby & A. J. Argyros. Madison, CT: International Universities Press.

Freud, A. (1936). *The Ego and the Mechanisms of Defense*. New York: International Universities Press.

——— (1954) The widening scope of indications for psychoanalysis: Discussion. *J. Amer. Psychoanal. Assn.*, 2:607–620.

Freud, S. (1891). *On Aphasia: A Critical Study.* New York: International Universities Press, 1953.

——— (1895a). Obsessions and phobias: Their psychical mechanism and their etiology. *Standard Edition,* 3:74–84. London: Hogarth Press, 1962.

——— (1895b). A reply to criticisms of my paper on anxiety neurosis. *Standard Edition,* 3:123–139. London: Hogarth Press, 1962.

——— (1896a). Heredity and the aetiology of the neuroses. *Standard Edition* 3:141–156. London: Hogarth Press, 1962.

——— (1896b). The aetiology of hysteria. *Standard Edition,* 3:191–221. London: Hogarth Press, 1962.

——— (1896c). Extracts from the Fliess papers. *Standard Edition,* 1:177–239. London: Hogarth Press, 1966.

——— (1896c). Letter to Fliess, December 6. *Standard Edition,* 1:233–239. London: Hogarth Press, 1950.

——— (1896d). Further remarks on the neuropsychoses of defense. *Standard Edition,* 3:162–185. London: Hogarth Press, 1962.

——— (1899). Screen memories. *Standard Edition,* 3:303–322. London: Hogarth Press, 1962.

——— (1900). The interpretation of dreams. *Standard Edition,* 5:339–625. London: Hogarth Press, 1953.

——— (1904). Freud's psychoanalytic procedure. *Standard Edition,* 7: London: Hogarth Press, 1953.

——— (1905). Fragment of an analysis of a case of hysteria. *Standard Edition,* 7:7–122. London: Hogarth Press, 1953.

——— (1910a). Five lectures on psychoanalysis. Fourth lecture. *Standard Edition,* 11:9–55. London: Hogarth Press, 1957.

——— (1910b). Five lectures on psychoanalysis. Fifth lecture. *Standard Edition,* 11:9–55. London: Hogarth Press, 1957.

——— (1910c). The future prospects of psycho-analytic therapy. *Standard Edition,* 11:139–151. London: Hogarth Press, 1957.

——— (1911). Formulations on the two principles of mental functioning. *Standard Edition,* 12:218–226. London: Hogarth Press, 1958.

——— (1912a). The dynamics of transference. *Standard Edition,* 12:97–108. London: Hogarth Press, 1958.

——— (1912b). Recommendations to physicians practicing psychoanalysis. *Standard Edition,* 12:109–120. London: Hogarth Press, 1958.

——— (1913a). On beginning the treatment (Further recommendations on the technique of psychoanalysis: I). *Standard Edition,* 12:121–144. London: Hogarth Press, 1958.

——— (1913b). Totem and taboo. *Standard Edition,* 13:1–161. London: Hogarth Press, 1955.

——— (1914a). On the history of the psychoanalytic movement. *Standard Edition,* 14:7–66. London: Hogarth Press, 1957.

——— (1914b). On narcissism: An introduction. *Standard Edition,* 14:73–102. London: Hogarth Press, 1957.

————— (1914c). Remembering, repeating and working through (Further recommendations on the technique of psychoanalysis: II). *Standard Edition*, 12:145–156. London: Hogarth Press, 1958.

————— (1915a). Observations on transference-love (Further recommendations on the technique of psychoanalysis: III). *Standard Edition*, 12:157–171. London: Hogarth Press, 1958.

————— (1915b). *A Phylogenetic Fantasy: Overview of the Transference Neuroses*, ed. I. Grubrich-Simitis (trans. A. Hoffer & P. T. Hoffer). Cambridge, MA: Harvard University Press, 1987.

————— (1917). Introductory lectures on psychoanalysis. *Standard Edition*, 16:243–463. London: Hogarth Press, 1963.

————— (1918). From the history of an infantile neurosis. *Standard Edition*, 17:7–122. London: Hogarth Press, 1955.

————— (1920a). Beyond the pleasure principle. *Standard Edition*, 18:7–64. London: Hogarth Press, 1955.

————— (1920b). The psychogenesis of a case of homosexuality in a woman. *Standard Edition*, 18:145–172. London: Hogarth Press, 1955.

————— (1922). The libido theory. *Standard Edition*, 18:255–25. London: Hogarth Press, 1955.

————— (1925 [1924]). An autobiographical study. *Standard Edition*, 20:7–74. London: Hogarth Press, 1959.

————— (1926a). The question of lay analysis. *Standard Edition*, 20:183–258. London: Hogarth Press, 1959.

————— (1926b [1925]). Psychoanalysis. *Standard Edition*, 20:263–270. London: Hogarth Press, 1959.

————— (1926c [1925]). Inhibitions, symptoms and anxiety. *Standard Edition*, 20:87–175. London: Hogarth Press, 1959.

————— (1930 [1929]). Civilization and its discontents. *Standard Edition*, 21:64–145. London: Hogarth Press, 1961.

————— (1937a). Constructions in analysis. *Standard Edition*, 23:255–269. London: Hogarth Press, 1964.

————— (1937b). Analysis terminable and interminable. *Standard Edition*, 23:216–253. London: Hogarth Press, 1964.

————— (1939 [1934–1938]). Moses and monotheism: Three essays. *Standard Edition*, 23:7–137. London: Hogarth Press, 1964.

————— (1940 [1938]). An outline of psychoanalysis. *Standard Edition*, 23:144–207. London: Hogarth Press, 1964.

————— (1941 [1938]). Findings, ideas, problems. *Standard Edition*, 23:299–300. London: Hogarth Press, 1964.

Friedman, L. (1996). Overview: Knowledge and authority in the psychoanalytic relationship. *Psychoanal. Quart.*, 65:254–265.

————— (1999). Book review of I. Z. Hoffman's *Ritual and Spontaneity in the Psychoanalytic Process. J. Amer. Psychoanal. Assn.*, 47:891–898.

————— (2000). Modern hermeneutics and psychoanalysis. *Psychoanal. Quart.*, 69:225–264.

Friedman, R. C. & Downey, J. I. (1995). Biology and the Oedipus complex. *Psychoanal. Quart.*, 64:234–264.

Fromm, E. (1941). *Escape from Freedom*. New York: Rhinehart.

Gabbard, G. O. (1994). Sexual excitement and countertransference love in the analyst. *J. Amer. Psychoanal. Assn.*, 42:1083–1106.

—— (1997). Discussion. *Psychoanal. Inq.*, 17:371–386.

—— (1998). Discussion of papers by L. Hoffman, J. Davies, P. Fonagy and L. Shengold. Symposium of the Journals of the CD ROM, February 28–March 1, New York.

—— & Lester, E. P. (1995). *Boundaries and Boundary Violations in Psychoanalysis*. New York: Basic Books.

Ganzarin, R. (1991). Extraanalytic contacts: Fantasy and reality. *Internat. J. Psychoanal.*, 72:131–140.

Gay, P. (2000). Against postmodernism. In: *Changing Ideas in a Changing World: The Revolution in Psychoanalysis. Essays in Honour of Arnold Cooper*, ed. J. Sandler, R. Michels & P. Fonagy. London: Karnac, pp. 247–254.

Gedo, J. (1999). *The Evolution of Psychoanalysis: Contemporary Theory and Practice*. New York: Other Press.

—— & Goldberg, A. (1973). *Models of the Mind*. Chicago: University of Chicago Press.

Geller, J. & Farber, B. A. (1993). Factors influencing the process of internalization in psychotherapy. *Psychother. Res.*, 3:166–180.

Gerson, M. (1993). Sullivan's self-in-development. Family context and patterning. *Contemp. Psychoanal.*, 29:197–218.

Gill, M. (1982). *Analysis of Transference, Vol. 1: Theory and Technique. Psychological Issues, Monogr. 53*. New York: International Universities Press.

—— (1991). Indirect suggestion: A response to Oremland's *Interpretation and Interaction*. In: *Interpretation and Interaction: Psychoanalysis or Psychotherapy?* by J. D. Oremland. Hillsdale, NJ: The Analytic Press, pp. 137–163.

—— (1993). One-person and two-person perspectives: Freud's *Observations on Transference-Love*. In: *On Freud's Observations on Transference-Love*, ed. E. S. Person, A. Hagelin & P. Fonagy for the International Psychoanalytical Association. New Haven, CT: Yale University Press, pp. 114–129.

—— (1994). *Psychoanalysis in Transition: A Personal View*. Hillsdale, NJ: The Analytic Press.

—— & Hoffman, I. Z. (1982). A method for studying the analysis of aspects of the patient's experience of the relationship in psychoanalysis and psychotherapy. *J. Amer. Psychoanal. Assn.*, 30:137–167.

Glenn, J. (1986). Freud, Dora, and the maid: A study of countertransference. *J. Amer. Psychoanal. Assn.*, 34:591–606.

Glover, E. (1937). The theory of the therapeutic results of psychoanalysis. Symposium. *Internat. J. Psychoanal.*, 18:125–132.

—— (1955). *The Technique of Psychoanalysis.* New York: International Universities Press, 1958.

Goldberg, A. (1997) Plenary Address, New York, December 19, American Psychoanalytic Association.

Goode, E. (1999). Mozart for baby? Some say maybe not. *The New York Times*, August 3, p. D1.

Gould, S. J. (1997). Reply to S. Pinker. *The New York Review of Books*, 44:56–58.

—— (2000). The human nature of science. Case Western Reserve University, March 25.

—— (2001). Humbled by the genome's mysteries. Op-ed, *The New York Times*, February 19, p. A15.

Green, A. (2000a). What kind of research for psychoanalysis? In: *Clinical and Observational Research: Roots of a Controversy. Psychoanalytic Monographs, no. 5*, ed. J. Sandler, A.-M. Sandler & R. Davies. London: Karnac Books, pp. 21–26.

—— (2000b). Response to Robert S. Wallerstein. In: *Clinical and Observational Research: Roots of a Controversy. Psychoanalytic Monographs, no. 5*, ed. J. Sandler, A.-M. Sandler & R. Davies. London: Karnac Books, pp. 32–37.

—— (2000c). Science and science fiction in infant research. In: *Clinical and Observational Research: Roots of a Controversy. Psychoanalytic Monographs, no. 5*, ed. J. Sandler, A.-M. Sandler & R. Davies. London: Karnac Books, pp. 41–72.

Greenberg, J. (1996). Psychoanalytic interaction. *Psychoanal. Inq.*, 16:25–38.

—— (1997). Analytic authority and analytic restraint. Presented at meeting of the Division of Psychoanalysis (39), American Psychological Association, Denver, CO.

Greenson, R. R. (1967). *The Technique and Practice of Psychoanalysis, Vol. 1.* New York: International Universities Press.

Greenspan, S. (1997). *The Growth of the Mind and the Endangered Origins of Intelligence.* Reading, MA: Addison-Wesley.

Gribinski, M. (1994). The stranger in the house. *Internat. J. Psychoanal.*, 75:1011–1021.

Grubrich-Simitis, I. (1985). Métapsychologie et métabiologie. In: S. Freud (1915), "Vue d'ensemble des névroses de transfert." Paris: Gallimard, 1986.

—— (1986). Six letters of Sigmund Freud and Sándor Ferenczi on the inter-relationship of psychoanalytic theory and technique. *Internat. Rev. Psychoanal.*, 13:259–277.

Grünbaum, A. (1990). "Meaning" connections and causal connections in the human sciences: The poverty of hermeneutic philosophy. *J. Amer. Psychoanal. Assn.*, 38:559–577.

—— (1993). *Validation of the Clinical Theory of Psychoanalysis: A Study in the Philosophy of Psychoanalysis. Psychological Issues,* Monograph 61. Madison, CT: International Universities Press.

——— (1997) One hundred years of psychoanalytic theory and therapy: Retrospect and prospect. In: *Mindscapes: Philosophy, Science, and the Mind,* ed. M. Carrier & P. Machamer. Pittsburgh: University of Pittsburgh Press.

——— (1999). The hermeneutic versus the scientific conception of psychoanalysis: An unsuccessful effort to chart a *via media* for the human sciences. In: *The White Book of "Einstein Meets Magritte,"* ed. D. Aerts et al. Dordrecht: Kluwer, pp. 219–239.

——— (2000). Reply to symposium on the Grünbaum debate. *Psychoanal. Dial.,* 10:335–342.

Hamburg, D. A., Bibring, G., Fisher, C., Stanton, A., Wallerstein, R., Weinstock, H. & Haggard, E. (1967). Report of ad hoc committee on central fact-gathering data of the American Psychoanalytic Association. *J. Amer. Psychoanal. Assn.,* 15:841–861.

Hartmann, H. (1939). *Ego Psychology and the Problem of Adaptation,* trans. D. Rapaport. New York: International Universities Press, 1958, pp. 114–129.

——— (1964). *Essays on Ego Psychology: Selected Problems in Psychoanalytic Theory.* New York: International Universities Press.

Heimann, P. (1950). On counter-transference. *Internat. J. Psychoanal.,* 31:81–84.

Hellhammer, D. H. & Wade, S. (1993). Endocrine correlates of stress vulnerability. *Psychother. Psychosom.,* 60:8–17.

Hesse, E. & Main, M. (1999). Second-generation effects of unresolved trauma in nonmaltreating parents: Dissociated, frightened and threatening parental behavior. *Psychoanal. Inq.,* 19:481–540.

Hewitt, J. K., Stunkard, A. J., Carroll, D. & Turner, J. R. (1991). A twin study approach towards understanding genetic contributions to body size and metabolic rate. *Acta Geneticae Medicae et Gemellologiae: Twin Research,* 40:13–146.

Hilts, P. J. (1997). Listening to the conversation of neurons. *The New York Times,* May 27, Science, pp. B7, B9.

Hinshelwood, R. D. (1999). Countertransference. *Internat. J. Psychoanal.,* 80:797–818.

Hirsch, E. (1967). *Validity in Interpretation.* New Haven, CT: Yale University Press.

Hirschmüller, A. (1989). *The Life and Work of Josef Breuer.* New York: New York University Press.

Hoffman, I. Z. (1991). Discussion: Toward a social-constructivist view of the psychoanalytic situation. *Psychoanal. Dial.,* 1:74–105.

——— (1996). The intimate and ironic authority of the psychoanalyst's presence. *Psychoanal. Quart.,* 65:102–136.

——— (1999). Responses to Book Reviews by J. Benjamin, L. Friedman & L. A. Sass. *J. Amer. Psychoanal. Assn.,* 47:907–920.

Holinger, P. C. (1989). A developmental perspective on psychotherapy and psychoanalysis. *Amer. J. Psychiat.*, 146:1404–1412.

Holt, R. R. (1986). Some reflections on testing psychoanalytic hypotheses. Commentary/Grünbaum: *Foundations of Psychoanalysis. Behavioral and Brain Sciences*, 9:242–244.

———— (1989). The current status of psychoanalytic theory. In: *Freud Reappraised: A Fresh Look at Psychoanalytic Theory.* New York: Guilford.

Horney, K. (1939). *New Ways in Psychoanalysis.* New York: Norton.

Horowitz, M. J. (1995). Defensive control of states and person schemas. In: *Research in Psychoanalysis: Process, Development, Outcome*, ed. T. Shapiro & R. N. Emde. Madison, CT: International Universities Press, pp. 67–89.

Inderbitzin, L. B. & Levy, S. T. (2000). Regression and psychoanalytic technique: The concretization of a concept. *Psychoanal. Quart.*, 49:195–223.

Jackson, D. D. & Haley, J. (1963). Transference revisited. *J. Nervous & Mental Diseases*, 137:363–371.

Jacobs, T. J. (1995). In search of the mind of the analyst: Progress report. Plenary Address, Annual Meeting of the American Psychoanalytic Association, December 15, New York.

Janet, P. (1907). *The Major Symptoms of Hysteria.* New York: Macmillan, 1920.

Jones, E. (1953). *The Life and Work of Sigmund Freud, Vol. I: The Formative Years and the Great Discoveries.* New York: H. Wolff.

Jones, S. (1997). Go milk a fruit bat! Why is sex fun? The evolution of human sexuality. *The New York Review of Books*, 44(12):39–41.

Joseph, B. (1985). Transference: The total situation. *Internat. J. Psychoanal.*, 66:447–454.

Kagan, J. (1998a). *Three Seductive Ideas.* Cambridge, MA: Harvard University Press.

———— (1998b). Biology and the child. In: *Handbook of Child Psychology, Vol. 3: Social, Emotional and Personality Development*, ed. N. Eisenberg. New York: Wiley, pp. 177–236.

———— & Moss, H. A. (1962). *Birth to Maturity.* New York: Wiley.

———— & Zentner, M. (1996). Early childhood predictors of adult psychopathology. *Harvard Rev. Psychiat.*, 3:341-350.

Kantrowitz, J. L. (1986). The role of the patient-analyst "match" in the outcome of psychoanalysis. *The Annual of Psychoanalysis*, 14:273–297. New York: International Universities Press.

———— (1995). The beneficial aspects of the patient-analyst match: Factors in addition to clinical acumen and therapeutic skill that contribute to psychological change. *Internat. J. Psychoanal.*, 76:299–313.

———— Katz, A. L., Greenman, D. A., Morris, H., Paolitto, F., Sashin, J. & Soloman, L. (1989) The patient-analyst match and the outcome of psychoanalysis: A pilot study. *J. Amer. Psychoanal. Assn.*, 37:893–919.

———— ———— & Paolitto, F. (1990a). Follow-up of psychoanalysis five to ten years after termination. I: Stability of change. *J. Amer. Psychoanal. Assn.*, 38:471–496.

———— ———— & ———— (1990b). Follow-up of psychoanalysis five to ten years after termination. II: Development of the self-analytic function. *J. Amer. Psychoanal. Assn.*, 38:637–654.

———— ———— & ———— (1990c). Follow-up of psychoanalysis five to ten years after termination. III: The relation between resolution of the transference and the patient-analyst match. *J. Amer. Psychoanal. Assn.*, 38:655–678.

———— ———— ———— & Soloman, L. (1987a). Changes in the level and quality of object relations in psychoanalysis: Follow-up of a longitudinal prospective study. *J. Amer. Psychoanal. Assn.*, 35:23–46.

———— ———— ———— & ———— (1987b). The role of reality testing in psychoanalysis: Follow-up of 22 cases. *J. Amer. Psychoanal. Assn.*, 35:367–385.

———— Paolitto, F., Sashin, J., Soloman, L. & Katz, A. (1986). Affect availability, tolerance, complexity, and modulation in psychoanalysis: Follow-up of a longitudinal prospective study. *J. Amer. Psychoanal. Assn.*, 34:529–559.

Kardiner, A. (1977). *My Analysis with Freud: Reminiscences.* New York: Norton.

———— Karush, A. & Ovesey, L. (1959). A methodological study of Freudian theory. 1. Basic concepts. 2. The libido theory. *J. Nervous & Mental Diseases,* 129:133–143.

Kellert, S. H. (1993). *In the Wake of Chaos: Unpredictable Order in Dynamical Systems.* Chicago: University of Chicago Press.

Kennedy, H. (1971). Problems in reconstruction in child analysis. *The Psychoanalytic Study of the Child,* 26:286–402. New Haven, CT: Yale University Press.

Kernberg, O. F. (1975). *Borderline Conditions and Pathological Narcissism.* New York: Aronson.

———— (1986). Institutional problems of psychoanalytic education. *J. Amer. Psychoanal. Assn.*, 34:799–834.

———— (1987). An ego psychology-object relations theory approach to the transference. *Psychoanal. Quart.*, 56:197–221.

———— (1993). The current status of psychoanalysis. *J. Amer. Psychoanal. Assn.*, 41:45–62.

———— (1994). Love in the analytic setting. *J. Amer. Psychoanal. Assn.*, 42:1137–1157.

———— (1999). Psychoanalysis, psychoanalytic psychotherapy and supportive psychotherapy: Contemporary controversies. *Internat. J. Psychoanal.*, 80:1075–1091.

Kerr, J. (1994). *A Most Dangerous Method: The Story of Freud, Jung, and Sabina Spielrein.* New York: Vintage Books.

Knoblauch, S. H. (1999). The third, minding and affecting: Commentary on paper by L. Aron. *Psychoanal. Dial.*, 9:41–51.

Knowlton, L. (1997). Psychoanalysis and pharmacotherapy—Incompatible or synergistic? *Psychiatric Times*, 14:60–61.

Kobak, R. (1999). The emotional dynamics of disruptions in attachment relationships: Implications for theory, research, and clinical intervention. In: *Handbook of Attachment: Theory, Research, and Clinical Applications*, ed. J. Cassidy & P. R. Shaver. New York: Guilford Press, pp. 21–43.

Kravis, N. M. (1992). The "prehistory" of the idea of transference. *Internat. Rev. Psychoanal.*, 19:9–22.

——— & Zentner, M. (1996). Early childhood predictors of adult psychopathology. *Harvard Rev. Psychiatry*, 3:341–350.

Kris, A. O. (1985). Resistance in convergent and divergent conflicts. *Psychoanal. Quart.*, 54:537–568.

Kubie, L. S. (1950). *Practical and Theoretical Aspects of Psychoanalysis*, 2nd rev. ed. New York: International Universities Press, 1975.

Kuhn, T. (1962). *The Structure of Scientific Revolutions*, 2nd ed. Chicago: University of Chicago Press.

Kurth, S. B. (1970). Friendships and friendly relations. In: *Social Relationships*, ed. G. J. McCall. Chicago: Aldine, pp. 136–170.

Lachmann, F. M. & Beebe, B. (1995). Self psychology: Today. *Psychoanal. Dial.*, 5:375–391.

Lampl-de Groot, J. (1954). Problems of psychoanalytic training. *Internat. J. Psychoanal.*, 35:184–187.

——— (1976). Personal experience with psychoanalytic technique and theory during the last half century. *The Psychoanalytic Study of the Child*, 31:283–296. New Haven, CT: Yale University Press.

Laplanche, J. & Pontalis, J. B. (1973). *The Language of Psychoanalysis*. New York: Norton.

Levine, H. B. (1997). Difficulties in maintaining an analytic stance in the treatment of adults who were abused as children. *Psychoanal. Inq.*, 17:312–328.

——— (1998). L'engouement du psychanalyste. *Trans. Revue Psychanalyse*, 8:55–78.

Levine, H. R. & Friedman, R. J. (2000). Intersubjectivity and interaction in the analytic relationship: A mainstream view. *Psychoanal. Quart.*, 49:63–92.

Levy, S. T. & Inderbitzin, L. B. (2000). Suggestion and psychoanalytic technique. *J. Amer. Psychoanal. Assn.*, 48:739–758.

Lewin, K. (1935). *A Dynamic Theory of Personality*. New York: McGraw-Hill.

Lewis, M. (1997). *Altering Fate: Why the Past Does Not Predict the Future*. New York: Guilford Press.

Lewis, P. (2001). Herbert A. Simon dies at 84; won a Nobel for economics. *The New York Times*, February 10, p. A13.

Lichtenberg, J. D. (1998). Experience as a guide to psychoanalytic theory and practice. *J. Amer. Psychoanal. Assn.*, 46:17–36.

——— Lachmann, F. M. & Fosshage, J. L. (1992). *Self and Motivational Systems: Toward a Theory of Psychoanalytic Technique*. Hillsdale, NJ: The Analytic Press.

Lipsyte, R. (2000). Outside the norm: The mind-set of the elite athlete. *The New York Times* sports section, February 6, pp. 30, 36.

Loewald, H. (1962). Internalization, separation, mourning, and the superego. *Psychoanal. Quart.*, 43:483–504.

—— (1971). The transference neurosis: Comments on the concept and the phenomenon. *J. Amer. Psychoanal. Assn.*, 19:54–66.

—— (1986). Transference-countertransference. *J. Amer. Psychoanal. Assn.*, 34:275–287.

Lothane, Z. (1999). The perennial Freud: Method versus myth and the mischief of Freud bashers. *International Forum of Psychoanalysis* (Stockholm), 8:151–171.

Luborsky, L. (1996). *The Symptom-Context Method: Symptoms as Opportunities in Psychotherapy*. Washington, DC: American Psychological Association.

—— (2000). Psychoanalysis and empirical research: A reconciliation. In: *Changing Ideas in a Changing World: The Revolution in Psychoanalysis. Essays in Honour of Arnold Cooper*, ed. J. Sandler, R. Michels & P. Fonagy. London: Karnac.

—— & Crits-Christoph, P. (1990). *Understanding Transference: The Core Conflictual Relationship Theme Method*. New York: Basic Books.

—— & Schaffler, P. (1990). Illustrations of the CCRT scoring guide. In: *Understanding Transference—The CCRT Method*, ed. L. Luborsky & P. Crits-Christoph. New York: Basic Books, pp. 51–81.

Lykken, D. T. & Tellegen, A. (1996) Happiness is a stochastic phenomenon. *Psycholog. Sci.*, 7:186–189.

Macalpine, I. (1950). The development of the transference. *Psychoanal. Quart.*, 19:501–539.

—— (1973). Tribute to Freud. In: *Freud: Modern Judgments*, ed. F. Cioffi. London: Macmillan, pp. 125–137.

Macmillan, M. B. (1976). Beard's concept of neurasthenia and Freud's concept of the actual neuroses. *J. History Behavioral Sci.*, 12:376–390.

—— (1991). *Freud Evaluated: The Completed Arc*. North Holland: Elsevier Science.

—— (1992). The sources of Freud's methods for gathering and evaluating clinical data. In: *Freud and the History of Psychoanalysis*, ed. T. Gelfand & J. Jerr. Hillsdale, NJ: The Analytic Press, pp. 99–151.

Mahler, M. S. & Kaplan, L. J. (1977). Developmental aspects in the assessment of narcissistic and so-called borderline personalities. In: *Borderline Personality Disorders: The Concept, the Syndrome, the Patient*, ed. P. L. Hartocollis. New York: International Universities Press, pp. 71–85.

Main, M. (1995). Recent studies in attachment. Overview with selected implications for clinical work. In: *Attachment Theory: Social, Developmental and Clinical Perspectives*, ed. S. Goldberg, R. Muir & J. Kerr. Hillsdale, NJ: The Analytic Press.

Makari, G. J. (1992). A history of Freud's first concept of transference. *Internat. Rev. Psychoanal.*, 19:415–432.

———— (1998). Dora's hysteria and the maturation of Sigmund Freud's transference theory: A new historical interpretation. *J. Amer. Psychoanal. Assn.*, 45:1061–1096.

———— (2000). Change in psychoanalysis: Science, practice and the sociology of knowledge. In: *Changing Ideas in a Changing World: The Revolution in Psychoanalysis. Essays in Honour of Arnold Cooper*, ed. J. Sandler, R. Michels & P. Fonagy. London: Karnac, pp. 255–262.

Malan, D. H. (1976). *Toward the Validation of Dynamic Psychotherapy*. New York: Plenum.

Malin, B. D. (1998). Psychoanalysis and medication. Epilogue. *Psychoanal. Inq.*, 5:746–762.

Mangelsdorf, S., Gunnar, M., Kestenbaum, R., Lang, S. & Andreas, D. (1990). Infant proneness to distress temperament, maternal personality, and mother-infant attachment. *Child Development*, 61:820–831.

Margolis, M. (1997). Analyst-patient sexual involvement: Clinical experiences and institutional responses. *Psychoanal. Inq.*, 17:349–370.

Marmor, J. (1986). The question of causality. Commentary/Grünbaum: *Foundations of Psychoanalysis. Behavioral and Brain Sciences*, 9:249.

Masson, J. M. (1985). *The Complete Letters of Sigmund Freud to Wilhelm Fliess*, 1887–1907. Cambridge, MA: Harvard University Press.

Matthews, S. H. (1986). *Friendships Through the Life Course: Oral Biographies in Old Age*. Beverly Hills: Sage.

May, U. (1999). Freud's early clinical theory (1894–1896): Outline and context. *Internat. J. Psychoanal.*, 80:769–781.

McGinn, C. (1999). Freud under analysis. *The New York Review of Books*, 46(17):20–24.

McGuire, W. (1974). *The Freud/Jung Letters*, trans. R. Mannheim & R. F. C. Hull. Princeton, NJ: Princeton University Press.

Meehl, P. E. (1994). Subjectivity in psychoanalytic inference: The nagging persistence of Wilhelm Fliess's Achensee question. *Psychoanal. & Contemp. Thought*, 17:3–82.

Meissner, W. (1992). The concept of the therapeutic alliance. *J. Amer. Psychoanal. Assn.*, 40:1058–1088.

———— (1996). Empathy in the therapeutic alliance. *Psychoanal. Inq.*, 16:39–53.

Michels, R. (1982). The relevance of infant observational research for clinical work with children, adolescents and adults. Discussion. Presented at a workshop sponsored by the American Psychoanalytic Association, Roosevelt Hotel, New York City, November 20–21.

———— (1994). Validation in the clinical process. *Internat. J. Psychoanal.*, 75:1133–1140.

———— (1998). Discussion of papers by J. Arlow, M. Lionels, Ornstein, and S. Dowling. Symposium of the Journals of the CD ROM, February 28–March 1, New York.

———— (2000). The case history. *J. Amer. Psychoanal. Assn.*, 48:355–375.

Miller, D. (1998). Neighbors. In *Time, Order, Chaos: The Study of Time IX*, ed. J. T. Fraser, M. P. Soulsby & A. J. Argyros. Madison, CT: International Universities Press, pp. 79–87.

Mitchell, S. A. (1988). *Relational Concepts in Psychoanalysis: An Integration.* Cambridge, MA: Harvard University Press.

—— (1993). *Hope and Dread in Psychoanalysis.* New York: Basic Books.

—— (1997). *Influence and Autonomy in Psychoanalysis.* Hillsdale, NJ: The Analytic Press.

Modell, A. H. (1990). *Other Times, Other Realities: Toward a Theory of Psychoanalytic Treatment.* Cambridge, MA: Harvard University Press.

—— (1995). *Metaphor and Mind.* Plenary Presentation, The American Psychoanalytic Association, New York, December 14.

Moi, T. (1900). Representations of patriarchy: Sexuality and epistemology in Freud's Dora. In: *In Dora's Case: Freud-Hysteria-Feminism*, 2nd ed., ed. C. Bernheimer & C. Kahane. New York: Columbia University Press, pp. 181–199.

Mollon, P. (2000). The recovered memories controversy. *Internat. J. Psychoanal.*, 81:167–169.

Moore, B. E. & Fine, B. D., eds. (1990). *Psychoanalytic Terms and Concepts.* New Haven, CT: Yale University Press.

Mosher, P. (1990). Book review of *Chaos: Making a New Science*, by J. Gleick. *Bull. Assn. Psychoanal. Med.*, Nos. 1 & 2, pp. 95–96.

—— (1999). Suggestion and the placebo effect. Email, Members' List, September 23.

—— (2000). OPLN: Need for placebo groups in clinical studies demonstrated again. Email, Members' List, October 1.

Munder Ross, J. (1999). Once more onto the couch: Consciousness and pre-conscious defenses in psychoanalysis. *J. Amer. Psychoanal. Assn.*, 47:91–111.

Nachmias, M., Gunnar, M., Mangelsdorf, S., Parritz, R. H. & Buss, K. (1996). Behavioral inhibition and stress reactivity: The moderating role of attachment security. *Child Development*, 67:508–522.

Nader, K., Schafe, G. E. & Le Doux, J. E. (2000). Recall of auditory fear conditioning in rats. *Nature*, 406:722–726.

National Institute of Child Health and Human Development (NICHD) Early Child Care Research Network (1997). The effects of infant child care on infant-mother attachment security: Results of the NICHD study of early child care. *Child Development*, 68:860–879.

Nemiah, J. C. (1989). Janet Redivivus: The Centenary of *L'Automatisme Psychologique*. *Amer. J. Psychiat.*, 146:1527–1529.

Newton, P. M. (1995). *Freud: From Youthful Dream to Mid-Life Crisis.* New York: Guilford Press.

Norman, H. F., Blacker, K. H., Oremland, J. D. & Barrett, W. G. (1976). The fate of the transference neurosis after termination of a satisfactory analysis. *J. Amer. Psychoanal. Assn.*, 24:471–498.

Nowotny, H. (1998). Times of complexity. In: *Time: The Modern and Post-modern Experience*, ed. J. T. Fraser, M. P. Soulsby & A. J. Argyros. Oxford: Polity Press, pp. 91–107.

Ogden, T. (1994). The analytic third: Working with intersubjective clinical facts. *Internat. J. Psychoanal.*, 75:3–19.

Opatow, B. (1999). On the scientific standing of psychoanalysis. *J. Amer. Psychoanal. Assn.*, 47:1107–1124.

Oremland, J. D., Blacker, K. H. & Norman, H. F. (1975). Incompleteness in "successful" psychoanalyses: A follow-up study. *J. Amer. Psychoanal. Assn.*, 23:819–844.

Orgel, S. (2000). Letting go: Some thoughts on termination. *J. Amer. Psychoanal. Assn.*, 48:719–738.

Pally, R. (1997). I. How brain development is shaped by genetic and environmental factors. *Internat. J. Psychoanal.*, 78:587–593.

Palombo, S. R. (1999). *The Emergent Ego: Complexity and Coevolution in the Psychoanalytic Process*. Madison, CT: International Universities Press.

Panel (1958). Technical aspects of regression during psychoanalysis. *J. Amer. Psychoanal. Assn.*, 6:552–589.

——— (1969). Problems of termination in the analysis of adults. *J. Amer. Psychoanal. Assn.*, 17:222–237.

——— (1986). Borderline personality disorders: Research issues and new empirical findings. *J. Amer. Psychoanal. Assn.*, 34:179–192.

——— (1989). Evaluation of outcome of psychoanalytic treatment. Should follow-up by the analyst be part of the posttermination phase of analytic treatment? *J. Amer. Psychoanal. Assn.*, 37:813–822.

——— (1995a). Enactments of boundary violations. *J. Amer. Psychoanal. Assn.*, 43:853–868.

——— (1995b). Classics revisited: Freud's papers on technique. *J. Amer. Psychoanal. Assn.*, 43:175–186.

——— (1995c). Classics revisited: Heinz Kohut's *The Analysis of the Self*. Discussion by S. T. Levy. *J. Amer. Psychoanal. Assn.* 43:187–195.

Parens, H. (1997). The unique pathogenicity of sexual abuse. *Psychoanal. Inq.*, 17:250–266.

Pelli, D. G. (1999). Close encounters: An artist shows that size affects shape. *Science*, 285:844–846.

Pelze, D. & Mastroni, N. (1989). *Putt Like the Pros*. New York: Harper Perennial.

Perelberg, R. J. (1999). The interplay between identifications and identity in the analysis of a violent young man: Issues of technique. *Internat. J. Psychoanal.*, 80:31–45.

Person, E. S. (1993). Introduction. In: *On Freud's "Observations on Transference-Love,"* ed. E. S. Person, A. Hagelin & P. Fonagy. New Haven, CT: Yale University Press, pp. 1–14.

Peskin, M. M. (2000). Through the looking glass: Psychoanalysis, conceptual integration, and the problem of the innate. In: *Changing Ideas in a*

Changing World: The Revolution in Psychoanalysis. Essays in Honour of Arnold Cooper, ed. J. Sandler, R. Michels & P. Fonagy. London: Karnac, pp. 229–236.

Pfeffer, A. Z. (1959). A procedure for evaluating the results of psychoanalysis: A preliminary report. *J. Amer. Psychoanal. Assn.*, 7:418–444.

——— (1961). Follow-up study of a satisfactory analysis. *J. Amer. Psychoanal. Assn.*, 9:698–718.

——— (1963). The meaning of the analyst after analysis: A contribution to the theory of therapeutic results. *J. Amer. Psychoanal. Assn.*, 11:229–244.

Phillips, A. (1996). *Terrors and Experts*. Cambridge, MA: Harvard University Press.

Pine, F. (1990). *Drive, Ego, Object and Self: A Synthesis for Clinical Work*. New York: Basic Books.

——— (1994). Multiple models, clinical practice, and psychoanalytic theory: Response to discussants. *Psychoanal. Inq.*, 14:212–234.

Pizer, S. A. (1999). Commentary on paper by L. Aron. *Psychoanal. Dial.*, 9:61–68.

——— (2000). A gift in return. The clinical use of writing about a patient. *Psychoanal. Dial.*, 10:247–259.

Polland, W. S. (1992). Transference: "An original creation." *Psychoanal. Quart.*, 61:185–205.

Ponsi, M. (1999). Email. On Psychoanalysis—Psychoanalytic Broadcast, October 31.

Pope, K. S. & Vetter, V. (1991). Prior patient-therapist sexual involvement among patients seen by psychologists. *Psychotherapy*, 28:429–438.

Popper, K. R. (1972). *Objective Knowledge: An Evolutionary Approach*. London: Oxford University Press.

Prigogine, I. (1997). *The End of Certainty: Time, Chaos, and the New Laws of Nature*. New York: Free Press.

Quinodoz, J-M. (1997). Transitions in psychic structures in the light of deterministic chaos theory. *Internat. J. Psychoanal.*, 78:699–718.

Rádl, E. (1909). *The History of Biological Theories*. London: Oxford University Press, 1930.

Rangell, L. (1963). On friendship. *J. Amer. Psychoanal. Assn.*, 11:3–54.

——— (1978). On understanding and treating anxiety and its derivatives. *Internat. J. Psychoanal.*, 59:229–236.

——— (2000). Psychoanalysis at the millennium: A unitary theory. *Psychoanal. Psychol.*, 17:451–466.

Raphling, D. L. & Chused, J. F. (1988). Transference across gender lines. *J. Amer. Psychoanal. Assn.*, 36:77–104.

Rawlins, W. K. (1992). *Friendship Matters: Communication Dialectics and the Life Course*. New York: Aldine de Gruyter.

Reich, A. (1958). A special variation of technique. *Internat. J. Psychoanal.*, 39:230–234.

Renik, O. (1996). The analyst's self-discovery. *Psychoanal. Inq.*, 16:390–400.
———— (1999). Playing one's cards face up in analysis: An approach to the problem of self-disclosure. *Psychoanal. Quart.*, 48:521–539.
Richards, A. (2000). Theory as part of compromise formation. Email: *JAPA NETCAST@psychoanalysis.net* (A moderated discussion exploring matters of mind.) November 26.
Rind, B., Tromovitch, P. & Bauserman, R. (1998). A meta-analytic examination of assumed properties of child sexual abuse using college samples. *Psycholog. Bull.*, 124:22–53.
Ritvo, L. (1990). *Darwin's Influence on Freud: A Tale of Two Sciences.* New Haven, CT: Yale University Press.
Roazen, P. & Swerdloff, B. (1995). *Heresy: Sándor Rado and the Psychoanalytic Movement.* Northvale, NJ: Aronson.
Robinson, P. (1993). *Freud and His Critics.* Berkeley: University of California Press.
Rogers, C. (1989). *Carl Rogers: Dialogues. Conversations with Martin Buber, Paul Tillich, B. F. Skinner, Gregory Bateson, Michael Polanyi, Rollo May, and Others,* ed. H. Kirschenbaum & V. L. Henderson. Boston: Houghton Mifflin.
Rubin, L. B. (1981). Sociological research: The subjective dimension. The 1980 SSSI Distinguished Lecture. *Symbolic Interaction,* 4:97–112.
Rubovits-Seitz, P. (1998). *Depth-Pschological Understanding: The Methodologic Grounding of Clinical Interpretations.* Hillsdale, NJ: The Analytic Press.
Russell, B. (1953). On the notion of cause, with applications to the free-will problem. In: *Readings in the Philosophy of Science,* ed. H. Feigl & M. Brodbeck. New York: Appleton-Century-Crofts, pp. 387–407.
Russel, D. E. (1986). *The Secret Trauma.* New York: Basic Books.
Rutter, M. (1987). Temperament, personality and personality disorder. *Brit. J. Psychiat.,* 150:443–458.
———— & Rutter, M. (1993). *Developing Minds: Challenge and Continuity Across the Life Span.* New York: Basic Books.
Sagi, A., van IJzendoorn, M. H. & Koren-Karie, N. (1991). Primary appraisal of the Strange Situation. *Developmental Psychol.,* 27:587–596.
Sandell, R., Blomberg, J., Lazar, A., Carlsson, J., Broberg, J. & Schubert, J. (2000). Varieties of long-term outcome among patients in psychoanalysis and long-term psychotherapy: A review of findings in the Stockholm outcome of psychoanalysis and psychotherapy project (STOPPP). *Internat. J. Psychoanal.,* 81:921–942.
Sandler, J. (1990). On internal object relations. *J. Amer. Psychoanal. Assn.,* 38:859–889.
———— Kennedy, H. & Tyson, R. L. (1980). *The Technique of Child Psychoanalysis: Discussions with Anna Freud.* Cambridge, MA: Harvard University Press.

———— & Sandler, A-M. (1987). The past unconscious, the present unconscious and the vicissitudes of guilt. *Internat. J. Psychoanal.*, 68:331–341.

———— & Sandler, A-M. (1994). Theoretical and technical comments on regression and anti-regression. *Internat. J. Psychoanal.*, 75:431–439.

———— Holder, A., Dare, C. & Dreher, A. U. (1997). *Freud's Models of the Mind: An Introduction*. London: Karnac Books.

Sass, L. A. (1999). Book review of I. Z. Hoffman's *Ritual and Spontaneity in the Psychoanalytic Process*. *J. Amer. Psychoanal. Assn.*, 47:899–906.

Schachter, J. (1990). Post-termination patient-analyst contact: I. Analysts' attitudes and experience; II. Impact on patients. *Internat. J. Psychoanal.*, 71:475–486.

———— (1992). Concepts of termination and post-termination patient-analyst contact. *Internat. J. Psychoanal.*, 73:137–154.

———— (1994). Abstinence and neutrality: Development and diverse views. *Internat. J. Psychoanal.*, 75:709–720.

———— & Luborsky, L. (1998). Who's afraid of psychoanalytic research? Analysts' attitudes towards reading clinical versus empirical research papers. *Internat. J. Psychoanal.*, 79:965–969.

———— & Brauer, L. (in press). The effect of the analyst's gender and other factors on post-termination patient-analyst contact: A confirmation questionnaire study. *Internat. J. Psychoanal.*

———— Martin, G. C., Gundle, M. J. & O'Neil, M. K. (1997). Clinical experience with psychoanalytic post-termination meetings. *Internat. J. Psychoanal.*, 78:1183–1198.

Schafer, R. (1977). The interpretation of transference and the conditions for loving. *J. Amer. Psychoanal. Assn.*, 25:335–362.

———— (1983). Psychoanalytic reconstruction. In: *The Analytic Attitude*. New York: Basic Books, pp. 193–203.

———— (1990). The search for common ground. *Internat. J. Psychoanal.*, 71:49–52.

———— (1994). The conceptualisation of clinical facts. *Internat. J. Psychoanal.*, 75:1023–1030.

Schlessinger, H. J. (1995). The process of interpretation and the moment of change. *J. Amer. Psychoanal. Assn.*, 43:663–688.

Schlessinger, N. & Robbins, F. P. (1983). *A Developmental View of the Psychoanalytic Process: Follow-up Studies and Their Consequences*. Madison, CT: International Universities Press.

Schuker, E. (1996). Toward further analytic understanding of lesbian patients. *J. Amer. Psychoanal. Assn.*, 44(Suppl.):485–508.

Scott, A. O. (1999). Looking for Raymond Carver. *New York Review of Books*, 46(13):52–59.

Scott, J. (2000). A bull market for Grant, a bear market for Lee. *The New York Times*, September 30, pp. A17, A19.

Seitz, P. (1966). The consensus problem in psychoanalytic research. In: *Methods of Research in Psychotherapy*, ed. L. Gottschalk & A. Auerbach. New York: Appleton-Century-Crofts.

Seligman, S. (1996). Commentary on P. Wolff's "The irrelevance of infant observation for psychoanalysis." *J. Amer. Psychoanal. Assn.*, 44:430–446.

Shapiro, A. K. & Shapiro, E. (1997). *The Powerful Placebo from Ancient Priest to Modern Physician.* Baltimore, MD: Johns Hopkins University Press.

Shapiro, T. (1981). On the quest for the origins of conflict. *Psychoanal. Quart.*, 50:1–21.

Shengold, L. (1998). A view of severely traumatized patients: Soul murder victims. Symposium of the Journals of the CD ROM, February 28–March 1, New York.

Siegel, D. J. (1999). *The Developing Mind: Toward a Neurobiology of Interpersonal Experience.* New York: Guilford Press.

Silverman, D. K. (1981). Some proposed modifications of psychoanalytic theories of early childhood development. In: *Empirical Studies of Psychoanalytic Theories, Vol. 2*, ed. J. Masling. Hillsdale, NJ: The Analytic Press.

Simon, B. (1991). Is the Oedipus complex still the cornerstone of psychoanalysis? Three obstacles to answering the question. *J. Amer. Psychoanal. Assn.*, 39:641–668.

Skolnikoff, A. Z. (2000). Seeking an analytic identity. *Psychoanal. Inq.*, 20:594–610.

Spence, D. P. (1982). *Narrative Truth and Historical Truth: Meaning and Interpretation in Psychoanalysis.* New York: Norton.

———— (1994). *The Rhetorical Voice of Psychoanalysis: Displacement of Evidence by Theory.* Cambridge, MA: Harvard University Press.

———— (1995). When do interpretations make a difference? A partial answer to Fliess' Achensee question. *J. Amer. Psychoanal. Assn.*, 43:689–712.

Spezzano, C. (1998). The triangle of clinical judgment. *J. Amer. Psychoanal. Assn.*, 46:365–388.

———— (2000). Another comment on Arnie's comment. Email: *JAPA NET-CAST@psychoanalysis.net* (A moderated discussion exploring matters of mind). November 26.

Spillius, E. B. (1999). Book review of *Freud's Models of the Mind: An Introduction by J. Sandler, A. Holder, C. Dare & A . U. Dreber. Internat. J. Psychoanal.*, 80:825–828.

Squire, L. R. (1992). Memory and the hippocampus: A synthesis from findings with rats, monkeys and humans. *Psychol. Rev.*, 99:195–231.

Stein, M. H. (1981). The unobjectionable part of the transference. *J. Amer. Psychoanal. Assn.*, 29:869–892.

Stern, D. N. (1985). *The Interpersonal World of the Infant: A View from Psychoanalysis and Developmental Psychology.* New York: Basic Books.

———— (2000). The relevance of empirical infant research to psychoanalytic theory and practice. In *Clinical and Observational Psychoanalytic Research: Roots of a Controversy*, ed. J. Sandler, A.-M. Sandler & R. Davies. London: Karnac Books, pp. 73–90.

Stoller, R. J. (1979). *Sexual Excitement: Dynamics of Erotic Life.* New York: Pantheon.

Stone, A. A. (2000). Beauty and redemption. *Boston Review,* 25:50–51.

Stone, L. (1984). The psychoanalytic situation and transference: Postscript to an earlier communication. In: *Transference and Its Context: Selected Papers on Psychoanalysis.* New York: Aronson, pp. 73–118.

Stoppard, T. (1993). *Arcadia.* Boston: Faber & Faber.

——— (1997). *The Invention of Love.* New York: Grove Press.

Strenger, C. (1999). Why constructivism will not go away: Commentary on paper by Mauricio Cortina. *Psychoanal. Dial.,* 9:609–616.

Sullivan, A. (1999). Counter culture: The assault on good news. *The New York Times Magazine,* November 7, Section 6, pp. 38–40.

Sulloway, F. J. (1979). *Freud, Biologist of the Mind: Beyond the Psychoanalytic Legend.* New York: Basic Books.

——— (1998). Darwinian virtues. Book review of *The Origins of Virtue: Human Instincts and the Evolution of Cooperation,* by M. Ridley. *The New York Review of Books,* 45(6):34–39.

Swales, P. (1989). Freud, cocaine and sexual chemistry: The role of cocaine in Freud's conception of the libido. In: *Sigmund Freud: Critical Assessments, Vol. 1,* ed. L. Spurling. London: Routledge.

Thomä, H. & Cheshire, N. (1991). Freud's *Nachträglichkeit* and Strachey's "deferred action": Trauma, constructions and the direction of causality. *Internat. Rev. Psychoanal.,* 18:407–427.

Thomas, R. M. (1998). Jack Streit, a Guardian of matzoh's traditions, is dead at 89. *The New York Times,* February 6, p. C18.

Thompson, R. A. (1999). Early attachment and later development. In: *Handbook of Attachment: Theory, Research, and Clinical Applications,* ed. J. Cassidy & P. R. Shaver. New York: Guilford Press, pp. 265–286.

——— (2000). The legacy of early attachments. *Child Development,* 71:145–152.

——— Connell, J. P. & Bridges, L. J. (1988). Temperament, emotion, and social interactive behavior in the Strange Situation. *Child Development,* 59:1102–1110.

Ticho, E. A. (1972). Termination of psychoanalysis: Treatment goals, life goals. *Psychoanal. Quart.,* 41:315–333.

Tögel, C. (1999). "My bad diagnostic error": Once more about Freud and Emmy v. N. (Fanny Moser). *Internat. J. Psychoanal.,* 80:1165–1173.

Tuckett, D. (1994). The conceptualization and communication of clinical facts in psychoanalysis. *Internat. J. Psychoanal.,* 75:865–870.

——— (2000). Theoretical pluralism and the construction of psychoanalytic knowledge. In: *Changing Ideas in a Changing World: The Revolution in Psychoanalysis. Essays in Honour of Arnold Cooper,* ed. J. Sandler, R. Michels & P. Fonagy. London: Karnac, pp. 237–246.

Tulving, E. (1983). *Elements of Episodic Memory.* Oxford: Oxford University Press.

Turner, J. R. & Hewitt, J. K. (1992). Twin studies of cardiovascular response to psychological challenge: A review and suggested future directions. *Ann. Behavioral Med.*, 14:12–20.

Tyson, P. (1998). Developmental theory and the postmodern psychoanalyst. *J. Amer. Psychoanal. Assn.*, 46:9–15.

van den Boom, D. (1994). The influence of temperament and mothering on attachment and exploration: An experimental manipulation of sensitive responsiveness among lower-class mothers with irritable infants. *Child Development*, 65:1457–1477.

van der Kolk, B. A. & van der Hart, O. (1989). Pierre Janet and the breakdown of adaptation in psychological trauma. *Amer. J. Psychiat.*, 146:1530–1540.

van IJzendoorn, M. H., Goldberg, S., Kroonenberg, P. M. & Frenkel, O. J. (1992). The relative effects of maternal and child problems on the quality of attachment: A meta-analysis of attachment in clinical samples. *Child Development*, 63:840–858.

Vaughan, S. C., Spitzer, R. Davies, M. & Roose, S. (1997). The definition and assessment of analytic process: Can analysts agree? *Internat. J. Psychoanal.*, 78:959–973.

Vaughn, B. E. & Bost, K. K. (1999). Attachment and temperament: Redundant, independent, or interacting influences on interpersonal adaptation and personality development? In: *Handbook of Attachment: Theory, Research, and Clinical Applications*, ed. J. Cassidy & P. R. Shaver. New York: Guilford Press, pp. 198–225.

Vidal, G. (1999). Chaos. *The New York Review of Books*, 46(20):39–40.

Viederman, M. (1991). The real person of the analyst and his role in the process of psychoanalytic cure. *J. Amer. Psychoanal. Assn.*, 39:451–489.

——— (1995). The reconstruction of a repressed sexual molestation fifty years later. *J. Amer. Psychoanal. Assn.*, 43:1169–1195.

Wagner-Jauregg, J. (1950). *Lebenserinnerungen*, ed. L. Schönbauer & M. Jantsch. Vienna: Springer.

Wallerstein, R. S. (1986). *Forty-Two Lives in Treatment: A Study of Psychoanalysis and Psychotherapy*. New York: Guilford Press.

——— (1988). Psychoanalysis and psychotherapy: Relative roles reconsidered. *The Annual of Psychoanalysis*, 16:129–151. New York: International Universities Press.

——— (1990). Psychoanalysis: The common ground. *Internat. J. Psychoanal.*, 71:4–20.

——— (1999a). The Generations of Psychotherapy Research: An Overview. Plenary Lecture to the Rapaport-Klein Study Group meeting at Austen Riggs Center, Stockbridge, MA, June 11.

——— (1999b). *Psychoanalysis: Clinical and Theoretical*. Madison, CT: International Universities Press.

——— & Sampson, H. S. (1971). Issues in research in the psychoanalytic process. *Internat. J. Psychoanal.*, 52:11–50.

Wampold, B. E. (2001). *The Great Psychotherapy Debate: Models, Methods and Findings*. Mahwah, NJ: Lawrence Erlbaum Associates.

Watillon, A. (1998). Vulnerabilities in the training situation. Presented to the Third EPF Conference of Training Analysts, Amsterdam.

Weinshel, E. & Renik, O. (1991). The past ten years: Psychoanalysis in the United States, 1980–1990. *Psychoanal. Inq.*, 11:13–29.

Westen, D. (1999). The scientific status of unconscious processes: Is Freud really dead? *J. Amer. Psychoanal. Assn.*, 47:1061–1106.

————— & Gabbard, G. O. (2001). Developments in cognitive neuroscience. II: Implications for theories of transference. *J. Amer. Psychoanal. Assn.*, In Press.

Wieseltier, L. (1970). When a sage dies, all are his kin. *The New Republic*. December 1, pp. 27–31.

Wilgoren, J. (1999). Quality daycare, early, is tied to achievements as an adult. *The New York Times*, October 22, p. A16.

Wilson, A. (1996). Commentary on P. Wolff's "The irrelevance of infant observation for psychoanalysis." *J. Amer. Psychoanal. Assn.*, 44:454–464.

Winnicott, D. (1955). Metapsychological and clinical aspects of regression within the psycho-analytical set-up. *Internat. J. Psychoanal.*, 36:16–26.

Wolff, P. H. (1996). The irrelevance of infant observations for psychoanalysis, and Response. *J. Amer. Psychoanal. Assn.*, 44:369–392, 464–474.

————— (1998). Response. *J. Amer. Psychoanal. Assn.*, 46:274–278.

Wright, L. (1997). *Twins and What They Tell Us About Who We Are*. New York: Wiley.

Wzontek, N., Geller, J. D. & Farber, B. A. (1995). Patients' posttermination representations of their psychotherapists. *J. Amer. Acad. Psychoanal.*, 2:395–410.

Yalom, I. D. (1980). *Existential Psychotherapy*. New York: Basic Books.

Zilboorg, G. (1941). *The History of Medical Psychology*. New York: Norton.

SUBJECT INDEX

AUTHOR INDEX

A

Abend, S., 54
Adler, N. E., 81, 111
Akhtar, S., 156
Albus, K. E., 86
Alexander, F., 164, 166–167
Allport, G., 25
Andersson, O., 39
Andreas, D., 86
Anzieu, D., 127
Arlow, J. A., 11, 57, 62–63, 146, 153, 222, 223, 227
Aron, L., 156, 158, 161, 163, 173–174, 191, 224
Auden, W. H., 230

B

Bachant, J., 48, 111
Bachrach, H. M., 8
Balaban, E., 102
Baranger, M., 134
Baranger, W., 134
Barratt, B. B., 74, 103
Barrett, W. G., 203
Bauer, G. P., 195
Bauserman, R., 78, 114
Beebe, B., 158
Belsky, J., 88
Bergmann, M. S., 31, 203, 214
Bird, B., 51, 168
Blacker, K. H., 53, 203
Block, J., 81

Blomberg, J., 224, 226
Blum, H. P., 48, 77, 167
Böhm, T., 158
Bollas, C., 56
Bonaparte, M., 213
Bost, K. K., 85
Boswell, J., 212
Bowlby, J., 111, 146–147, 212
Boyce, T., 81
Brauer, L., 4, 5, 207, 209
Brenner, C., 11, 121, 196, 222
Breuer, J., 17, 22, 31, 33, 38, 49, 56
Brickman, H. R., 149, 208
Bridges, L. J., 86
Briere, J., 78
Britton, R., 3
Broberg, J., 224, 226
Bronstein, H., 92
Brooks Brenneis, C., 142
Brown, R., 162
Browne, A., 78
Buckley, P., 54, 201
Bukerton, D., 114
Butler, S., 226–227
Buxbaum, E., 206

C

Campbell, R., 41
Canestri, J., 224
Carlsson, J., 224, 226
Carroll, D., 85
Carter, K. C., 16